'In *Remembering the Future*, Melinda Hinkson takes us on an engaging journey through a process of visual repatriation that not only traces a path of Warlpiri drawings from the 1950s back to their communities, but to the imaginations of the descendants of the artists. Throughout, she preserves the essentially enigmatic and open possibilities of the archive, and of drawing as a mode of recording, representing and communicating. With eloquence and insight she reveals the frameworks of interpretation that have contained the drawings, exposing the limits of our understanding, and breaking open these frameworks to the activities and lives of real people, past and present.' — Professor Fred Myers, Silver Professor of Anthropology, New York University

'This will be the first study to explore the significance of Aboriginal drawing and Warlpiri visuality in a systematic fashion. In doing so, Melinda Hinkson opens up several new paths of inquiry and wonder at the sophistication and beauty of Indigenous art. This landmark book breaks new ground in exploring Aboriginal visual culture and will serve as an important touchstone in years to come.' — Professor Jane Lydon, Wesfarmers Chair of Australian History, University of Western Australia

'More than an art book, the text constitutes a major insight into the history and current circumstance of the Warlpiri themselves … a fresh reflexive and multi-perspectival approach to the analysis of visual representation not found in many "art" books… it marks a generational change and a new approach to scholarship.' — Dr Luke Taylor, Adjunct Professor, Australian National University

To the memory of Japangardi Poulson

Remembering the future

Warlpiri life through the prism of drawing

Melinda Hinkson

Aboriginal Studies Press

First published in 2014
by Aboriginal Studies Press

Aboriginal Studies Press is the publishing arm of the
Australian Institute of Aboriginal and Torres Strait Islander Studies.
GPO Box 553, Canberra, ACT 2601
Phone: (61 2) 6246 1183
Fax: (61 2) 6261 4288
Email: asp@aiatsis.gov.au
Web: www.aiatsis.gov.au/asp

National Library of Australia
Cataloguing-In-Publication data:

Author: Hinkson, Melinda, author.

Title: Remembering the future : Walpiri life through the prism of
drawing/Melinda Hinkson.

ISBN: 9781922059673 (paperback)

ISBN: 9781922059680 (ebook)

Notes: Includes index.

Subjects: Warlpiri (Australian people) — Art. Warlpiri (Australian people)
— Social life and customs. Warlpiri (Australian people) — Intellectual life.
Warlpiri (Australian people) — Kinship. Warlpiri (Australian people) —
Religion. Warlpiri (Australian people) — Rites and ceremonies. Warlpiri
(Australian people) — History. Aboriginal Australians — Northern
Territory — Art. Ethnology — Australia, Central. Race relations —
Australia.

Dewey Number: 305.89915

Design and typsetting by Christine Bruderlin, Bruderlin MacLean
Publishing Services

Cover design by Christine Bruderlin

Front cover: Larry Jungarrayi, The spearing of a man at Yuendumu native
settlement, Hooker Creek 1953–4. (Drawing #48, Meggitt Collection,
AIATSIS).

Endpapers: Larry Jungarrayi, *Bush*.

Printed in Hong Kong by Phoenix Offset Pty Ltd

Contents

Preface

In early 2001, while working at the Australian Institute of Aboriginal and Torres Strait Islander Studies (AIATSIS) and having recently completed a doctoral thesis on Warlpiri people's engagements with visual media, I learned of the crayon drawings that comprise the Meggitt Collection. The drawings were filed as research materials when Meggitt deposited them with the Institute in 1965 before he relocated from Australia to the United States. During a survey to value the Institute's art and artefacts, consultants Jon Altman and Chris Fondum were given free reign to browse the Institute's diverse material culture holdings. They later recalled their surprise and delight on opening a filing cabinet drawer and laying eyes on the first of the drawings Meggitt had collected. The valuers proclaimed the Warlpiri drawings to be works of considerable significance, recommended their reclassification from 'research materials' to 'art', and suggested they be listed on the Institute's assets register with a conservative value of $250,000.[1]

Much beguiled by the drawings during my short time at the Institute, I pitched a research project dealing with them as part of a successful application for a postdoctoral fellowship at the then Centre for Cross-Cultural Research at the Australian National University (ANU). On taking up the fellowship in mid-2001 I had second thoughts and negotiated with the Centre's then director Howard Morphy to pursue a different project. I owe Howard a debt of thanks for inadvertently helping the potentiality of the drawings project stew for another decade while I pursed other interests and developed a teaching program in the School of Archaeology and Anthropology.

Research towards this book started in early 2011 as a collaborative effort between ethnomusicologist Stephen Wild, who first worked with Warlpiri people at Lajamanu in 1969, and me. Stephen undertook crucial early discussions with senior Warlpiri men to ensure they approved of the drawings being brought out of the archive to become subjects of new research.

He oversaw the introduction of copies of the drawings to people at Lajamanu and collected newly made drawings from them while I undertook similar work at Yuendumu. Stephen retired in 2012, at which time he decided to withdraw from research in favour of more leisurely interests. I am grateful for his sensitive diplomacy and important early contribution. This shift in the project after its commencement explains something of a skew in focus of this book. Yuendumu and Lajamanu are separated by 600 kilometres of unsealed track which is prone to flooding after heavy rain. Time and other logistical constraints meant I was only able to visit Lajamanu on two occasions so the vantage point adopted in the chapters that follow is more Yuendumu-centric than it might otherwise have been. The story of Warlpiri experience over the period under investigation is vast and diverse. As is the case in any ethnographic endeavour, the perspectives adopted in this book are the outcome of various contingencies, as circumstances have resulted in my interactions with particular people at particular places and particular times.

There has been a special poignancy in reintroducing the drawings made in the early 1950s to Warlpiri people in the 2010s. As recounted in the pages that follow, the post-war period was a turbulent time in Warlpiri history. The drawings have been re-introduced to Warlpiri communities during another period of upheaval. Across three years of visits to Central Australia I have been regularly struck by the fortitude, grace and resilience of Warlpiri friends, many living under circumstances of considerable stress. My aspiration in writing this book has been to take up the drawings as a prism through which to explore something of these circumstances, while maintaining a focus on the creative drive that is apparent in so many Warlpiri people's attitudes and ways of acting in the world. I have been most fortunate in the enthusiasm, generosity, guidance and support I have enjoyed along the way.

First and foremost I am grateful for the hospitality, friendship and wise counsel of Tess Napaljarri Ross, Otto Jungarrayi Sims, Alma Nungarrayi Granites, Ormay Nangala Gallagher, Thomas Jangala Rice, Maxine Nungarrayi Spencer, April Napaljarri Spencer, Valerie Napaljarri Martin, Alice Napurrurla Nelson, Jerry Jangala Patrick, Wanta Steven Jampijinpa Patrick, Biddy Napaljarri Timms, Jeannie Nungarrayi Herbert, Elizabeth Nungarrayi Herbert, and two late great men: Paddy Japaljarri Stewart and Neville Japangardi Poulson. As will become clear, Japangardi's thoughtful interventions before his death in July 2013 have shaped my enquiry in significant ways. In dedicating this book to Japangardi I record my gratitude for his generosity in sharing an incisive way of looking at the world as well as his passion for working towards a more productive relationship between Warlpiri and non-Aboriginal people.

Hannah Quinliven provided outstanding research assistance, was an incomparable travelling companion and a highly insightful interpreter of events and drawings. This book would have been a different beast without Hannah's involvement. Joan Meggitt, widow of Mervyn, has been remarkably open and trusting in sharing memories of life with her late husband and her time at Hooker Creek. David Tunley enthusiastically shared drawings, slides and memories of his time at Yuendumu.

At Yuendumu and Lajamanu Cecilia Alfonso and Louisa Erglis, as managers of Warlukurlangu Aboriginal Artists Association and Warnayaka Art and Cultural Aboriginal Corporation, provided warm hospitality and support. They facilitated various elements of the research, along with Gloria Morales, Frank Baarda, Wendy Baarda, Jeff Bruer at Pintupi Anmatyerre Warlpiri Media and Rachel O'Connell at Yuendumu's Bilingual Resources Development Unit.

The intellectual shape of this book has benefitted from interactions with many friends and colleagues. I am particularly grateful to Andrew Sayers and Jennifer Deger for substantial creative and critical engagements of various kinds. Jane Lydon, Mandy Paul, Jeremy Beckett, Nicolas Peterson, Petronella Vaarzon-Morel and Diana Young provided thoughtful comments on draft chapters as well as more wide ranging stimulations. Paul Carter, David Brooks, David Nash, Ute Eickelkamp, Nina Fischer, Sarah Holcombe, Fiona Jenkins, Philip Jones, Desmond Manderson, Maria Nugent, Debjani Ganguly, Margaret Jolly, Martin Thomas, Yasmine Musharbash, Wally Caruna, Judith Ryan, Simone Dennis, Alison French and Åse Ottosson have lent further ideas, guidance and encouragement. Early drafts were written in two creatively inspiring environments, the Humanities Research Centre at ANU during a six-month internal fellowship in the second half of 2012, and in the home of good friends Tim Bonyhady and Nicole Moore during a period of house-minding in 2013. Core ideas and ethnographic writings have been tested in seminars and conference presentations in Canberra, Brisbane, Melbourne and San Francisco, and in one substantial article 'Back to the future: Warlpiri encounters with drawings, country and others in the digital age', *Culture, Theory and Critique*.

The project was initially funded by an AIATSIS grant, with supplementary funds granted by the Research School of Humanities and the Arts and the School of Archaeology and Anthropology. The School and the Humanities Research Centre supported two crucial semesters of teaching relief. At the Australian Institute of Aboriginal and Torres Strait Islander Studies I thank Luke Taylor for his keen interest in this project. David Jeffery oversaw complex arrangements for the reproduction of images with meticulous attention. Barry Cundy, Eleanor Galvin and staff of the library and access unit responded to my requests with great efficiency and good humour. Rhonda Black, Director of Aboriginal Studies Press, has been enthusiastic since our first discussions. I thank Rachel Ippoliti for overseeing the book's production, Christine Bruderlin for its handsome design and Margaret McDonell for her careful subediting.

Remembering the Future has been written in tandem with the development of an exhibition I have curated for the National Museum of Australia, the idea for which first arose in 2011 in discussions with Andrew Sayers during his period as Director. I am grateful to the Museum for funding three trips to Central Australia and for allowing photographic work undertaken for the exhibition to be shared in the production of this book.

For permission to reproduce photographs, drawings and other images I thank Vanessa Bertagnole, Jol Fleming, Joan Meggitt, Hannah Quinliven, David Tunley, Jon Altman, Warlukurlangu Artists Association, Mitchell Library and Newspix. For his patience and meticulous map making skills I thank Francis Markham.

Finally, I thank Jon Altman, who read various drafts of this manuscript and was a constant source of support and encouragement throughout its development. Jon, Oskar and Tess Altman cheerfully endured my absences and prolonged periods of obsessive focus away from family life. For their energy, love and good humour I say thanks.

Melinda Hinkson
Canberra, January 2014

Note on names and orthography

Across the Warlpiri community individuals are addressed and referred to by a variety of names, depending on occasion, stage of life and interpersonal relationship. Names in this sense are used in highly relational and dynamic ways.

A system of eight categories, subsection terms, or 'skin names' as they are commonly referred to, socially locates all members of the community in relation to each other. These names organise kin-based groupings along matrilineal (mother's side), patrilineal (father's side) and generational lines. They animate a reciprocal order of social expectations surrounding marriage that maps onto inheritance of country and bodies of ceremonial law. Warlpiri also bestow these names upon strangers who enter into relationships with them. In the extended forms of relatedness reproduced in this system, one has, for example, a biological mother, as well as mother's sisters and more socially distant classificatory mothers who share the same skin name. Women identified as Napaljarri, for example, may be actual sisters, they may be daughters of biologically related brothers, or they may be more distantly related as daughters of Jungarrayi men. While more specific kin terms and other names are commonly used in interpersonal interaction, skin terms are widely adopted as a mode of public address.

Nampijinpa / Jampijinpa	Napangardi / Japangardi
Nangala / Jangala	Napanangka / Japanangka
Napurrurla / Jupurrurla	Nungarrayi / Jungarrayi
Nakamarra / Jakamarra	Napaljarri / Japaljarri

Warlpiri skin terms arranged in patricouples. (N designates female and J designates male.)

Throughout this book persons are identified by their most-often used personal name and Warlpiri skin name. In respect of persons who have recently died Warlpiri custom requires that the term *kumunjayi*, which translates as 'no name', be substituted for all personal names. This is a crucial and sensitive element of face-to-face communication, especially when close relatives of the recently deceased are present. However, at Yuendumu in particular, there is growing support of the publication of personal names as well as photographs of recently deceased persons to ensure legacies are recognised into the future in the ever-expanding social world in which Warlpiri participate. Where recently deceased people are identified in the text by their personal names I do so with the approval of close relatives. In a small number of cases individuals' identities are deliberately obfuscated by the use of skin name only.

Throughout the book Warlpiri spellings have been standardised wherever possible to conform to the orthography of the Warlpiri dictionary.[2]

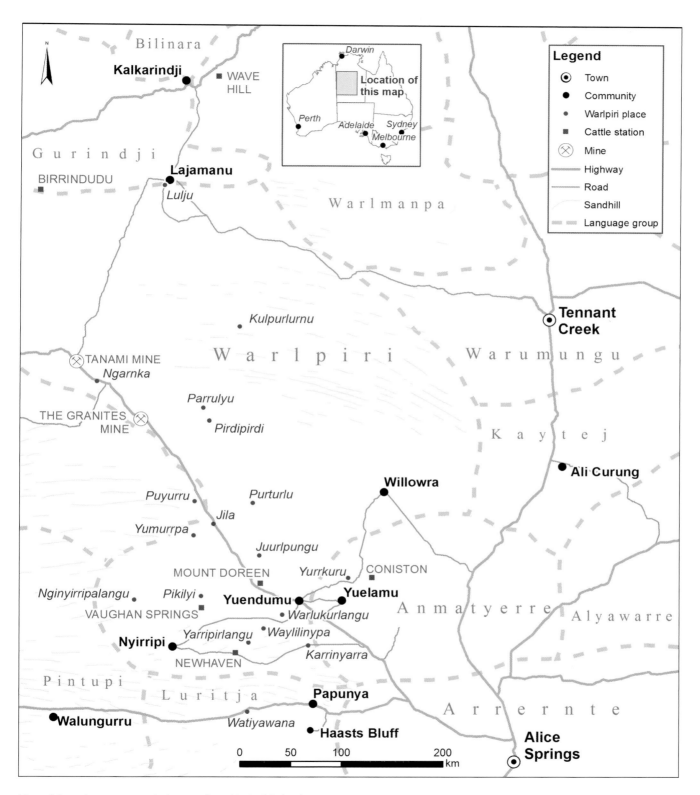

Map of the primary area and places referred to in this book.

The relation between what we see
and what we know is never settled.

John Berger, *Ways of Seeing*

Introduction
Clearing the ground

Larry Jungarrayi called upon Mervyn Meggitt one evening in 1953, some time into the anthropologist's ten-month stay at Hooker Creek, and presented him with this drawing (figure 1). Handing over the sheet of card, Jungarrayi asked his researcher-friend if he knew what the drawing was. Meggitt eyed the picture and shook his head. As recalled sixty years later by Joan Meggitt, Jungarrayi looked at her husband with utter astonishment, as if he were a fool. 'What is it?' asked the anthropologist. 'It's the *malaka*'s house!' Jungarrayi exclaimed.[1]

Twelve years later, when he documented the drawings he had collected at Hooker Creek in discussion with friend Peter Hamilton, Meggitt described Jungarrayi's 'extremely interesting' drawing thus:

> It's impressionism of a high order. It looks like an aerial view of rice fields in green with black borders. In fact it is Larry's version of the superintendent's house. He said the most striking thing about the house was the flywire that screened it. By drawing the flywire as he's done here, he's indicated the house.
>
> *Peter Hamilton*: 'Is this flywire of one window?'
>
> *Mervyn Meggitt*: 'It's . . . all the windows put together and that's the house. You don't need anything else.'[2]

Here we encounter a picture and two brief stories about it. Each story encourages us to look at Larry Jungarrayi's drawing in different ways. The second directs our attention, showing us *how* to look, what to see in the drawing. The first reveals this way of looking did not arise spontaneously. While Mervyn Meggitt's description of the picture provides the text that would become the authoritative interpretation

of Larry's drawing, Joan Meggitt's recollection of the moment of interchange between the men, as the picture changed hands, alerts us to the problem of seeing.

We meet the picture with which this book opens framed by the discussions that accompanied its exchange between maker and collector, collector and colleague, in two key moments that punctuated its passage from Larry Jungarrayi's camp at Hooker Creek on the northern edge of the Tanami Desert where it was made, to the Australian Institute of Aboriginal and Torres Strait Islander Studies in Canberra where it was archived. These two moments have been made visible by acts of memory and recording while many others lie beyond reach.

Figure 1:
Larry Jungarrayi:
The malaka's (superintendent's) *house*, Hooker Creek 1953.
(Drawing #63, Meggitt Collection, AIATSIS.)

Malaka is a term that was widely used across northern Australia to refer to the white boss.

1

Figure 2:
Larry Jungarrayi:
Pikilyi, Hooker Creek 1953–4.
(Drawing #42, Meggitt Collection,
AIATSIS.)

'It's rain snakes. You have the two
sinuous rain snakes realistically
depicted and beside them red sand
hills and blue trees on top of the
sand hills' (Mervyn Meggitt).

This book is interested in how pictures acquire stories, are interpreted and provoke discussions. Some ways of seeing pictures become authoritative, true stories, while others slip away or are marginalised. The enquiry the book pursues reveals there is much at stake in the stories we tell about pictures; these stories do not stop with the pictures themselves, they get applied to the makers of those pictures. Stories about pictures structure relationships between people, across time and place.

A collection of drawings made at Hooker Creek in 1953 and 1954 has been brought out of the archive, digitised and introduced to descendants of the men and women who made them. Across three years of research the drawings have been taken up in a new round of discussions, they have become subjects of new stories and interpretations. The drawings and the responses they have stimulated have been displayed in an exhibition at the National Museum of Australia. This book tracks the social life of these drawings[3] over six decades, approaching them as a prism through which to explore Warlpiri lives and ways of seeing across a momentous period of change.

The starting point for this enquiry is the impossibility of recovering a singular true account for these pictures. All of the men and women who made the drawings are deceased, none can describe what they intended or saw in the pictures they made. So we approach the drawings from a number of distinct vantage points — contemporary Warlpiri responses, Meggitt's descriptions and interpretations, the wider scholarship on Aboriginal visual culture of the period, archival documents and writings that allow us to glimpse the turbulent events that preceded the transportation of Warlpiri to the place where they made the drawings, and my own propositions.

The significances found for these drawings in the pages that follow reflect the journey of the research. Following these different lines of enquiry, we will have cause to return to Larry Jungarrayi's picture *the malaka's house* a number of times throughout this book. *The malaka's house* is what visual culture scholar WJT Mitchell[4] would call our *metapicture* — a picture with layers of significance, a picture that not only depicts something, but comments on and poses questions about the process of picturing itself. By his committed attention, by the care he took in making this picture; his layered, experimental, working up of colour and use of the entire space of the page, as well as the angle and proximity of his perspective, Larry Jungarrayi's picture establishes a series of interests this book shall explore.

Central Australian Aboriginal people's pictures of their ancestral countries have long been recognised as a distinct genre of cultural creativity. In accounts of the vital painting movements that emerged from desert communities from the 1970s the irrepressible drive to picture absent country, the places from which Aboriginal people were increasingly separated from the 1920s and to which some would later return, is a clear and constant theme, as it shall be in this book. Many drawings in the Meggitt Collection enact this abiding imperative (for example figure 2). But Larry Jungarrayi's drawing pushes to the surface another set of concerns that is less frequently written of — questions of how those same people saw, pictured, made sense of the new surroundings, new architecture, new regimes of work and daily life, the new world order that settlement life brought into being. In the very act of drawing the superintendent's house, Larry Jungarrayi declares these interests.

Taking up the 1950s drawings as a prism through which to explore Warlpiri experience, I make a claim at the outset about the crucial role of images and the practice of looking and being looked at in structuring distinctive relations between people.[5] How and what did Warlpiri *see* in the landscape of Hooker Creek, the new settlement to which they were forcibly moved just months before Mervyn Meggitt arrived to conduct research? How were Warlpiri *seen* by the settlers who dispossessed them of their lands and the government agents who would adopt responsibility for their welfare and administration? How did they envisage the life they had left behind and the future they faced? In the enquiry undertaken by this book, Larry Jungarrayi's drawing stimulates consideration of such questions and helps shape a broader exploration of transformations in Warlpiri life following their relocation to government settlements. Through the eyes of Warlpiri people in the present what do the 1950s drawings reveal? What

Figure 3:
Paddy Japaljarri: *Maliki-jarra Jukurrpa* (Two Dingoes Dreaming), Hooker Creek 1953–4. (Drawing #1, Meggitt Collection, AIATSIS.)

The first drawing Meggitt collected. '. . . [A]n episode or a place from the dreaming track of the two dingoes. It refers to the eaglehawk camp and also to the *yinirnti*, or bean trees . . . this illustrates part of the track followed by the two dingoes as they pursue this line of advance between the mountains from one waterhole to the next and the bean trees are around' (Mervyn Meggitt).

discussions do they trigger? What life stories and wider interpretations emerge from interactions with the drawings?

Traces of picturing

Mervyn Meggitt destroyed his Warlpiri field notes and research materials prior to his death, concerned about what might come of that material in the future. The only documentation for the drawings was edited from a recorded interview Meggitt made with friend Peter Hamilton, in 1965 just prior to depositing the drawings with the Australian Institute of Aboriginal Studies. Meggitt's own documentation indicates that we should be cautious of any authoritative claims in respect of the drawings. In relation to several drawings he remained intrigued, bemused, unsure of subject matter or significance. Meggitt's delight and thoughtful engagement with the drawings are apparent in his animated discussion with Hamilton, but as will become clear he also imposes classifications that go against the grain of Warlpiri principles.

Contemporary Warlpiri responses throw some of Meggitt's documentation into question. In a small number of cases they also suggest his identifications were just plain wrong. Other factors compound the need for intelligent speculation and uncertainty in

respect of these drawings. In early 2011 a man who would die just months later was adamant he was the maker of one drawing, but equally sure he was not at Hooker Creek during the Meggitts' residency. He recalled having produced drawings as part of an adult education program. Joan Meggitt, Mervyn's widow, is just as certain her husband only acquired drawings directly from the men who produced them. The fragile and complex workings of memory run as a thread through the chapters that follow.

What kinds of things are drawings? A number of scholars see drawing as a universal human activity.[6] But tempering such claims is the recognition that drawing occurs in an array of vastly different situations. Desert dwelling Warlpiri people commonly draw with their hands in the sand, seated among others on the ground, recounting all manner of stories from ancestral events to neighbourhood gossip. One set of questions to be explored in this book is to do with the activity of drawing itself — how should we compare drawings made in sand by a person engaged in social interaction with others, with those made in more solitary circumstances with crayon on paper?

Grappling with this question requires holding in mind three interrelated levels of approach to the practice of drawing itself — in the first, drawing is sense making of a highly personal kind. One of the distinguishing characteristics of drawing for John Berger, who has written widely and eloquently about drawing as a modern practice, is that it is private work.[7] Drawing of the kind Berger has in mind is not undertaken in anticipation of a public audience; it is not intended to communicate. It is rather the imaginative activity of a person making sense of the environment and their place within it at a particular moment. In this sense drawing is an individual but also thoroughly *relational* activity, it enacts the spatial relationship between a person who draws and an object seen. In drawing something, the drawer attempts to get the measure of that thing. Drawing anchors its maker in the world. A drawing of a tree, Berger tells us pointedly, is not a tree, but 'a tree being looked at'.[8]

At the second level of engagement with drawing and continuing with Berger we might ask, *how* do Warlpiri people look at trees? It will be seen that this is an especially poignant question to pose, one that will be fully explored in Chapter 5. While the Warlpiri drawings seem to confirm many of the ideas Berger puts forward, they were produced in a very different context to that which he has in mind. Are there distinctive elements of a Warlpiri way of picturing and if so, what does this reveal of how Warlpiri people see their place in the world? How does a cultural attitude to images make itself apparent in the drawings made by individual persons?

At the third level of engagement, this book is concerned with the intercultural context in which these drawings were produced. Mervyn Meggitt provided card and crayons, in the first instance to Warlpiri men. In distributing these materials and inviting his informants to draw, Meggitt followed a well-established trajectory of research in Aboriginal Australia. Joan Meggitt recalls that Mervyn 'wanted to find out how they saw things'. When he came to formally document the drawings more than a decade after they were made Meggitt articulated his intentions more tightly. Meggitt's research focus, as was common during this period, took him into the Warlpiri ceremonial realm. Crayon drawing emerged as an ideal medium in which Meggitt could ask men to depict elements of ritual knowledge he was trying to understand. Drawing was introduced as part of

a methodological toolkit with a set of wider aims and questions. What were these aims and questions and how did they influence what Meggitt saw in the drawings?

In response to his request, the men in the main produced pictures of the places and related ritual knowledge trajectories they were enacting in the ceremonies Meggitt attended. The majority of the drawings depict events and itineraries of ancestral creation (figure 3), they give shape and form and colour to Warlpiri ritual knowledge, they visualise Warlpiri places. These places and the Dreamings through which they were created were the focus of discussion between Meggitt and his informants; places from which Warlpiri were now separated, located across the vast expanse of the Tanami Desert hundreds of kilometres to the south and south-west of Hooker Creek. The drawings enact relationships: relationships between people and places, between people who share authority and compulsion to reproduce the potency of their countries and in the process sustain themselves, and between those men and the anthropologist who sought to understand their way of life. The drawings materialise traces of this research relationship, the full shape of which we can never recover, but the general trajectory we might deduce from the core themes and interests of Meggitt's published work.

Delimiting contexts

Recognising that Meggitt was engaged with Warlpiri men on ritual practices, songs, narratives, knowledge that was restricted in its circulation, it makes sense to see the drawings not as a set of individual pictures but a series of interrelated threads or a mosaic of intersecting stories, ancestral itineraries, visual distillations of places.

In 1980, ethnomusicologist Stephen Wild, who had a longstanding research relationship with Warlpiri men at Hooker Creek, now Lajamanu, returned on behalf of the Institute with copies of the drawings and sought senior men's advice on how they should be treated. The outcome of this consultation was the division of the drawings into two classes, those regarded as appropriate for public circulation and

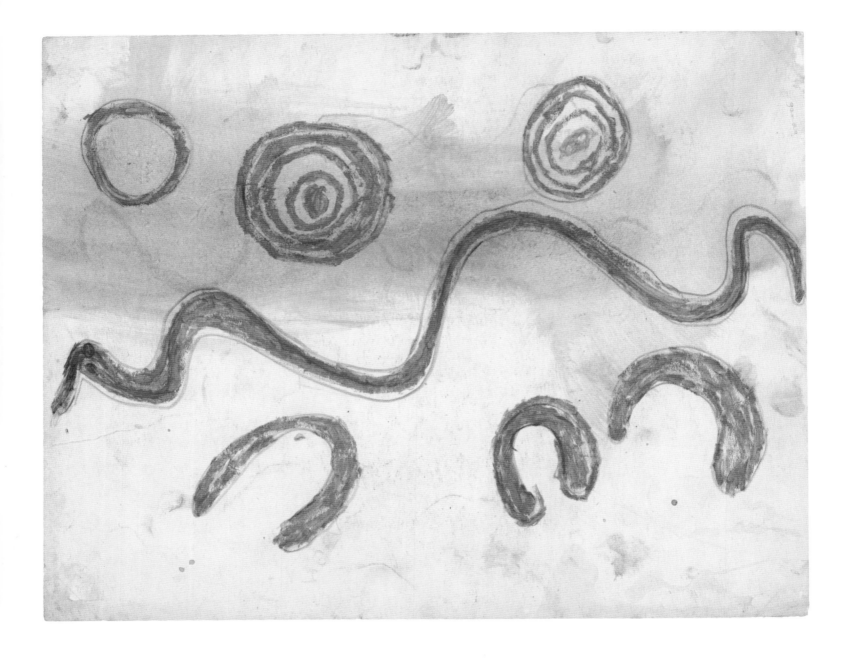

Figure 4:
Larry Jungarrayi:
Warnayarra (Rain Snake),
Hooker Creek 1953–4.
(Drawing #45, Meggitt Collection,
AIATSIS.)

'A depiction of the rain snake with
concentric circles for waterholes.
The half circles have a double
meaning as seated men and rain
clouds' (Mervyn Meggitt).

those deemed restricted, suitable to be seen only by initiated men.

The 1980 report is illuminating for what it also reveals of attitudes to another class of images, photographs. Meggitt took hundreds of photographs during his Warlpiri fieldwork. As the drawings were assembled as a collection, along with the documentation Meggitt produced in discussion with Peter Hamilton, photographic portraits of the makers of the drawings were also identified and mounted on a series of slides. The men instructed Wild that:

> if this [report] is published, no photographs of living people should be included because they may die at any time. However, photographs of those who are already deceased may be included because they have all died sufficiently long ago for there to be no objection. Any photographs of people, living or dead, may be put on display on condition that the photographs do not go to the NT.[9]

Thus the men made clear the display and circulation of photographs of persons was a matter of great concern, requiring as much care and consideration as the drawings themselves. Here lie traces of a distinctively Warlpiri way of seeing. Pictures in Warlpiri reckoning are not pictures *about* things but rather retain an essential connection to the thing or person pictured, this is the case whether a picture is produced by camera, crayon or paint. A picture of a place is inextricably tied to the people of that place; the two are treated in relational terms. Acts of picturing are acts of making and remaking these relationships. A picture of a place signals the authority of specific persons to draw, paint, sing and dance particular Dreamings, ancestral bodies of law, and their related tracts of country. A portrait of a person points not only to the portrayed individual but to a related group of people and the country to which they are inextricably tied. The making, display and circulation of pictures are thus matters of high order significance; Warlpiri pictures enact principles of the wider Warlpiri social order.

At the conclusion of Wild's consultation, men directed that copies of the drawings identified as suitable for public circulation be deposited with the Lajamanu Council office (where many of the men served as councillors). Wild was instructed to remove the remaining prints to Canberra for safe storage.[10]

By 2011, when I commenced research towards this book, all of the men consulted in 1980, including four makers of the 1950s drawings, had died. Undertaking preliminary work for the current project Wild again consulted senior men to secure their approval for the drawings to be circulated publicly. Discussions at Lajamanu and Yuendumu resulted in the directive that the drawings identified as restricted in 1980 should remain so. Significantly this decision was taken without viewing those drawings. The 119 drawings identified in 1980 as suitable for public circulation were reviewed. In a small number of cases men at Yuendumu deferred to the authority of men at Lajamanu for directives on the appropriate status of drawings, at the end of this process no further drawings were added to the restricted list.

The 1980 classification produces a particular kind of archive, one marked by significant absences. Twenty-one men and three women produced drawings for Meggitt. Of these, the works made by four men, Freddy Jangala, Jack Jakamarra, Louis Jupurrurla and Cookie Jampijinpa are all restricted. All but one of the seventeen drawings by Paddy Japaljarri are restricted. Seven of fifty-two drawings made by Larry Jungarrayi are restricted. Three of six produced by Ginger Japangardi and one of two drawings each produced by brothers Paddy Jupurrurla and Charlie Jupurrurla are restricted. The corpus that remains is like a tapestry with significant sections cut out and the contributions of several makers missing. Yet rather than approaching the collection as a jigsaw puzzle lacking crucial pieces, the chapters that follow take the drawings up as a palimpsest, a set of layers and traces of a body of knowledge, relationships, memories, creative explorations of places and what anthropologist Nancy Munn terms 'Warlpiri world theory',[11] across time. Like any archival research, particular drawings will stimulate lengthy exploration, while others will go unexamined.

Research for this project has brought further collections of Warlpiri drawings to light — drawings collected in the early 1930s by Olive Pink and drawings made in the Yuendumu school in the 1960s. Since 2011 Warlpiri people have made hundreds of drawings responding to the 1950s drawings. In the pages that follow, this larger corpus is selectively drawn upon to help amplify the enquiry.

Lines of inheritance, lines of enquiry, lines in the sand

This book takes a speculative approach to the drawings, the intellectual justification for which is provided by Clifford Geertz, who promoted anthropology as an exercise in 'guesses at guesses'.[12] But the primary motive for such an approach lies with the drawings themselves. The 1950s drawings invite speculative attention not simply because of the absence of a comprehensive account produced at the time of their making, but because, as responses to them reveal, images are highly malleable and dynamic things. Framed and encountered in different media and circumstances, taken up by different hands at different times and places, images work differently.

I am interested in how the drawings are seen, what gets seen through them, the debates they provoke, the wonder they stimulate, as well as the silences

they meet. Collectively and one by one the drawings produce an excess of stimulation; they continue to produce questions, they refuse to be tied down to a single or final explanation.

Recording practices — whether drawing, writing, or photography — by their very nature give attention to certain events and perspectives at the expense of others. They produce truths and silences. The photograph of Meggitt on horseback (figure 5) is of the classic kind chosen to denote the authoritative researcher 'in the field'. Indeed it has been called upon to do this kind of work.[13] Yet Joan Meggitt recalls Mervyn was a poor rider, and not mechanically oriented. He did not drive a car. By some accident in the developing process, the photograph carries a shadowy trace of another; in the image file I look at on my computer screen the shadowy spectre of a Warlpiri man looms large, hovering over the figure of Meggitt. Each of these two small observations destabilises the photograph in terms of any clear message it might convey. Like the anecdotes that introduced Larry Jungarrayi's drawing *The malaka's house*, these observations affect the way we look at this photograph. They remind us that pictures, whether photographs or drawings or paintings, never just show what they appear to show.

Speculative discussion of the kind that is invited by the drawings had no place in the anthropology pursued by Meggitt. Anthropologists of the mid-twentieth century were occupied by different questions. Like others of his generation Meggitt's ethnography gives only limited attention to the colonial context in which he encountered the Warlpiri at Hooker Creek. Chapter Two of *Desert People* compellingly unfolds the layers of conflict, political and climatic pressure that led Warlpiri people to leave their nomadic existence for a profoundly different life in settlements. Having dealt with this 'background' he quickly moves on to the main task at hand, detailing Warlpiri social organisation, kinship, life cycles of men and women. It is a paradox of anthropology of this period that while aspiring to record and describe the cultural life of peoples in the present, the questions that framed much anthropological research had the effect of placing the people who were the subjects of that research outside of time, and

Figure 5:
Mervyn Meggitt preparing to ride to Wave Hill Station to borrow flour, imposed over a second unidentified photograph, Hooker Creek 1953. (Photograph: Joan Meggitt, Mervyn Meggitt Collection AIATSIS N390.134.)

Figure 6:
Artist unknown:
Subject unknown, Hooker Creek
1953–4.

(Drawing #100, Meggitt Collection, AIATSIS.)

This is the only drawing Meggitt collected that remained unidentified. He speculated that Abe Jangala had started the drawing, thrown it away, after which it was retrieved by and worked on by Alecky II Japaljarri. Meggitt had no idea of the drawing's subject matter.

more specifically outside of the shared time–space of anthropologists' own society. Johannes Fabian describes this as the 'denial of coevalness'; a refusal to see European and non-European peoples as occupying shared social space.[14]

Larry Jungarrayi's drawing and his reported surprise at Meggitt's failure to identify its subject matter make a compelling statement on this very theme. Meggitt's numbering system suggests Jungarrayi made twenty-five other drawings before this one, many responding directly to the request to draw cosmological themes. So why break the mould? What motivated Larry Jungarrayi to shift focus from distant ancestral country and Dreamings to the here and now of the settlement? Could it be that he drew *The malaka's house* in an attempt to instigate a new kind of conversation with Meggitt, a conversation focused on matters beyond the anthropologist's tightly established interests, matters Larry Jungarrayi saw as pressing, matters dealing with the here and now of colonial relations and the uncertain future Warlpiri people faced?

Picturing beyond the visual

Joan Meggitt recalls that her husband's motivation for encouraging the men to draw was that he 'wanted to find out how they saw things'. Can a distinctive Warlpiri way of seeing be identified? Above I touched upon the way places and related persons are conjoined in Warlpiri responses to pictures made by other Warlpiri people. The question most

Figure 7:
Curtis Jampijinpa
Fry, Warlukurlangu
Aboriginal Artists
Association, Yuendumu
February 2011.
(Photograph: Vanessa
Bertagnole.)

consistently asked of the 1950s drawings was, 'Who made that picture?' On many occasions I have been reminded that neither picture makers nor viewers are ever neutrally positioned. While recounting his recollections of the early settlement, a senior man made a portrait of a striking figure of authority recalled from his childhood. Another man later voiced his disapproval — 'Who made this picture? Why is [that person] making a picture of that man? He is not his family.' Such are the structuring constraints that characterise what might be termed a classical Warlpiri way of seeing. An attitude to images goes hand in hand with the maintenance of social order. Yet all communities have members who actively push against such attitudes.

In Warlpiri ritual, image making is part of an interwoven set of communicative acts between persons, country and spirit beings related in particular ways. The force of images as powerful markers of identity is felt in the constellation of activity that brings them into being and shows their beholders *how* to look at, embody and care for images as part of a deeply held sense of who a person is. *This is your father's Dreaming. This is your Dreaming. These are the places created by this Dreaming. These are the designs that enact this Dreaming. These are the songs and dances that revitalise that Dreaming.* Historically Warlpiri pictures were performed and communicated in their making rather than stored for contemplation at a later time. Pictures are made in sand then dissolved by the wind; they are painted on bodies then blurred and rubbed by clothes, sweat, bodily movement. Even the ritual objects that are stored require the revitalising touch of human hands at each new encounter in order to keep their power alive.

Central Australian communities have distinctive visual languages; members of a community recognise pictures made by other members. Munn identified the circle and line as the primary units of Warlpiri image making.[15] Yet the same visual form in a picture may stand for a variety of phenomena; a circle may depict a waterhole, fruit, campfire, digging stick, cave, tree, the place from which new life emerges (female body or ground) or into which persons and spirit beings descend. Thus it has been suggested that, while classical Warlpiri pictures draw from a closed set of elements and established principles, it is not possible to interpret with certainty any picture without the input of the person who made it.[16]

To appreciate Warlpiri responses to the drawings in the 2010s involves recognising the complex visual cultural environment that has come to shape contemporary Warlpiri experience. Between the 1950s and the present the idea of what might pass for a 'Warlpiri image' has been increasingly expanded and complicated. From one direction an infinite range of visual material has flowed into Warlpiri townships, carried by state authorities, education programs, a multitude of visitors, as well as a raft of media including newspapers and magazines, films, television, video games, digital photographs, the internet and mobile phones. From another direction Warlpiri persons have attended school and acquired print literacy and techniques of administration; they have taken up video cameras and made films and animations as well as acrylic paintings for which they have become renowned. Warlpiri artworks adorn the walls of national and international galleries as well as the forecourt of Australia's federal Parliament House. Footage of revered Warlpiri Australian Football League players kicking game-winning goals is broadcast on national television, as are scenes of the same men fronting court on criminal charges.

The present project has involved returning 'new' pictures made in 'old' media, crayon on paper, into a highly dynamic visual environment. If Warlpiri men were concerned about the circulation of photographs of persons in 1980, what is the situation today? In 1985 Eric Michaels identified 'at least' four areas 'in which Aboriginal culture may be compromised and Aboriginal subjects offended when they become photographic subjects': unauthorized display of restricted material, violation of mortuary restrictions, invasions of privacy, and 'rhetorical devices' that 'constitute them as exotic'.[17] It was common through the 1990s to find the faces of recently deceased persons that appeared in books or community newsletters at Yuendumu scratched out with ink, and for locally produced videos to be removed to locked cupboards; two practices adopted as part of a wider set of prescriptions enabling the spirit of the deceased to make an unimpeded passage back to ancestral country.

By 2011 one man was utilising photographs to support his passion for making portraits of people. Members of one family were using mobile phones to circulate and store photographs of a recently deceased young boy following a tragic accident — in the midst of their grief, the precious photographs were spoken of as 'helping keep his memory alive'. Others were eager to watch video footage of their recently deceased father. Photographs were also being incorporated into mortuary practices, placed on top of coffins, with the adult children of one prominent woman keen to be photographed holding the photograph of their deceased mother at the conclusion of her funeral service.[18] These are brief traces of the highly dynamic visual environment that will be explored as part of the process of grappling with how Warlpiri people in the present behold the 1950s drawings.

Figure 8:
Donny Jungarrayi:
A place called Diri, west of Mt Doreen, where Donny was conceived, Hooker Creek 1953–4. (Drawing #131, Meggitt Collection, AIATSIS.)

'The Aboriginals in this area believe that a woman becomes pregnant by accidentally being at or near a totemic site' (Mervyn Meggitt).

Imagining Hooker Creek, remembering the future

The structure of this book follows the various strands of my speculative enquiry. Chapter 1 opens with the reintroduction of the drawings to Warlpiri people in 2011 and weighs one man's considered

Figure 9:
Crossing Hooker Creek
after rain, c. 1953–4
(Photograph: Mervyn
Meggitt, Mervyn Meggitt
Collection, AIATSIS
N390.342.)

responses against Meggitt's work and the wider scholarship of Aboriginal visual culture through the early-to-mid twentieth century. Chapter 2 tracks the crucial backstory to the drawings; the brutal frontier circumstances that precipitated Warlpiri people's movement out of the desert and into settlements. Chapter 3 explores the early world of the settlement and Warlpiri involvement in the construction of this radically new environment. Chapter 4 recounts a trip to the ancestral country of Larry Jungarrayi and contemplates his life through the lives of his brothers' descendants. Chapter 5 considers the conundrum posed by one series of drawings and looks (unsuccessfully) to Warlpiri post-colonial place-making practices in pursuit of a resolution. Finally, Chapter 6 examines the influence of school-based

education and technological change on how Warlpiri people picture past events, see themselves in the present and imagine a future.

Four interludes to the main chapters allow relevant threads to be pursued; the voices of Olive Pink and Warlpiri sisters Jeannie Nungarrayi Herbert and Elizabeth Nungarrayi Ross are given space here, as are my own ethnographic observations and consideration of Mervyn Meggitt's writings. The closer we come to the present the more voices of living people shape the journey. Throughout, my propositions are clearly distinguished from what Warlpiri people or other sources have to say.

Images appear in a number of guises and play a significant part in telling the story that follows. A selection of the 1950s drawings and Meggitt's annotations is reproduced throughout, while the full Meggitt Collection is catalogued at the back of this book. Reproductions of drawings made in the 1930s, 1960s and 2010s conjure up continuities and transformations in Warlpiri ways of seeing across eight decades of turbulent life. Photographs by Meggitt and others provide visual anchor points as well as stimulations. Contemporary photographs convey settings of the research. Images accompany, stimulate and disrupt the written narrative. They are never simply intended to show what they appear to show.

Significantly, images are the places where Warlpiri people and most other Australians meet. Our attitudes, expectations and ways of relating to each other get substantially shaped through our interactions with pictures found in books, films, news reportage.[19] Many images associated with Aboriginal people circulating in the public domain tend towards starkly negative or positive stereotypes. Images of Aboriginal art and culture have historically been glorified, while images of the many ways Aboriginal people fail to achieve according to mainstream expectations arouse criticism and disdain. Warlpiri pictures get taken up in this politics of representation as vehicles for circulating messages. One place where the implications of this process are clear is in the symbolic significance attached to acrylic painting. Acrylic paintings have become prime carriers for recognition of Central Australian Aboriginal people's place-based forms of identity. Yet certain public readings of these paintings as marking an authentic Aboriginality have loaded up the producers of those paintings with coercive expectations. In this way of seeing Warlpiri get wedged between abstract and ossified stereotypes, traditional Aborigine or modern Australian: they are never fully human.

Experience has given Warlpiri people a sophisticated awareness of this process, which bears down upon the way they remember the past in perhaps surprising ways, hence the title of this book. *Remembering the future* is born of my observation that Warlpiri acts of remembering occur against current concerns and in respect of the future. Acts of remembering are freighted with other people's judgments and expectations. Acts of remembering

can simultaneously amplify hope for a differently inflected future. This observation of memory's future-focused orientation has largely gone un-examined in the field of memory studies.[20] It also sits in tension with much that has been observed of the Dreaming, a world order characterised as orienting Aboriginal communities to the past rather than the future.[21] In the present, matters are not so straightforward.

The 1950s drawings were made as part of the creative social interchange between an anthropologist and the men and women who aided his research. Through such interactions lies potential to bring about new understandings as well as new, shared ways of seeing.[22] While Mervyn Meggitt's interactions with Warlpiri men were deeply interested and respectful of Warlpiri cultural life, any dialogue that might have ensued as a result of the making of the drawings seems not to have brought about such a transformed intercultural way of seeing. The strongest evidence of this is that as far as can be known Larry Jungarrayi did not make further drawings of a similar kind to *The malaka's house*.

Ultimately, it is in pursuit of an open-minded interaction with the Warlpiri drawings and their makers that I have written this book. Taking up drawing as a prism for exploring Warlpiri experience involves complex memory work and much tracking back and forth through time. Throughout these explorations the concerns of the present and hopes and fears for the future shape the way Warlpiri people picture the experience of early settlement and the actions of their forebears — in their own country, in the country of others, in the place of Australia.

INTERLUDE I
Regarding Nangala

Figure 1:
Abe Jangala:
Devils in sandhill country,
Hooker Creek 1953–4.
(Drawing #29, Meggitt
Collection, AIATSIS.)

1 February 2011

Rosie Nangala and I are seated on a mat outside the flat she occupies in the grounds of the Baptist Mission House, next door to Yuendumu's Warlukurlangu Arts Centre. She takes up a series of the laminated pictures I have brought with me and peruses them. Without a word she selects one of Abe Jangala's pictures (figure 1). She asks for paper to 'practice', producing a series of simple tree-like figures in black crayon on a page I have torn from my notebook. Then she sends me to collect small eucalyptus leaves from a young tree growing just over the Mission House fence. She traces the outline of the leaves with green crayon, asking me to hold the leaf still for her while she marks a wobbly outline.

Nangala's right hand is thickly wrapped in a fresh white bandage, injured and swollen with infection as a result of some recent but now forgotten incident. She is finding the crayon unwieldy and difficult to handle. Unprompted, she tells me it is the 'first time' she has used crayons and the 'first time' she has drawn leaves. She draws short lines running outwards from the edge of the leaf and then into its interior. As she does so her drawing acquires a double perspective — it becomes both leaf and tree, depending on how one looks at it. I observe that Nangala's attention has been drawn not to the figures that to my eye dominate Abe Jangala's composition, the vital red *jarnpa* devil figures, but rather the delicate branches of little red flowers, identified by Meggitt as *ngulmana*, scattered across the outer field of the drawing.

Incrementally, this simple drawing of 'a leaf' becomes 'a flower' and emerges to take the recognisable visual attributes of Warlpiri *Jukurrpa* painting. Nangala executes this transformation as she shifts seamlessly from drawing with crayon to drawing with paint. Dissatisfied with the lack of pigment density she is getting from the crayon Nangala begins dipping the crayon into one of the pots of paint sitting beside her on the edge of the mat. In vivid green she paints strong wavy lines through the middle of the leaf. 'Ah, now that's lifting up', Nangala smiles with some satisfaction. She returns to crayon to apply yellow flower roundels to the edges of the leaves/braches, but having put down the crayon forgets it and returns to her pots of paint. Eventually the simple and uncertain outlines of green crayon are filled out and overwhelmed by

Figure 2:
Rosie Nangala and Melinda Hinkson, Yuendumu February 2011. (Photograph: Vanessa Bertagnole.)

Figure 3:
Rosie Nangala as a
young woman at work
in the Mission House,
Yuendumu c. 1960s.
(Photograph: Tom
Fleming, courtesy of Jol
Fleming.)

paint, by dots, by the marks that indicate *yankirri wirliya*, emu tracks. Nangala's drawing becomes a painting, the medium that over the past thirty years has steadily accrued intercultural status as *the* medium for picturing country and Dreamings. Across this period painting has come to proclaim something basic about how Warlpiri people wish to have their priorities, imperatives and place in the world recognised.

As she draws and paints, Nangala speaks, unprompted, of her life working as a domestic helper 'long time ago' for the missionaries. She speaks of the significance of living in this house again now, full of memories — as the place where Warlpiri people used to come to shower before going to school. 'See that concrete over there? That's where they used to come to "shop" for clothes, all the naked people. See that tree stump, people would sit under that tree. When did that tree get cut down?' She asks herself several times and looks puzzled. She speaks of 'all' her country Warlukurlangu, where she tells me she now takes 'all the *kardiya* ladies who come to look at art'. She speaks of how she is living alone in this house, waiting for her granddaughter (who Nangala raised at

Yuendumu), now living in the Western Australian town of Halls Creek. 'She might come, anytime.' Nangala also speaks of her brothers who were due to come here, 'any day', for a mining royalties meeting.

Nangala has dementia and her stories are repeated over and over. The images she carries in her mind, these memories to which she gives voice throughout the day to any white person who will listen, are what she dwells with in the present. While other residents of Yuendumu live life at a rapid pace, Nangala's age and dementia have carried her into a more contemplative and at times unhinged disposition. Women speak of her yelling out in the night things she should not speak. But a quieter demeanour colours her picture making, which is deeply attentive, meditative, undistracted by the demands and pressures that are primary concerns for others. In the fast-paced blur of activity that characterises the daily scene at the art centre, Nangala is often a pillar of serenity, working away largely oblivious to the tensions that swirl around her.

The stories she tells locate Nangala in the establishment of Yuendumu. They also mark her as an unusual senior woman, residing on her own in the grounds of the Mission

House rather than in the company of other women in the widow's camp. Long ago she was married to Jimija Jungarrayi, a Warlpiri man renowned for his status as intercultural leader as well as for the brutal treatment he sustained as a young man at the hands of the pastoralist who ran Mt Doreen Station, a lease that takes in country Warlpiri refer to today as their heartland. But Nangala does not speak of her deceased husband.

The living area in which Nangala spends the most time is her outside studio — a bamboo mat, tins of brushes, plastic pots of paint — surrounded by a perimeter of diverse objects piled high: containers, plastic sheeting, metal frames and poles, materials which to an unknowing eye appear as a jumbled pile of junk. In the days that follow she sends me to these piles to retrieve various items — tarpaulin and cardboard to sit on, crowbars, billycans, an axe head, storage containers for a hunting trip.

The curtains are drawn on the windows of Nangala's bedsit; these internal spaces are functional, not lived in. The living room provides storage, holding empty flour drums, crowbars, paint supplies, old shopping bags with unknown contents, clothes, blankets but no furniture; the bedroom contains a mattress and bedclothes.

This modest dwelling has a history of being occupied by intercultural brokers of considerable standing. Before Nangala came to live in the flat her classificatory father resided here — Darby Jampijinpa Ross, stockman, ritual leader, Churchman, great painter and storyteller. Darby died in 2005 at the age of 100. His life is memorialised in Liam Campbell's biography of the same name.[1]

Later Nangala calls me over to show me a leak in her shower — a rusty exposed pipe protrudes from the wall where the arm of the showerhead should be. Water trickles steadily down the besser brick wall. We look up at the large pool of water spreading across a ceiling bubbling and straining under its weight. The mission staff are away on leave. Nangala wonders out loud who might come and fix this for her. I tell her I will ask at the women's centre.

The following morning Nangala has no recollection of having made her drawing/painting. I retrieve its slightly crumpled and dew dampened form from the margins of her camp. Scanning recently produced work on the walls of the art centre later that day my eye is caught by a screen print made two years earlier by Nangala — a picture of simple tree-like figures closely resembling those she drew for me yesterday 'for the first time'.

Over the course of the next two weeks I see Nangala every day. I watch her emerge from the interior of her flat into the morning sun and make her way across the yard to the art centre. She often has breakfast there, waited upon by attentive art centre staff and a steady flow of short-term volunteers, and then later in the day by people delivering meals on wheels. There is much affection and concern among Warlpiri and other residents for Nangala's wellbeing, and gentle scolding of her for working too hard, staying up late cleaning and not getting the rest she needs.

Nangala's difficult grappling with crayons, her continual reversion to paint and to *Jukurrpa* mark a point of difference with the freer, easy-handed and quick work of younger people aged into their fifties. For these people European schooling has brought familiarity with the ideas and technology of drawing vernacular experience.

While watching Nangala paint and draw and listening to her stories, my attention is drawn to her feet. Bunions have forced both her big toes back across her feet at sharp angles. Having spent the majority of her life bare-footed, Nangala's feet have acquired a shape and toughness that indicates life lived on the ground. Her feet remind me of those of an emu. A blurred memory comes to me of a hunting trip with a group of women fifteen years earlier. That particular day was windy and unsettled and there was a sense of volatility in the air. We were in the vicinity of Warlukurlangu, Nangala's emu country. Suddenly Nangala adopted the disposition of an emu. As she made the moves and sounds of this 'cheeky' and unpredictable animal, a sparkling look of wickedness came across her face. Captivated by this compelling transformation I was momentarily disoriented, the world seemed to tip sideways. Just as quickly Nangala resumed the demeanour of a Warlpiri woman and we went about the business of tracking goanna.

Driving out of Yuendumu several days after our interactions in her camp over drawing, I listen in as Nangala encourages the young French volunteer seated next to her on the back seat to pronounce the Warlpiri names of the various species of trees she spies rushing past the car window. I watch the two of them later, once

Figure 4:
Rosie Nangala painting/
drawing, Warlukurlangu
Aboriginal Artists
Association, Yuendumu
February 2011.
(Photograph: Vanessa
Bertagnole.)

we've arrived at our destination, the volunteer trailing along behind Nangala as she wanders through the spinifex scrub with a look of deep concentration on her face, plucking flowers which she tucks behind her ear, reciting further names for her young charge to copy — 'wanakiji . . . yakajirri . . . wurrpardi — we gotta hold all those names'.

Four months later I am in Manchester, England, standing in a travel agency waiting to purchase train tickets. A brochure for Intrepid Tours catches my eye, its front cover adorned with an image of a mischievous looking young Aboriginal girl in the foreground of Uluru. Flicking through the pages as I wait in line I land upon a promotion for tours to art-producing communities of the Northern Territory — and there is Nangala, sitting against the red ochre-coloured wall of the Warlukurlangu Arts Centre, porridge bowl beside her, arms linked and in easy conversation with a visiting tourist.

Back at Yuendumu for a brief research visit in May 2013, Nangala greets me as a friendly stranger over her fence. 'I'm always living here, one woman, I came back to this place . . . ' The life narrative remains close to the surface, albeit expressed this time in tighter form. I notice a new addition to her yard, a large metal shelf neatly holding various lengths of wood and other materials. Her outdoor studio is transformed. One of the art centre managers tells me there have been problems with cockroach and mice infestation of Nangala's camp. As a result her 'hoarded' materials are now regularly cleared from the yard. Nangala has been given a new bed and base and freshly painted walls inside her 'house'. She is escorted away and distracted during these cleaning incursions, and reportedly notices nothing new on her return.

Stories always, and inevitably, draw
together what classifications split apart.

Tim Ingold, *Lines*

Chapter 1
Locating the Warlpiri drawings

Late one afternoon in early February 2011 I am sitting in the yard of the *yarlu-kuru* widows' camp at Yuendumu as dramatic storm clouds form overhead. A senior woman takes a mobile phone from the hands of a younger woman and thrusts it towards me. The screen displays a satellite image of Cyclone Yasi, which is hurtling towards the Queensland coast, thousands of kilometres to the northeast. 'Look', she urges, pointing to 'ears' on either side of the 'head' of this beast. '*Mamu*' (monster). Later that night Warlpiri children dive under beds in terror as alarming sounds and pictures of cyclone warnings are televised — the television station in question broadcasts to Queensland, but its satellite footprint extends into the Northern Territory, confirming some Warlpiri viewers' fears that the cyclone is bearing down upon them. The following morning old women tell me they prayed through the night for the people of Queensland.

The timing of the trip to instigate research with the Warlpiri drawings coincided with a series of dramatic events — social as well as climactic. A protracted inter-family feud had broken out at Yuendumu, following the death of a young man four months earlier during a drunken fight in an Alice Springs town camp. Three young men were in prison awaiting trial on charges relating to the death. In the aftermath of violent retribution that followed, a group of some 100 relatives of the men in prison had left Yuendumu and sought refuge nearly two thousand kilometres to the south, in Adelaide. Those who remained in the township lived with daily eruptions of fighting, constraints on their ability to move around the town, an increased police presence and frequent arrests of people on charges of assault. Tensions were high with much of the productive activity of the town as well as

school attendance deeply affected. One of the three men in prison is the son of one of my closest friends, herself a granddaughter of the late Jimmy Jungarrayi, the man whose photographic portrait graces the cover of Mervyn Meggitt's Warlpiri ethnography, *Desert People*.

＊　　＊　　＊

Six decades earlier, this is how Meggitt described the circumstances that governed the making of drawings at Hooker Creek:

> In no case had an artist drawn with crayon prior to this occasion. For the most part no informant saw the work of other informants and it can be taken that each informant's response reveals his own ability and ingenuity in adapting to this new medium. No informant placed particular significance on the drawings and if not collected then and there, were discarded.[1]

Meggitt's brief note conveys the feel of a tightly controlled scientific experiment. It is a narrative commonly encountered in descriptions of similar exercises undertaken by anthropologists between the 1930s and 1950s, including the Berndts who collected drawings from Aboriginal people, some of them Warlpiri, at Birundudu Station not far from Hooker Creek, a decade before Meggitt.[2] The producers of the drawings, so we are told, are introduced to the medium of crayon and paper *for the first time*. They are socially isolated to ensure they do not influence each other, allowing the researcher to gauge individual skills and capacities. The purity of the experiment seems confirmed in the men's apparent lack of interest in the objects they produce; on completion the drawings are left to the wind.

Under these circumstances at Hooker Creek, and unbeknownst to them, emerge two 'true artists', Larry Jungarrayi and Abe Jangala, who, Meggitt observed, 'went on drawing for the pleasure of drawing'. Art and pleasure in these tales are the unintended and, as we will see, difficult-to-deal-with consequences of research.

The journey tracked in this chapter looks to situate the Warlpiri drawings through two kinds of response — in the thoughtful engagement of one senior Warlpiri man, and in mid-twentieth century scholarship on Aboriginal visual culture. To understand what Meggitt did and did not do with the drawings he collected and to make sense of his ways of speaking about them requires a consideration of the approaches of other anthropologists in the same period. What kinds of things were drawings and how did their production and circulation contribute to wider understandings of Aboriginal societies and cultures? What questions and interests framed anthropologists' writings on visual production at the time Meggitt was working and what silences remained? In what ways have Warlpiri people responded to and internalised those forms of anthropological attention?

Drawings to make white people happy

If the circumstances of the drawings' production were as tightly controlled as Meggitt suggests, the introduction of their copies to a new generation of Warlpiri image makers six decades later could not have been more different. The community art centres, Warlukurlangu Aboriginal Artists Association of Yuendumu and Warnayaka Art and Cultural Aboriginal Corporation of Lajamanu, each established in the 1980s, provided the institutional conduit and locations for the first public introduction of the drawings to Warlpiri people in early 2011. The concurrent death of a senior man at Lajamanu and the protracted inter-family feud at Yuendumu meant that the potential size of these publics were considerably smaller in both places than might otherwise have been the case. At Lajamanu Stephen Wild, an advisor to the project, displayed images of the drawings for a group of about 40 people assembled in the art centre, by way of a digital slide show. At Yuendumu our attempts to do the same failed as a result of a technical hitch. So, instead, sitting out the back on the concrete verandah among some dozen middle-aged and older female painters who were at work on their variously sized canvases, research assistants Hannah Quinliven, Otto Jungarrayi Sims and I handed around laminated prints of the drawings, arbitrarily selected from a pile.

As we explained something of the context of the drawings' production and the research we hoped to conduct, pictures changed hands quickly, amid expressions of curiosity, delight and some emotion. '*Wiyarrpa*' — dear one, dearly missed — some women greeted the pictures as traces of lost relatives. A short period of conversation followed, questions put to us, who made this picture? What is this? And then one by one the women got back to the business at hand, painting.

At Yuendumu we introduced copies of the drawings to people in various ways and contexts over the following two weeks. For four mornings we pinned a selection of prints to the external walls of the art centre (figure 1), so they would catch the attention of people coming to and from the building. On the second morning a senior man arrived and paused to look at the pictures on display. A retired schoolteacher, sometime painter, ritually active man, Neville Japangardi Poulson is an acute interpreter of Warlpiri history and keen observer of the world at large. His eyes scanned the images briefly. He shook his head and smiled. 'They're only for making white people happy', he told me. When I asked him what he meant Japangardi went on to distinguish 'cheap'

Figure 1:
Warlukurlangu Arts Centre, Yuendumu February 2011.
(Photograph: Vanessa Bertagnole.)

Figure 2:
Larry Jungarrayi,
Yankirri (Emu), Hooker Creek
1953–4.
(Drawing #90, Meggitt Collection,
AIATSIS.)

'A magnificent drawing of a red emu on a green and yellow background. When I pointed out to Larry that emus are not red, he replied that red is an important colour, it's the colour of blood, the colour of ochre. Emus are important birds; therefore emus are red. And that was the end of the argument' (Mervyn Meggitt).

drawings (for example, figure 2) from those he saw as valuable, pointing out several examples of each.

Japangardi's distinction seemed to turn upon two criteria — first, whether a drawing depicted its subject as it was seen or deployed classical Warlpiri iconography, and second, whether it appeared to have been completed with care ('neat work') or was roughly drawn. Japangardi indicated which works fell into each category. I was bewildered by some of his identifications, as I knew the subject matter of several he placed in the 'whitefella' camp to be treatments of important ritual themes. But on reflection I could see what Japangardi was doing, he was distinguishing images that presented objects as able to be apprehended by the European eye from those that followed Warlpiri conventions of picture making, wherein the most potent social-spiritual forces are rendered and understood to lie beneath the surface of visibility, accessible only to those educated in how to read them, most properly in ritual contexts.

In elaborating on his distinction between drawings made to make white people happy and those that were important to Warlpiri, Japangardi spoke about cave paintings and engravings as being the 'really important' pictures. Then discussion ensued between us on the question of quality in production of art objects for sale. Japangardi told me that he was critical of people bringing in 'rough work' to the art centre — boomerangs and other wooden objects that were not finely worked, not properly planed or sand-papered. He suggested 'you can tell by looking at something' whether it has been made 'just for money'. The key marker of quality, Japangardi proposed, is care — one can clearly see when a wooden object or painting has 'truly been cared for' by its maker. The ultimate significance of such an attitude, Japangardi said, was that only when one cares for that picture, really thinks about what one is doing and handles the material with sustained attention, only then can one feel good about oneself.

Japangardi's considered response to the drawings brings a number of issues to the fore. Against Meggitt's suggestion that at least two of the makers were swept up in the pleasure of drawing itself, Japangardi gives us the possibility that a considerable number of these works may have been made to placate the imagined desires of the anthropologist — *these are only for making white people happy*. The segue in our conversation implies that these pictures were not significant; they were not made with care. The challenge of trying to understand the drawings from a vantage point six decades removed quickly emerges as a complicated exercise. Two questions immediately follow: what is it in the style of pictures that makes them amenable to such interpretation? Why would Warlpiri people want to produce drawings to make white people happy? These questions will command our attention across the pages and chapters that follow.

Japangardi's reflection on classification, motivation and care stimulates further questions about what kinds of things the drawings are. Meggitt's comments would have us approach them as pure forms of experimental picturing, acts of image making undertaken within the carefully governed confines of a research activity. But the fact that Meggitt did not write about the drawings suggests they did not sit easily within his research agenda. Japangardi's response displaces the drawings into an intercultural field of interaction, exactly the murky terrain that classical anthropology struggled with and ultimately failed to account for.

The problem of classification

Significantly, on the face of it Japangardi's distinction seems to echo a classification adopted by Meggitt himself. In his discussion of the long series of drawings made by Abe Jangala and Larry Jungarrayi, Meggitt distinguished 'straightforward totemic' designs from those he described as 'representational pictures', 'just pictures', 'simply' drawings, or objects 'just there' receiving the artist's attention.

At the outset we are presented with a quandary in trying to make sense of some puzzling elements of Meggitt's descriptions — are the annotations of this 'simply decorative drawing' (figure 3) transcribed from what Abe Jangala told Meggitt, or are they Meggitt's own interpretations? What is the relationship between text and picture?

Figure 3:
Abe Jangala:
Desert landscape,
Hooker Creek 1953–4.
(Drawing #37, Meggitt Collection,
AIATSIS.)

'Again, the desert. You have by now very sophisticated use of red, yellow and black in patterns to produce massed effects of colour and these for Abe are representing stylised hills and stylised perspective. Naturalistically done are two trees with red flowers. I think these are meant to be a kind of grevillea like the desert version of a silky oak. Again, this simply is a decorative drawing' (Mervyn Meggitt).

Figure 4:
Larry Jungarrayi:
Pulalypa (goanna),
Hooker Creek 1953–54.
(Drawing #52, Meggitt
Collection, AIATSIS.)

Writing of the process of collecting drawings from Aboriginal communities in Central Australia, Charles Mountford observed that men would move through a series of stages, with 'representational' picturing identified as the first, culturally shallow stage of working with crayon and paper.[3] Meggitt recorded the order in which the Warlpiri men made their drawings and this order suggests a different scenario to that described by Mountford. Abe Jangala, like Larry Jungarrayi, produced a series of ritually significant drawings before he began to picture objects 'as they are seen' in the landscape or in ways that Meggitt suggests 'looks good'. Seven of the first eight drawings Abe Jangala made for Meggitt are restricted men's drawings. Moreover, Larry Jungarrayi and Abe Jangala's 'representational' pictures reveal considerable effort in their making. These were not 'quick pictures'. It would seem to follow that they dealt with more than shallow concerns.

Meggitt's distinction between drawings of ritual significance and experimental picturing is also challenged by the subject matter of some of the supposedly insignificant pictures. For example, Meggitt describes Larry Jungarrayi's goanna (figure 4) as 'a *pulalypa* goanna. An experiment in style. The goanna has no particular significance, other than being highly prized food'.[4] Yet once it is known that Goanna is the principal Dreaming of Jungarrayi's paternal country Yarripirlangu, Meggitt's attribution appears bewildering. Rather than picturing something of 'no particular significance' it seems Larry Jungarrayi was experimenting with *alternative way of picturing* significant phenomena. How are we to understand his move to do so?

Meggitt devoted considerable focus to documenting ritual activity at Hooker Creek where senior Warlpiri men revealed to him the ceremonial life at the heart of their sacred world order. On numerous occasions he was exposed to the rich iconography of ceremonial painting with its restricted palette and designs. Yet a concern with visual production featured only as a marginal aspect of Meggitt's interest in Warlpiri social organisation. His ethnography includes little reference to Warlpiri image making beyond cursory descriptions of sacred objects. Yet, Meggitt's documentation of drawings now classified as restricted makes clear that he recognised several layers of symbolism at work in Warlpiri drawings, the most valuable of these lying well below the surface of what could be seen.

The tendency to presume that recognisable objects lie outside of the realm of significance is an unsurprising outcome of an anthropology directed to an appreciation of high culture. As he approached images as a subset of ritual rather than a pervasive visual language, it seems Meggitt's eyes were simply not attuned to seeing the connected significances across the many kinds of pictures the men produced for him. It is only in the audio recording made to document the drawings that talk of 'art' emerges. Consider his description of the drawings produced by Abe Jangala:

> ❧ . . . you'll see that Abe starts off drawing very standard totemic patterns to illustrate particular incidents from myths for points that we'd been discussing. After he had done a number of these you will find that the drawings get slightly wild and representational items such as human or anthropomorphic figures of demons come in (demons with boomerangs) and then beyond that Abe starts to become interested in colour. He attempts, what I think is, to depict perspective. He starts drawing different coloured hills, one behind the other and different coloured soils. And then you get very decorative patterns of snakes and wells and sand hills and bushes. The whole thing becomes particularly interesting because you start to move on to red and yellow and black which would be delightful as patterns for curtains and fabrics. These are very sophisticated indeed. Beyond that you get into straight impressionism of just colour been put together to provide a pattern. So this is one of the very interesting series that I did get of *a man who, starting with his own cultural matrix, artistically moves beyond that in response — I think — to the stimulus of drawing materials that are easy to use and he simply enjoyed this and went on with it.*[5] ❧

The language Meggitt uses to describe the drawings displaces them from the realm of specifically located ethnographic interest to a much wider and less certain field of artistic experimentation.

On closer attention we can read Meggitt as deploying the loose language of a popularised art history. In his commentary on some of the drawings Meggitt steps outside of the anthropological analysis so meticulously maintained across his ethnographic writing. In some instances Meggitt identifies elements of symbolic significance and experimentation at work in the same drawing. He takes these as transitional drawings, moments at which artistic sensibility emerges (for example figure 5). The activity of drawing is seen as propelling these men beyond the imperatives of culture, in the process leaving the anthropologist with little expertise to make sense of their creative work.

Meggitt's interpretive approach seems at one level to echo writing by the Berndts and Mountford, who similarly distinguish pictures they collected of 'just animals' or depictions of 'scenes from daily life', from 'totemic drawings'. He identifies pleasure at work in those pictures that involve experimentation. Tindale and Mountford had similarly reflected upon the pleasure their informants took in using crayon and paper.[6] Berndt, however, is suspicious of interpretations that mark the creative or pleasurable aspects of art production as autonomous of, 'or a departure from, if not a reaction against, traditionalism'.[7] Explicitly against Mountford's claims that one of the motivations for Arnhem Land painting is 'sheer pleasure', Berndt suggests the matter is not so clear-cut. 'Pleasure' and 'creative' are identified as concepts that point to something beyond the social world. If the suggestion is that this 'is a spontaneous, or primarily personal affair, with no social pressures involved, then it is hardly applicable to the Australian Aboriginal'.[8]

The argument implied here is that if innovation, creativity, pleasure, experimentation are attributed to the makers of these works then there are clear consequences for the way we understand their cultural identity. Under the spectre of assimilation, mid-twentieth century opinion had it that Aboriginal society faced an inevitable demise — the older generations of 'full-blooded' Aborigines would die out, younger people would progressively adopt the ideals of mainstream Australia, inculcated particularly through the education system and a wider suite of

Figure 5:
Abe Jangala:
Walpirinpa, Hooker Creek 1953–4.
(Drawing #32, Meggitt Collection,
AIATSIS.)

'This is a place called Walpirinpa, a big hill near Tanami and it's the Dingo Dreaming. On this you can see Abe . . . is depicting a landscape in many different colours and he's attempting by varying his colours to show you perspective, to show you the way the hills stretch away into the distance (and you can see hills laid out in the different colours the countryside takes through distance). This is Abe, I think, starting as an artist.'

Peter Hamilton: 'And the foreground?'

Mervyn Meggitt: 'Topographical detail, I don't know what. It's probably a waterhole.'

Peter Hamilton: 'And this dividing?'

Mervyn Meggitt: 'Wouldn't have a clue. A lot of these things are of no individual significance, they're just part of a general pattern . . . it's there because it looks good'. (Mervyn Meggitt).

government programs. Drawings made 'to make white people happy' would be an inevitable outcome of the transformations that would follow colonisation. There was little scope for imagining a more optimistic and productive interaction between Aboriginal and European Australians and their symbolic orders.

Yet Neville Japangardi's observation unsettles such a vision of seamless cultural transformation. The day after he dismissed the drawings as only for making white people happy, this man came to speak to me again. 'I've been thinking about this some more', he told me, 'and I've changed my mind. Those drawings are important ones. All of them. I'm going to show you why.' Over the next three days he mounted a forceful argument in both spoken and illustrated form for reinterpreting some of the apparently secular or 'cheap' drawings, drawings which Meggitt had described as objects 'just there' receiving the artist's attention, as in fact dealing with Warlpiri high culture, with restricted men's sacred themes. He made a series of vivid depictions of ritual objects in order to make his point. While Japangardi was keen for his drawings to be publicly displayed in the exhibition arising from this research, other senior men disagreed. By way of his actions and the men's response, Japangardi transformed the status of the 1950s drawings; initially dismissed as cheap copies, they were now identified as significant works of cultural creativity with elements that must be withheld from public view.

In order to make sense of Japangardi's interpretive work we must track back to consider how the making and collection of drawings and scholarly responses to these took shape across the twentieth century. While Meggitt's statement that none of the men working with him had previously drawn with crayon and paper might be technically correct, art historical research, as well as Warlpiri memory, conveys a different sense of the situation.

Drawing as exchange in Australia

Drawing, in various forms and contexts, was an integral part of cross-cultural interaction and collecting practices in Australia from the earliest encounters between Aboriginal people and travellers,

missionaries, scientists and others. Both Phillip Jones and Andrew Sayers have written of eighteen coloured pencil drawings of animals and birds made by Aboriginal prisoners and employees of the Darwin prison that were included in what was possibly the first exhibition of Aboriginal visual production *as art* in Australia, 'The Dawn of Art' in Adelaide in the late 1880s.[9] The Deputy Sheriff of Palmerston (soon to be Darwin) JG Knight, who was responsible for this exhibition, similarly included Aboriginal drawings in the display he mounted in the Northern Territory Courts for the great Centennial International Exhibition in Melbourne in 1888.[10] Knight reported that the drawings had received strong positive responses from the visiting public:

> As I predicted, the drawings made by Billamuc, Davey, Jemmy Miller, Paddy, Wandy and other native artists attract almost undue attention, especially from real artists. The other evening Mr. Folinsby, a painter of some renown, after a careful inspection of the original works declared that the executants were all worthy of being made honorary members of the Australian Academy of Arts.[11]

Earlier still, Sayers writes of the Methodist missionary Reverend LE Threlkeld's collection of drawings from Awabakal people in the Newcastle region of New South Wales between 1825 and 1841.[12] Carol Cooper observes that Aboriginal Protector William Thomas collected drawings from Warwoorong and Boonwoorong people of the Yarra River and coastal Port Phillip and Western Port areas, from the 1840s.[13] Four decades earlier, drawings were collected by the Baudin expedition that visited Australia between 1801 and 1803. Stylistically these images were said to share striking similarities with the rock engravings that Aboriginal people of the Sydney area made in great numbers across the sandstone platforms and shelters they occupied around Sydney harbour.[14]

In the period of colonial encounter and the violent dispossessions that often followed, picture making functioned as part of a process of coming to terms with and communicating with others about the rapidly changing world order. Cooper writes that a significant component of the visual culture of

Figure 6:
Johnny:
*Portrait of von Guérard
sketching*, Kangatong
1855.

(Mitchell Library, State
Library of New South
Wales, PXA 606/f.3.)

south-east Australia in the nineteenth century was
concerned with the arrival of whites. On the other
side of the exchange, Sayers suggests that Europeans
collected Aboriginal drawings with two interests in
mind — as sources of information and as evidence of
Aborigines' aptitudes and capacities; in short, their
facility to adapt or be assimilated to European life.[15]
But Knight's recording of the appeal of prisoners'
drawings to the public also hints at another kind of
appreciation which was likely always present at least
to some degree in the visual exchanges between black
and white — a fascination with what these pictures
could provide by way of unprecedented access to
the distinctive ways of seeing, the inner lives, of their
producers.

On occasion drawing was a medium for deeply
interested cross-cultural interaction. In the winter
of 1855 artist Eugene von Guérard spent a month
at Kangatong near Warnambool, at the invitation
of wealthy squatter James Dawson. While painting
on Dawson's property von Guérard met Dawson's
teenage stock keeper, 'Black Johnny'. Two small
drawings, one made by each man of the other,
published in the opening pages of Sayers' *Aboriginal
Artists of the Nineteenth Century*, leave visual traces

of their meeting. Von Guérard's sketch of Johnny is
a clear, confident pencil drawing of the features of a
handsome male face. Johnny's sketch of the painter
(figure 6) is made in coloured pencil; it depicts the
whole physical person, the painter's dress, the detail
of his hat, and captures well von Guérard's bodily
disposition as he sits at work on a chair, legs crossed,
drawing tool in one hand, paper in the other.[16]

Johnny gives special attention to the technology
that mediates the European artist's experience of
the landscape — his chair, his drawing materials,
his dress. Von Guérard meanwhile works in the
tradition of life drawing, focusing his attention on the
precise depiction of his subject's head. In both cases
drawing indicates the distinctive modes of attention
and attempts of each man to grasp something of the
other's view of the world. Sayers observes that this
encounter in drawings is marked by its particular
circumstances.[17] The meeting of these two men was
not accidental; they came together on the property
of Dawson who was renowned for his sympathetic
treatment and genuine engagement with local
Aboriginal people, and from whom Johnny acquired
employment and his European name. Their exchange
stands as a potent example of the reciprocity John
Berger sees as inherent in drawing.[18] Place making
and empathetic regard come together, are realised, in
the activity of drawing.

Australian anthropology and drawing

While the men and women who made drawings
for Meggitt may have had their first encounter with
paper and crayon in 1953, theirs were by no means
the first Warlpiri crayon drawings. At least one man
working with Meggitt, Paddy Japaljarri, had been
at Birundudu a decade earlier when the Berndts
collected drawings. Warlpiri women at Lajamanu
recall drawing for Olive Pink when she camped with
them at Pirdipirdi in the Tanami Desert in the 1940s.
While these drawings seem not to have survived,
a small number of others made a decade earlier by
senior men and young boys at Yunmaji have been
preserved among Pink's papers. Pink, herself an avid
maker of many drawings and watercolours, was so
taken by the pictures she collected from Warlpiri
and Arrernte people that she imagined curating an

exhibition for the Tasmanian Museum and Gallery — she got as far as designing the poster she fancied would promote the show (figure 7).

Anthropologists' requests to Aboriginal people to draw, like the commissioning of paintings, moved Aboriginal visual production onto explicitly intercultural terrain. These were objects made *in and for* the research process. Norman Tindale, who sought advice directly from Spencer on how to go about ethnographic fieldwork[19] collected crayon drawings from Aboriginal people, including from Warlpiri and Anmatyerre people camped at Cockatoo Creek in 1931 (approximately 15 kilometres north-east of the site where Yuendumu would be established in 1946), at Haasts Bluff to the south, then again twenty years later at Yuendumu. The monumental mapping project for which Tindale is best known utilised crayon drawings as an integral part of the process of charting the points of connection between mythological trajectories and territorial boundaries across the nation. Philip Jones suggests Tindale had borrowed the technique from Daisy Bates and Herbert Basedow.[20] In the 1940s Charles Mountford would emerge as the greatest proponent of drawing. An energetic researcher who, despite his lack of anthropological training and uncertain standing among institutional authorities, managed to publish widely, especially on Aboriginal art forms, Mountford compiled a collection of some 1500 drawings from Aboriginal people in Central Australia across two decades of research.[21]

Like Meggitt, early advocates of drawing as a medium of research were keen to stress the scientific framing of the endeavour; Mountford claimed he did not dictate subject or palette — although his field notes suggest this may not have always been the case.[22] 'It was,' Mountford stated, 'especially desired that nothing external should influence the choice either of the subject, the colours chosen or the method of drawing'. The Aboriginal person 'was asked only to make marks (*walka*) on his paper'. Initially 'simple drawings of everyday things of aboriginal life were made, such as kangaroos, emus, trees, camps and waterholes' but after a period of days, confidence was gained and:

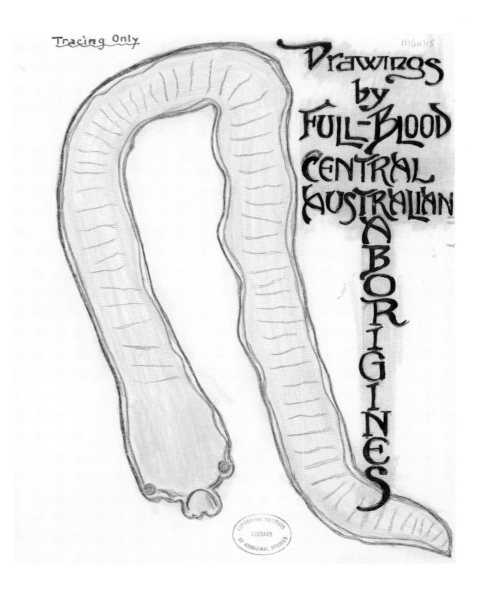

Figure 7:
Olive Pink's poster for the exhibition of drawings she imagined she would curate for the Tasmanian Museum and Art Gallery. Correspondence with the Gallery indicates no such exhibition was mounted. (Olive Pink Collection, AIATSIS.)

Figure 8:
Unidentified man drawing for members of the Tindale Expedition, Cockatoo Creek 1932.

(Screen grab from film footage, courtesy Jeff Bruer, Pintupi Anmatyerre Warlpiri Media Association; reproduced with permission of South Australian Museum.)

> drawings relating to the travels and exploits of the aboriginal's mythical ancestors began to be produced by the older men. From that time onward, no difficulty was experienced in obtaining designs, in fact, it was unfortunate that, as only a limited amount of time was available for interpretation of the detail, and the recording of the data, *the distribution of sheets had to be curtailed*.[23]

The size of the Warlpiri drawings, like those that anthropologists collected throughout Central Australia, was roughly equivalent in scale to the designs painted on ceremonial objects. Cardboard a little bigger than foolscap was reported by Meggitt to be the preferred size. The colours 'generally preferred' were bright red, yellow, blue and black (see for example figures 5 and 9). They were made on artist's paper until stocks were exhausted and thereafter on any material the men could get their hands on — any kind of cardboard, including empty food containers.[24] Drawings for these anthropologists provided portable distillations of particular ritual knowledge as well as an indication of the capacities of their makers. But Mountford hints that his informants took pleasure in this practice of image making, so much so that '*distribution of sheets had to be curtailed*'.

Ronald and Catherine Berndt collected drawings as part of the survey research they conducted across Aboriginal Australia. The Berndts engaged more deeply with visual cultural traditions than many of their contemporaries, their extensive ethnographic experience gave them a substantial handle on the place of art production in the context of social life:

> Traditionally, then, Aboriginal art was designed to communicate ideas to specific persons or groups of persons . . . it served as a vehicle through which a vision of the natural world could be conveyed — a world, however, seen through a mythological screen . . . It was not so much the 'actuality' of a situation with which an artist was concerned. Rather it was the essence, an attempt to obtain the essential elements which constituted a particular idea . . . an artist who depicted an aspect of nature was engaged in transforming it mythically, projecting its spiritual essence into the service of human beings.[25]

Mountford and the Berndts shared a fascination with image making, recognising it as the practice at the core of Aboriginal high culture. They also, along with Elkin, saw art in somewhat strategic terms, as a vehicle that could carry strands of that cultural life in elegant forms into the public arena and shift public sentiment towards Aboriginal people. But as Berndt observed, in the 1950s anthropological work on visual forms remained a marginal interest. He highlighted the 'uneasiness' that characterised anthropologists' approach to art through the mid-twentieth century, a pervasive fear that an interest in art would undermine the 'scientific approach' and draw the disparagement of the time — that one was an ethnographer with 'museum or "cultural" leanings'.[26] Nancy Munn, who undertook an extensive study of Warlpiri visual forms at Yuendumu just five years after Meggitt's research, wrote to Mountford from Canberra in 1956: 'there is no one here who both understands the problem of Aboriginal art (and of art in general) and who knows the Australian field; thus I am relying upon your knowledge and interest for guidance'.[27]

Where a substantial interest in religion or cosmology emerged, the question of image making, or of poetry, was never far away. In 1958, WEH Stanner embarked on a physically gruelling expedition to locate rock art sites in the isolated country of the Fitzmaurice region of north Australia. Stanner was at the time completing his most important work on Aboriginal religion. His pursuit of paintings in the rock country stemmed

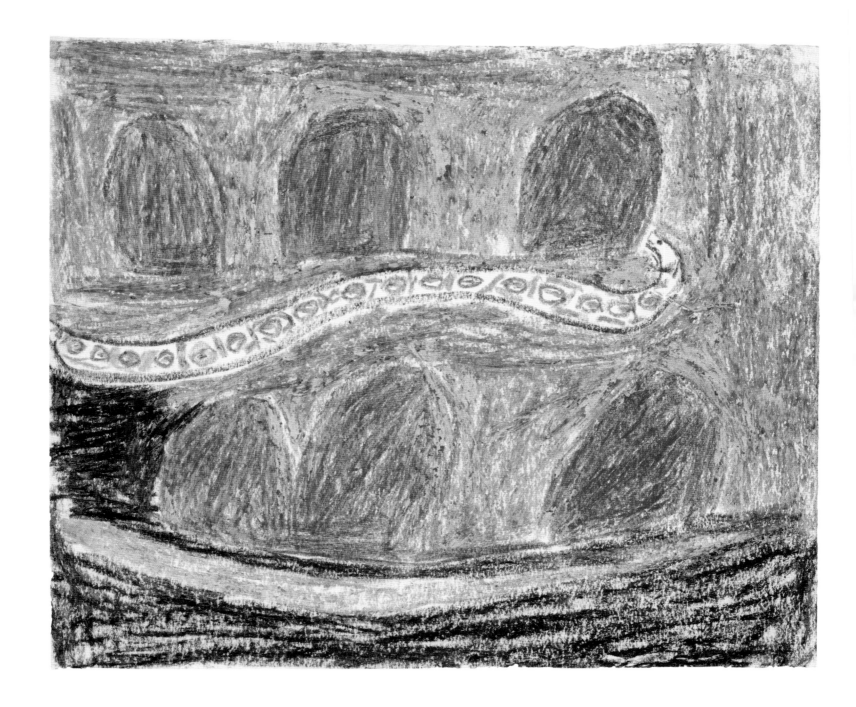

Figure 9:
Abe Jangala:
Luwindji, Hooker Creek 1953–4.
(Drawing #35, Meggitt Collection,
AIATSIS.)

'The sandhill country — dreaming is the *jutia* python snake. The place is called Luwindji. The big red spots indicate red sandhills, the blue indicates the rocks and the black, the bush. The black is here used for objects which because of the distance have no detail' (Mervyn Meggitt).

Figure 10:
Wally Japaljarri:
The Warna (snake) *at Karltarrangu*, Hooker Creek 1953–4.
(Drawing #122, Meggitt Collection, AIATSIS.)

'This is simply concentric circles again with squiggles that indicate two snakes going out looking for their food' (Mervyn Meggitt).

from a conviction that rock art galleries sedimented ancient cosmological truths, providing anchor points in deep time for the ritual events he had been witnessing on ceremonial grounds adjacent to Port Keats mission. Stanner's discovery of awe-inspiring rock art galleries, which he observed had been produced by 'men of genius', led him to pursue (but never achieve) 'a new classification', something more substantial than Mountford's work on the conjunction of myth, art, country that stretched across the north of Australia.[28]

Stanner's engagement with visual culture was fuelled by his aspiration to find a way of writing about Aboriginal religion that conveyed its emotion, drama, poetry and philosophical depth.[29] While he failed to fully achieve it, Stanner's work is indicative of a new humanism that emerged from this critique of

scientism, with an aspiration to produce scholarship that might engage the public imagination and favourably influence national thinking. Introduced to the public, Aboriginal visual culture could help stir a shift in sentiment as part of a growing anti-assimilation movement.[30]

If Stanner's work stands as one version of a new humanistic and humanitarian anthropology emerging through the mid-twentieth century, TGH Strehlow's writings stand as another. In Stanner's all-consuming pursuit of Fitzmaurice rock art lie traces of Strehlow's similarly solitary and obsessive pursuit over a longer time frame of Arrernte song. Strehlow wrote just one paper dealing with classical Arrernte visual culture[31] — possibly because from the late 1920s Arrernte forms had been dramatically displaced at Hermannsburg by the images of Lutheran

Christianity,[32] and then the new ways of seeing the desert produced in the watercolour landscapes of Albert Namatjira and those who followed him. Strehlow's literary tendencies led him to song, to ritual knowledge, to the textual forms of Arrernte culture. Sharing Stanner's disdain for desiccated scientism, Strehlow was driven by a deep poetic appreciation of Arrernte song and philosophy.[33] He revealed his literary tendencies in varied contexts, including in long lyrical field reports paying homage to the country through which he travelled as a patrol officer en route to enquire into the welfare of Warlpiri people; a style that greatly annoyed bureaucrats.[34]

Drawing beyond encounter

What if the Hooker Creek drawings are approached not via the context of their production but as continuous with a universal human practice? This is the way John Berger and Tim Ingold would have us approach them.[35] Berger puts forward the idea that drawing may be a response to an ontological question — where are we? 'Drawing,' Berger tells us, 'is a form of probing. And the first generic impulse to draw derives from the human need to search, to plot points, to place things and to place oneself'.[36]

Every drawing, Berger suggests, 'begins with a similar movement of the imagination'.[37] Line making is movement, movement of a person in an environment. Different writers associate drawing with different modes of mobility. Paul Klee, and after him Tim Ingold, see an affinity of drawing with walking — Klee puts forward the idea of drawing as 'taking a line for a walk'. Berger says drawing reminds him of bike riding. Michael Taussig sees drawing as akin to dancing.[38]

The activity of drawing is the basic enactment of a mimetic or imitative attitude, the making of a sympathetic copy.[39] Walter Benjamin describes mimesis, in its most potent form, as establishing a sensuous similarity between persons and elemental aspects of the environment that is experienced as a flash of recognition, a kind of 'sympathetic magic'. In ancient societies Benjamin suggests the mimetic faculty was a 'life-determining force',[40] a perceptual order that established proximate, empathetic relations between subjects and objects and lay at the heart of acts of creative production and ways of being human.

Writing of the image making practices of north-Central Australia, Berndt appears to endorse the ideas of these writers, describing the 'striking parallel' between the style of image making that enacts mythology, 'the basic designs of spirals and concentric circles' joined by 'meandering lines and/or linked meandering geometric patterns, signifying the wanderings of ancestral beings, the tracks of snakes, or masses of clouds . . . ' and everyday life of the people. 'Art style' emerges, in Berndt's words, 'as a kind of "short hand" summary of the particular society and culture in which it flourishes'.[41] For the visual language or iconography of Central Australia:

> the simple combinations of circles, semi-circles, spirals, concentric circles and lines, expresses the relative homogeneity of their society, the compactness of its structure, the intimacy of relationship among those within it.[42]

In everyday contexts Warlpiri make marks in the sand while talking, they perform stories with these marks, enacting the tracks and movements of people, animals, cars. There is a close affinity between this kind of mark making in sand and dancing which is similarly performed in sand, and often accompanied by singing. As they dance, dancers become their ancestors, mimicking the dispositions and bodily movements, transforming themselves recognisably.[43] This sympathetic magic by which a person establishes and is recognised as having deep and affective relationships with other beings and places lies at the heart of the Warlpiri worldview. It provides the ground from which all forms of image making take place.

Image making, dancing, storytelling are interwoven modes of expression through which relations between places and persons are reproduced and revitalised. In drawing a segment of a Dreaming track the maker enacts the journey, naming the places traversed, imagining the experience of taking the route, the pauses for rest or sustenance, the other beings encountered, the changes in environment and signs of life noticed along the way. The lines made are the traces of gestural movements of the hand as it

Figure 11:
Tess Napaljarri Ross:
Ngalyipi (snake vine) *at
Yarripirlangu*, 2011.

re-enacts the journeys taken by the ancestors along their world-creating paths. There are resonances here with Berger's description of storytelling:

> In following a story, we follow a storyteller, or, more precisely, we follow the trajectory of a storyteller's attention, what it notices and what it ignores, what it lingers on, what it repeats, what it considers irrelevant, what it hurries towards, what it circles, what it brings together. It's like following a dance . . . [44]

Working at Yuendumu in the late 1950s, Nancy Munn observed significant gendered differences in the storytelling gestures of Warlpiri men and women — women's stories focussed on the rhythms of family life, 'the activities of sleeping and eating that are localized in the camp, the separation of men and women for hunting and foraging activities and their reunification at night within the camp. Over and over again', she observed, women's stories 'reiterate the microtemporal rhythms of the daily cycle'.[45] Men's image making practices, on the other hand, utilised a visual language for the 'macrotemporal rhythms of nomadic movement from place to place "following the water holes" (and implicitly the food and game)'. In men's drawings:

> The circular "camp" connotes the vital activities of eating, sleeping (dreaming), and sexuality of the family camp; similarly the track line expresses movement toward and away from the camp, with its connotations of following game and food.[46]

The core marks of Warlpiri men's images, *kuruwarri*, are, in Munn's words,

> visual sedimentations of a movement connecting individual consciousness of bodily being and the outer, social world. They are both the body's interiorized life energy and the 'transbodily' social forms that objectify this energy.[47]

This analysis of Warlpiri mark making in terms of movement and a distinctive social order resonates with what Ingold writes of perception as a function of movement.[48] Ways of moving, ways of knowing, ways

Figure 12:
Bulbul Japaljarri and Clem
Jungarrayi: *Ibis Dreaming at
Yulpawarnu*, Hooker Creek 1953–4.
(Drawing #111, Meggitt Collection,
AIATSIS.)

A collaboration between father and son. Bulbul Japaljarri
drew the central ceremonial design; his son Clem
Jungarrayi added in grey pencil the trees across the
top of the picture and the boomerang-shaped hill to
the left. Meggitt interpreted the division of labour and
the apparently marked difference in visual forms as
appropriate to the men's relative ritual status.

of describing — for Ingold these are parallel facets of the same process. He uses the term wayfaring to describe the 'fundamental mode by which living beings inhabit the earth'. The inhabitant in this context is 'one who participates from within the very process of the world's continual coming into being and who, in laying a trail of life, contributes to its weave and texture'.[49] In Barbara Glowczewski's observation Warlpiri paintings are open, with 'no end, no beginning'.[50]

If wayfaring might be taken as a mode of habitation that can be found across societies, the rise of transport, navigation and print literacy are the technologies that uproot it. With the rise of technologically mediated mobility, Ingold argues, the line is 'gradually shorn of the movement that gave rise to it', and the movement of walking is replaced by assembly.[51]

In the present Warlpiri people contend with the competing claims made upon them by the social forms of wayfaring and transport. The most basic level at which this can be observed is in competing forms of instruction for life.

One afternoon in February 2011, I sit with Neville Japangardi on the concrete porch of his house, watching as he makes drawings to demonstrate his proposition about the 'important' status of the 1950s drawings. His small granddaughter is close by, similarly working with crayon and paper. 'Put your Dreaming', Japangardi tells her, 'only your Dreaming, and your name, your full name'. In the next breath Japangardi goes on to speak at length about his aspirations for his children and grandchildren —

> If they want to live in the world [they] got to go to school, to read and write. Only *kardiya* style . . . you got to try and be with the world. Like, if I went to the moon, you got to get different kinds of clothes to live there. Same in *kardiya* world . . . one thing I've learned is, when you drive a car, you've got to follow that road — you worry about that bump, for tree, fence, rock. But, you cannot control people's minds.
>
> . . . nowadays, I don't see *kardiya* put their effort into *yapa*, only in Catholic schools *yapa* are really taught. Because the Church really helps *yapa*. In government school it's different. They don't give what *yapa* wants, no. In their mind, *kardiya* is frightened. [They are thinking, if] we give more for *yapa*, they might become more powerful. In my days they gave us everything. School in my time was better than today. Because, my age group, you can see today, [we] are not frightened of cities, towns, [we] speak good English, because . . . good teachers . . . taught us . . . Two girls I've got . . . I send them to *kardiya* schools . . . [I say to them:] 'You got to go on time, like *kardiya*. You got to catch the bus, like *kardiya*. You come to school right on time. You make sure you study, you got to study yourself . . . ' [I say to my daughter] 'You will never see me, but you have to learn to catch the bus, read and write, be with them. No matter what *kardiya* are, they're human beings, just different colour. But in your mind, you've got to grow, be clever.' And today when they grow up now, they're not frightened.[52]

By the doubled nature of his actions and words, drawing ceremonial headdress and instructing his granddaughter while engaged in this monologue, Japangardi indicates the two directions in which young Warlpiri people must simultaneously commit themselves if they are to succeed in the contemporary world with a confident and grounded sense of self.

In the 1950s Meggitt observed that white men were regarded as holding 'almost unlimited wealth and power'. This power was seen to have many expressions, including the ability to 'manipulate symbols on paper so that other people (especially Aborigines) are made to act in ways often uncongenial to them'.[53] An appreciation of the power vested in print-literate processes has expanded across subsequent decades and is clear in Japangardi's criticism of recent attitudes observed in government schools, which he interprets ultimately as the wilful withholding of power from Warlpiri people. Part of the story told in this book is about the ways such concerns resonate at the level of cross-cultural image making and interpretation. Japangardi's suggestion that some of the 1950s drawings may have been made *only for making white people happy* is one indication of this complex politics of representation. He gives us a sense of a kind of doubling of mimetic attitudes in the present, as Warlpiri seek strength in two directions, through the re-enactment of ancestral order *and* in securing recognition in the terms of white Australia. Is it possible to be a wayfarer and a navigator simultaneously?

Drawings of settlement architecture, recalled events, experiments with colour and texture lay beyond the interests and conceptual capacities of mid-twentieth century anthropology. Berndt suggests that Central Australian iconography reveals conservatism and traditionalism. But such an interpretation wishes away the world-changing impacts of colonialism. A number of drawings made by Larry Jungarrayi appear to directly challenge such attribution and demonstrate clear engagement with the pressures and interests of his transforming world. Does this suggest that the experiments with form, content, colour (for example figure 13), are expressions of artistic autonomy of the kind that Berndt refers to, indicating the drawings' makers to be emerging as newly cultured individuals? Or is it a matter of needing to differently conceptualise cultural process itself? Is Japangardi right, were these drawings made to make white people happy? If so, was this gesture a case of strategic positioning in a colonial environment? Or was it the case that Warlpiri were more open to the transforming world and the new ways of seeing called out by those circumstances than structuralist readings of their classical forms of image making suggest? If some of these drawings were made to make white people happy, was it a matter of meeting expectations of the more powerful in order to be left alone, or an attempt to engage *kardiya* in serious dialogue? In the words of anthropologist Jennifer Biddle, who writes of more recent Warlpiri acrylic painting, could it be that these drawings were made to engage the bodily senses of *kardiya*, to make us *feel* and thus engender a sympathetic response?[54]

Research with neighbouring Arrernte and Pitjantjatjara people over the same timeframe indicates similar tensions at work between creative practice and the trajectories of scholarly interpretation. In the 1940s Ronald and Catherine Berndt collected drawings from children at Hermannsburg. They noted but did not analyse the influence of school (and Church) in these pictures.[55] In 1940 at Ernabella, Mountford collected some 300 drawings from children, which, to his 'satisfaction',

lacked 'signs of European influence'. He observed that 'school life and the illustrated papers would soon have shown the children new ways of depicting their mental images'.[56]

Writing more recently of the postcolonial adoption of brightly coloured clothing, objects, pastels and paint by members of this same Ernabella community, Diana Young shows that taking up bright colour has 'become integral to Anangu's conception of their own humanity in the contemporary world'. Young writes against the anthropology that identified conservatism as at the heart of visual languages of desert communities, observing that 'new ways of thinking accompanied the novel goods' that were introduced into the Anangu world. These new ways

Figure 13:
Larry Jungarrayi:
Green on yellow spinifex in the bush, Hooker Creek 1953–4.
(Drawing #68, Meggitt Collection, AIATSIS.)

of thinking emerged from the experience of working with new things — 'Anangu have learned virtuosity with colours through technical skill and practices'.[57] Significantly, 'new things' in this context remain relationally dependent upon pre-existing modes of identification; names for colours are drawn from localised, concrete forms — grasses and ochres, for example, rather than abstract categories.[58] But without doubt, Young suggests, the adoption of brightly coloured things has been part of the wider pursuit of stimulants that saw Aboriginal people voluntarily leave behind a nomadic life in the desert for the radically new life on settlements.[59]

Seeing a wider field

If drawing is movement that mimics the ways communities of people move in the world then might it be possible to track related transformations as people take up drawing on paper? Looking beyond the crude expectations of technological determinism, the argument that presumes every adoption of a new technology of seeing will involve a loss of an older one, what can we say about the pictures Meggitt collected that transcend the terms of classical Warlpiri image making?

One possible way forward emerges in Strehlow's writing on Albert Namatjira's paintings of the same period. Strehlow suggests that when landscape painters Rex Battarbee and John Gardner presented Arrernte with the pictures they had painted of their country, the 'old pictorial order' had revealed 'its highest stage of development'. The Aboriginal men marvelled at this new way of picturing their country for its new powers of suggestion — here for the first time they encountered art that had been 'freed of its dependence on the spoken word', an art form that could speak directly and unaided to its audience. They 'gazed with delight upon a world depicted as seen by eyes that have stopped staring at the ground in search of tracks and are looking instead at the landscape itself'.[60]

Strehlow's ultimate appraisal of these new works folds them back into the recognisable structures of feeling of Arrernte ritual forms. These new landscape paintings 'expressed through a pictorial

Figure 14:
Larry Jungarrayi:
Country, Hooker Creek
1953–4.
(Drawing #77, Meggitt Collection, AIATSIS.)

'Back to representationalism again. This is the countryside and it's done in sort of green on yellow on blue. Larry incidentally, unaided, discovered that blue and yellow will give you green. He made that discovery himself' (Mervyn Meggitt).

Figure 15:
Larry Jungarrayi:
Wangarla (black crow),
Hooker Creek 1953–4.
(Drawing #62, Meggitt Collection,
AIATSIS.)

Figure 16:
Larry Jungarrayi:
The malaka's house,
Hooker Creek 1953–4.
(Drawing #63, Meggitt
Collection, AIATSIS.)

medium the same kind of distinctive Arrernte feeling for balance, love of repetition and design, and same sense of rhythm, that give such glorious vitality to their best verse'.[61] In short, in Strehlow's eyes, innovation enabled Arrernte to transcend the frustration of a restricted visual language, allowing painters such as Otto Pareroultja to 'express himself with freedom and clarity', while remaining recognisably Arrernte. In the pages that follow Strehlow's observations, Battarbee remarks that the Ngalia (southern Warlpiri) were watching with some interest the Arrernte adoption of these new ways of painting the land.[62]

In chapters that follow I argue that a modest version of the process of stimulation and renewal Strehlow describes for Arrernte landscape paintings is at work in Larry Jungarrayi's energetic embrace of crayon and paper, specifically in the enlivened mottled green-blue grounds he develops through a series of experimental works and then repeats across a number of his

pictures (for example figures 14, 15, 16). Yet rather than simply enabling fresh depictions of an abiding world order, Jungarrayi's approach to drawing at a time of upheaval was directed not only to picturing ancestral potency, the vigorous charge of country, *but also* the new forms of power Warlpiri were subjected to and struggling to come to terms with.

My argument shares ground with Paul Carter's analysis of Albert Namatjira's practice. Against assessments that Namatjira's painting stood as a successful instance of assimilation, Carter proposes that the Arrernte man had adopted a style that the Lutherans and white community would recognise and make sense of, 'allegorically, as a prefiguring of somewhere else'. Might it be, Carter suggests, that rather than painting the landscape before him, Namatjira was conjuring up the Land of Promise, depicting it recognisably in the iconography of Bible illustrations? Namatjira, Carter proposes, 'not only mimicked Battarbee's style but the European way of seeing the ground in terms of representative images'.[63]

Here Carter might be read as identifying in Arrernte painting the same process of 'making white people happy' that Japangardi first saw at work in the Warlpiri pictures. The interpretive gaze of the European viewer is the ultimate target of Carter's proposition, as he asks why it is that attempts to make sense of Namatjira's works always refer back to his own country, rather than admitting the cross-cultural interactions of which his paintings were born. That we do not see in these works signs of the new religious order the mission imposed on the Arrernte, nor traces of the colourful picture books and pamphlets circulating through the community at Hermannsburg, and rather 'assume that he was painting, say, the MacDonnell Ranges', is a critical element of our own cultural attitude. It 'may illustrate', Carter suggests, 'how blind we are to the cultural blinkers that determine our seeing.'[64]

It is telling that missionaries and artists came to Central Australia equipped with the same technologies of easel and landscape (figure 17). While missionaries went about undermining the power of the ancestral order, Arrernte picture makers found ways to depict their own country *as well as* the Land of Promise, in the same way that Warlpiri people commonly invoke the power of God in concert with that of ancestral beings. In watercolour Namatjira and those who followed him revitalised their own tracts of Arrernte country while bringing into focus newly imagined countries as well. In the process of making these new pictures an enlarged world was brought into being.

Produced two decades before painting for the market emerged as a serious proposition in Warlpiri settlements, the drawings made for Meggitt distil a crucial moment in the history of Warlpiri visual cultural production. Elsewhere, such as Hermannsburg and Yirrkala where missionaries established economic exchange as a central feature of organised work, long histories of painting as a form of explicit and strategic action to engage whites have been observed.[65] The subsequent flourishing of Central Australian painting movements has been explained by Fred Myers in terms of a double set of aspirations: that painting could satisfy local Aboriginal imperatives to revitalise country at the

same time as finding a wider audience and market was crucial to its success.[66] To whatever extent the makers of the Warlpiri drawings might have imagined a future life for their pictures,[67] a wider sphere of reception beyond the here and now, surely their expectations would have been shaped by an understanding of the workings of their own public sphere — whereby images and associated forms of ritual knowledge were (at least before the introduction of photography, film, video) produced for and in the company of specific others, often in tightly controlled circuits of exchange.[68]

Yet by the time Meggitt arrived at Hooker Creek the turbulence of the previous decades had dealt a forceful blow to these circuits of exchange. Violent conflict and displacement but also openness to new experiences of travel, labour and interactions with others were factors in the expanding Warlpiri world and new ways of seeing that were taking shape. Japangardi's proposition regarding the drawings may have been neatly resolved by his change of mind; but his highlighting of unequal and uncertain relations between Warlpiri and Europeans demands further interrogation. So it is to the decades of the 1920s, 1930s and 1940s we now briefly turn our attention, pursuing the backstory to how and why Warlpiri came to be at Hooker Creek on Gurinji land producing drawings for Mervyn Meggitt.

Figure 17:
Religious instruction class, Mt Denison c. 1954. (Photograph: Tom Fleming, courtesy Jol Fleming.)

INTERLUDE II
Olive Pink's picnic

by Olive Pink [1]

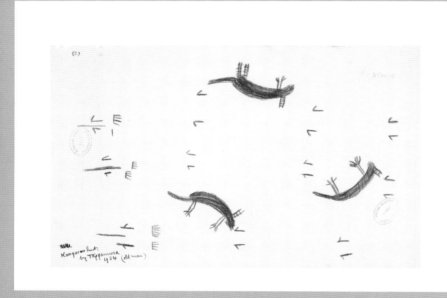

Figure 1:
Jakamarra, 'an old man': *Kangaroo hunt*, Tanami Desert c. 1934 (Olive Pink Collection, AIATSIS.)

It is not every day in the week that one can go for an (almost!) really stone-age picnic. But I was fortunate enough to do so, right out in the country so erroneously called spinifex desert by surveyors and others.

Really (except to the jaundiced eye of the would-be pastoralist — when he comes across it), it is really far from being 'desert'. That is in the conventional sense of that word. Except for the scarcity of water.

But given rain, flowers blossom on every bush. I saw it, so it is more than hearsay.

On the day of our picnic there was a fairly strong cool breeze blowing from the south so (except for my clothed self) all were carrying — although the small boys soon discarded theirs — glowing knobby burnt roots of 'fire sticks', which were blown on occasionally if required but held close to the navel as some kind of warmth most of the time, in their cloth-less state. Most of these bush natives had scars or sore places in this region of their bodies from too close an application of the fire stick.

We started about 11 o'clock and except for the additions I had made — all they had with them were entirely primitive picnic requirements. Fire sticks, yam sticks, two wooden food containers and for the boys toy shields and bark (or broken) boomerangs. The picnic party consisted of a very dignified big man of about 55, who as he had a yam stick as a kind of walking stick, and had my camera slung over one shoulder (in its leather case), looked quite like a retired General at the Melbourne Cup, instead of a picnic in the so-called 'Dead Heart' (which is so VERY <u>alive</u>!), and he one of those termed 'treacherous niggers'.

With him was his recently — within the year — acquired old wife, and her daughter of eight. The woman also had four sons but only one was at the camp and he not with us.

In addition there were three boys of almost the one age, about eight or nine too. One was my Cicerone's eldest brother's son — temporarily with him. Merry imps all three.

Our objective, or rather our original one, was the nearest rocky outcrop in the vicinity — some hills distant and quite invisible from my camp — from where I wanted to take photographs. In fact the only 'hills' I ever could see from there were in the early morning, a range of non-existent hills! (A mirage).

By Wailbri' boys 1933

B'ilda' (a species of lizard)

Figure 2:
Unidentified Warlpiri
boys: *Lizards*, Tanami
Desert c. 1933 (Olive
Pink Collection,
AIATSIS.)

The walk was through spinifex (a course spikey grass [sic] — this for the uninitiated!). How the Aborigines bare legs endure it I do not know. I had on leather leggings, and in another area to the South a white man had to be treated in hospital for septic legs after going about with them uncovered in that type of country. And yet the natives themselves have very soft skin. Or at least to the touch. (I have massaged both men and women so know from experience).

There was no formality about our picnic; we just straggled along as 'the fancy took us'. No sign of the fictional terrified stone-age woman walking behind her 'lord' . . . Who in this instance must have been six foot two or three, and as beneficent looking as he was tall, a man of fine character. They walked along like any white married couple going for a bush stroll — only that for the Aborigines the country they know is more like a town! (Invisible to us but ever present to them). With 'Cathedral' in one spot, historic highways, 'market' gardens: lizard, bandicoot, desert rat and other 'markets' or 'farms'. The difference being that they hunt for their food in these areas instead of buying it. But every one is known of these special grounds.

If the native wants yams today he or she goes straight there — not to the place where she or he looks for bandicoots. (I am writing now of the country they own. Their totemic clan estate — or even those of their near relatives, an associated group of Totemic Estates).

The one small girl and three small boys skipped in front or behind the adults, like white children do, and the boys throw bark or broken ('real') boomerangs at anything or everything — just like white boys use stones.

But with this difference.

Sometimes the dark boy is aiming with the object of getting a meal! It is not all the time just an outlet for too much vitality, as the other's stone throwing is. The nephew of the old man carries a cracked shield (adult) which is really too large for him. But of which he is naturally proud. The other two — less fortunate have sham ones — made from the green bark cut from a white gum tree or a bloodwood. And 'play boomerangs' of the same bark.

45

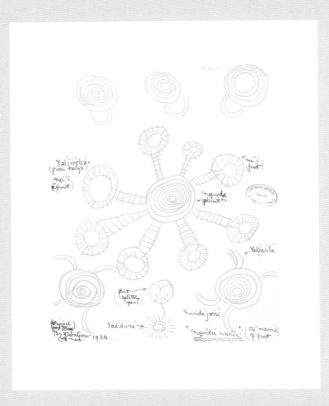

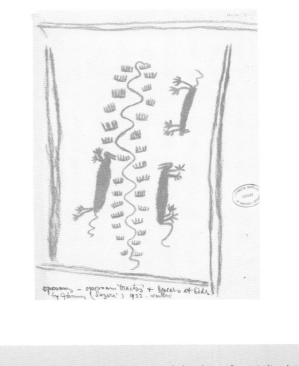

Aboriginal myths relate how the culture heroes — the boys of those days — used these even in the far past Dream Time. So we have that time and the present possibly linked in these little fellows using them in this twentieth century. The first thing we all go over to investigate (I also, trying to look at them would-be-intelligently!) is a Gum Tree where opossum's claw marks can be seen on the tree's bark — and on the ground nearby. But we do not find the toothsome 'tit-bit' we (or more truthfully they) had hoped for. I am usually thankful — although feeling selfish, when the prey escapes if I have to see the killing.

Then we go on to look if there is still any water in a rock hole. We, however, only find a mass of tiny convolvulus and no water or even dampness at all. From there the direction we take leads through more open country — where we see occasional yam plants (the one in this region is not a vine), but no yams. They have either been 'worked' as the deeply scarped pits indicate or are yet too young.

And some have seeds on them. All the time — en route — at any 'likely' spots there is what looks like at first glance, a ritual dance performed by the old wife and the girl and boys. It is however, superb bush-craft, not ritual of any kind.

They zigzag about in a limited area — a kind of run on their heels and stamping all the time, when they see certain tracks on the ground. They are locating the sound (and feel) the direction in which the tunnels run to the underground home of a lizard — prior to digging it out to add to the larder. When they do get a bag it is quite short but rather dainty looking, with a soft skin, pale underneath and coloured on top (if I remember correctly this species is salmon pink on top). But so far, we have had no luck this morning!

Suddenly a pounce! With a large foot thrust into a big tuft of grass, no word spoken, perfect coordination between man and woman but an anxious plunging in of the thin arm and skinny witch-like fingers of the old woman — the release of the foot and a bandicoot is hauled out by the legs, struggling desperately, and its head banged on the ground. The dead body is tossed into one of the two wooden food containers carried one in the other under the arm of the old wife. A first item for the picnic then!

The man brought no boomerang. His wife will provide the luncheon — not without a thought of my assistance too, as he is carrying a bag of mine as well as the camera — slung over his scarred brown back. Very honourable scars, most of them, I found, when much later I enquired and heard of their history. Chivalrous wounds in fact. We now have the nucleus of our 'meat ration' for the picnic lunch. Or so I thought!

My scout tempered his stride to mine most considerately, or I should soon have been left marooned.

After a most interesting detour we arrived back at my camp where my interpreter and his companion were having a . . . holiday in our absence — a hot wash of themselves and clothes and doing necessary patching — they being 'civilized' and so always patching in that clothes tearing type of country. The old man went away smiling with his tobacco gift.

And I into my tent — with a very happy memory stored away of a very smooth running picnic thanks to stone-age standards of courtesy to a stranger in their midst!

Figure 5:
Artist unknown:
Men hunting kangaroo with spears, spear throwers, boomerangs, Tanami Desert c. 1934. (Olive Pink Collection, AIATSIS.)

[B]lindness . . . was organic with the
European mind of the day.

WEH Stanner, *Religion, totemism and symbolism*

Chapter 2
Seeing the Warlpiri

In February 2011 I asked Paddy Japaljarri Stewart, at the time one of the oldest men at Yuendumu (and whose death was mourned in November 2013), to draw something, anything, from memory. Japaljarri quickly produced this sketch of a male and female figure, whom he identified as dingo trapper Fred Brooks and Warlpiri woman Marungali. It is a compelling sketch; two torsos oriented towards each other, the larger figure of the man looking down at the woman who looks on, her mind apparently elsewhere. There is nothing in the facial features or comportment or dress of either figure that makes them recognisable as Marungali and Brooks. The drawing provides no context, no ground for these figures apart from a smear of blue. It is a surprising depiction of the central characters involved in events that led to the deaths of a contested but ultimately unknown number of Anmatyerre and Warlpiri people, a drawing made by a man whose immediate family lived through those events. Japaljarri has simply placed the figures in space and invited the viewer to look upon them.

*   *   *

How do ways of seeing come into being? How are changes in attitude brought about? Olive Pink's 'native picnic', presented as the Interlude preceding this chapter, was probably penned in 1933. Pink's prose may read as quaint, indeed antiquated, from our vantage point eight decades removed, but it is heavily charged with aspiration to cultivate such change, willing her readers to see Warlpiri people as fully human, much closer to themselves than Aboriginal people were commonly seen at the time. Pink had a heightened sensitivity to such matters and research in her papers suggests her 'picnic' may have been written in response to a book she had recently

read, one that adopted a very different way of seeing Warlpiri, journalist FE Baume's *Tragedy track: the story of The Granites*. In this chapter I interrogate Baume's vision before tracing the broad contours of what happened in Warlpiri country between the 1920s and 1940s, the period in which settler–colonial interests fully established themselves in Central Australia. While such an exploration is not called out directly by the drawings Warlpiri people made for Meggitt in the 1950s, it provides the crucial backstory to how those people came to be at Hooker Creek. And as indicated by Paddy Japaljarri's spontaneous drawing (figure 1), as well as others we shall consider later, events of this period remain close to the surface of Warlpiri memory. Further, an examination of the attitudes that took shape in the 1920s is crucial to understanding the complex nature of intercultural relations in the present. In exploring how Warlpiri people were seen by miners, pastoralists, government

Figure 1:
Paddy Japaljarri Stewart: *Portrait of Fred Brooks and Marungali*, Yuendumu 2011.

agents and other strangers who intruded on their country and displaced them to settlements, we gain crucial insight into how Warlpiri people see their place in the world today.

Seeing the frontier, seeing the future

In 1932, news that gold had been discovered at The Granites triggered a rush of prospectors to the northern region of Warlpiri country. Journalist FE Baume immortalised a certain reading of these events in *Tragedy track*, a raw account of the near unbearable conditions under which miners toiled in pursuit of the dream of striking it rich, on what he described as the 'world's loneliest field'. Through Baume's eyes The Granites is cast as an intolerable place — searing heat, calcified water that stank and stimulated a torturous unquenchable thirst, dysentery, an onslaught of flies that were drawn to eyes, ears and mouths from first light until sundown. The Granites was reached via a roughly hewn road 300 miles from Alice Springs, a road punctuated by tree roots, potholes and sharp rocks that jarred bodies, pierced tires and routed engines. In this region's harsh climate, periods of prolonged dry heat gave way to torrential rain that bogged vehicles and washed away tents. The area was inhabited by hostile natives who were known to have killed and would kill again.

Baume's story is not simply an account of the dangerous seduction of gold, a melancholy tale of hopes dashed and lives lost. It is a romantic saga crafted to draw the curiosity of the metropolitan newspaper reader, providing a rare glimpse of a foreign world unknown to many Australians of some of the men and women eking out an existence in these unforgiving environs. The promise of gold was the promise of transformation — of personal circumstances as well as regional and national economies. Thus, The Granites swept up in its promise not only marginal prospectors but federal politicians, bank executives, business men and the postal service, all of whom were represented on the train journey Baume made from Adelaide to Alice Springs. The promise of gold had a lure much sharpened given this was 1932 and the country and global economy were in the grip of deep depression. That year the Australian stock market hit its lowest

level, export income plummeted and unemployment peaked at 30 per cent. Thousands of men were suffering post-war trauma. But that same year the Sydney Harbour Bridge was completed. The Australian Broadcasting Corporation was launched. Nation-making was occurring apace. And through the misty-eyed haze of the desert heat Baume, like so many other writers drawn to explore the inland in this period, appealed to his readers to embrace the centre, a new greenfields of adventure and unknown possibilities.

In recounting the 'tragedy' of The Granites, Baume conjures up the stoicism and heroism that lies at the heart of Australian settler mythology. Through his eyes we learn not only of the precarious circumstances of those who tried their luck on the goldfields, but of the lives of those individuals who subsisted on the cattle stations and settlement blocks along the Tanami Track. Baume reveals that his emotional interest lies entirely with the white settlers. By and large he makes no attempt to know Aboriginal people by their names, either by group or individual, and there are few signs of any kind of interchange with Aboriginal persons as he undertakes his journey up the Tanami. Aborigines in this account are simply 'myalls', dangerous and suspicious blacks who are said to have murdered at least two white men in the area in recent years. Through the eyes of those who furnish him with accounts of their character and misdeeds, Aborigines of the Tanami are savage, cruel, treacherous, unstable.[1]

From within this grim narrative two striking portraits of Aboriginal persons are presented. One is Worraborra, or 'Paddy' as the miners called him. Baume describes this 'giant' of a man coming into the mining camp, a 'lithe, tall, healthy warrior' who:

❝ scrounged from the cook a singlet, a shirt, a pair of elastic-sided boots and a felt hat. With these on he looked a cross between a negro comedian and an old clothes dealer. He panted in the heat, his feet swelled, he was in pain, but he stuck to those clothes. He drank billy tea and it burned his tongue. He gorged on salt beef. He was ill, but *he was aping the white man and boasting to his tribe at night*.[2] ❞

Baume draws wider consequences from Worraborra's actions and the transformation he reportedly underwent after just a few days residing on the goldfields:

> The chances are that some prospector will be murdered one day because all the native boys at the Granites are becoming "civilised" — the civilisation that leads to envy and greed and murder — because a myall wants a hat, a pair of boots or a flannel.[3]

The other portrait Baume presents is of a woman named Alice, 'a lubra of unusual education and intelligence', whom he observed at Coniston Station. Alice was camped with and cooked for pastoralist Randall Stafford, a man infamous for the part he played in the reprisal killings of Warlpiri and Anmatyerre people in 1928 that would come to be known as the Coniston massacres. Baume makes clear his deep sympathy and admiration for Stafford. Alice marks a lone celebrated Aboriginal figure in Baume's account, distinguished by her commitment to Stafford and adoption of the hallmarks of civilized culture. Baume describes Alice as wearing 'a felt hat, a quiet dress, long black stockings and black high boots'. She was said to have saved Stafford's life on several occasions, warning him of the impending arrival of members of 'one of the wildest tribes', her own people, from which Alice herself was said to have been banished. Alice was, Baume remarks in passing, 'especially interested in drawing'.[4]

These two portraits indicate a widely held attitude of the period: Aboriginal people with distinctive cultural ways of living were destined to die out. Moreover, they had to be *made* to vanish as their savage ways stood as a deterrent to civilization and development fully taking hold in the Northern Territory. Baume's description of Worraborra's garish mimicry conveys a sense of the multiple threats that Aboriginal people were imagined to pose to settler society if their separateness was not maintained. Local Aborigines were contaminating — they were infected with venereal disease (seemingly by their own actions), they polluted water supplies and threatened cattle and other livestock. They were crude and lacking in initiative, untrustworthy and likely to murder a man as much as look at him.

Such primitivist fantasies legitimise Aboriginal dispossession from the time of European arrival. Too primitive to develop the land, these poor wretches must be moved aside, they must be contained in ways that would enable the pioneers of the Territory to do their heroic work, unhampered. By the early twentieth century such ideas had been comprehensively laid down and would continue to shape policy making for decades to come: the idea that adult Aboriginal people could be classified as wards of the state, as they were officially declared to be from 1953, presumed they were childlike, unable to look after themselves, requiring protection. The work of researchers was by no means immune to such attitudes. Nicolas Peterson has written of the disjuncture between the compelling photographs Baldwin Spencer and Frank Gillen took of Arrernte ceremonies and their descriptions of 'naked, howling savages' — the 'prevailing framework for understanding otherness' at the turn of the twentieth century was so powerful that these men simply 'could not bring themselves to believe' what their photographs told them.[5]

The story of Alice that Baume presents might on first reading seem suggestive of a more sympathetic attitude, in contrast to the revulsion elicited by the figure of Worraborra. But the two portraits are continuous with a single way of seeing Aboriginal people. Alice embodies the only positive future imagined for her kind: she is celebrated for having left behind her own ways and her own people and for fully adopting the civilised and individualised habits of European Australia. Of particular interest, given the focus of our enquiry, is Baume's observance of Alice's keenness for drawing — presented here as the quiet composed activity that is a hallmark of civilised femininity.

It is unsurprising that the future for Aboriginal people invoked through these portraits is highly gendered. Aboriginal women are imagined as able to successfully make the transition, submitting to the authority and care and reproductive power of white men, showing loyalty to the white boss while acting traitorously to their own people, while virile Aboriginal men are seen as much more problematic, threatening, unpredictable. In this vision Aboriginal people are to be dealt with in one of two ways. They would be segregated until such time as they die out, or successfully lured away from their kin and disciplined in European ways. In the figures of Worraborra and Alice we are presented not simply with images of how Aboriginal individuals encountered in the Tanami were seen, but with an attitude that echoes through the distinct yet related policy positions of protection and assimilation that would be adopted in Aboriginal affairs across subsequent decades.[6]

These portraits also present us with two postures of mimicry and mimesis that are enacted cross-culturally again and again in accounts of colonial Australia — one posture draws revulsion and disparagement, the other is cause for admiration. Worraborra and Alice are flip sides of the same coin. In this brutal and suspicious environment any attempts at crossing the cultural divide to adopt the dispositions of the other were to be treated as yet further indications of barbarity and danger. In Baume's telling, there is no scope for imagining a space of interaction in which Worraborra's performance might have been understood as a good humoured or genuinely interested attempt at getting a feel for white man's ways. Rather, he is ridiculed. He is at once a bad performer, a garish mimic and a growing threat. As Europeans invaded Warlpiri country it is as if an unconscious response kicked in — shared social space was to be undermined in favour of enduring forms of separation or complete absorption.

The cultural politics of self-presentation was a preoccupation among the settler–colonial class. Ann McGrath recounts the tale of Jeannie Gunn who arrived at Elsey Station in the early 1900s. In working out the 'art' of handling black employees Jeannie took to dressing up to 'make herself attractive to the "camp lubras"', explaining, 'The power of inspiring others with a sense of superiority is an excellent trait to possess when dealing with a black fellow'.[7] Above all, the natural order of things, with its presumed racial hierarchy, had to be maintained. On such grounds

there was very little scope for a different kind of space for interaction to open up.

Yet buried in Baume's account are signs that the goldfields and the wider landscape of Central Australia did indeed play host to other, more interested and sympathetic kinds of intercultural relations than those he champions. He writes disapprovingly of the difference in treatment of the natives by the old prospectors and 'the new chums'. The old prospectors are admired for their sternness, their capacity to maintain the upper hand, to issue an order to an Aborigine and have it acted upon promptly. The 'new chums' are said to 'smile at the black' and to 'yabber' with him. In this merry scene, 'the black giggles in response', pleads for boots or tobacco and receives them.[8] The ordered separation is breached.

To what extent is this fiction of separation supported by what we know of events on the ground? A series of observations quickly unsettle Baume's picture — the widespread occurrence of venereal disease among Aboriginal people living proximate to cattle stations and mining camps, Warlpiri women's own fond memories of white boyfriends, and reports that by the late 1920s the proportion of white men to 'half-castes' in Central Australia was 2:1.[9] More bewildering are reports of men such as esteemed Warlpiri leader Darby Jampijinpa Ross returning to work alongside his 'friend', prospector and cattleman Jack Saxby, in the wake of Saxby's involvement in the Coniston killings.[10] Baume's image of stark racial separation unravels further when we learn that Darby was the grandson of Alice, Baume's heroine, and also lived and worked for Stafford on Coniston Station. Such shadowy traces of frontier life fly in the face of the idea that only renunciation of one's kin and cultural imperatives would bring about workable intercultural relations. Something more complicated was going on here.

Among the small number of drawings Meggitt collected from Warlpiri women is a sketchy picture (figure 2) of 'a camp scene at supper time'. Meggitt's annotation does not identify the figure walking toward the fire as female, but her dress clearly marks her gender. One senior man speculated in discussion

with me that this was a drawing of the gathering of 'shooting men' who led the reprisal killings through Coniston. But the presence of a female figure and a certain conviviality that the drawing seems to convey suggests otherwise. The attire of the figures makes clear their status as stockmen. What is less certain is whether these three figures are Warlpiri or mixed company, Meggitt does not say. In the period leading up to the Second World War, the figure of the Aboriginal stockman emerged as a new kind of character in Warlpiri life — the working Warlpiri man who was able to free himself up from the dense sociality of Warlpiri community in order to work alongside *kardiya*, often travelling vast distances together over lengthy periods.[11] This was exactly the relationship Darby and Saxby apparently shared.[12] In the same way that Larry Jungarrayi's picture *The malaka's house* distils a profound change in the Warlpiri universe, so too Elizabeth Napanangka's sketch of stockmen draws attention to significant transformations in Warlpiri experience.

Meggitt's annotation suggests Napanangka who made the drawing was just thirteen years old. The presence of a woman in the drawing begs the question, is this picture drawn from memory? Is it autobiographical? A feature of the early pastoral movement in Australia was the role played by young women who posed as 'drover's boys', dressing and presenting as 'boys' as cover for their true identity as a stockman's lover, a story immortalised in a song, 'The drover's boy', by Ted Egan, balladeer and one-time Administrator of Yuendumu and more recently of the Northern Territory as a whole. Napanangka's 'girl' appears to cart water, bringing a billy to place on the fire for the two seated men. In the situation Egan sings of, and older Warlpiri women recall with fondness and humour, such a woman would have been waiting on her white boyfriend.

The sociality of stock work brought Warlpiri men and white drovers together in new situations of adventure, cooperation and mutual dependence. Between the 1920s and 1950s a new class of Aboriginal worker was emerging and being recognised as pivotal to the viability of the pastoral industry. In the process a social gulf was opening up between two kinds of Aboriginal subjects, those who were productive and those who were dependent and received only begrudging, if any, support from station managers.[13]

Figure 2:
Elizabeth Napanangka:
Stockmen's camp,
Hooker Creek 1953–4.
(Drawing #167, Meggitt
Collection, AIATSIS.)

'Bullocks and blacks don't go together'

From the 1870s pastoral interests and missionaries progressively moved into the Northern Territory, the former seizing Aboriginal land and installing mobs of wandering cattle on hunting grounds, the latter setting up missions and attempting to convert souls. Through the 1880s and 1890s conflicts between Aboriginal people and settlers intensified, with many incidents of injury and death. The character of interactions across Warlpiri country in the decades that followed was significantly shaped in this earlier period. The culture of the frontier was aided by a relative lack of government attention and support, or what MC Hartwig describes as governance at a distance.[14] Such distance went hand in hand with a wider culture that encouraged authorities to turn a blind eye to the violence and results of dispossession, allowing the logic of colonialism to play out.

Economic and moral dimensions were entangled. By 1928, Hartwig writes, 'not a penny' of government money had been spent drilling bores through the Tanami region, the most basic and crucial infrastructure required to subsist in the desert. Under-resourced, with just seven police allocated to the vast region of Central Australia, settlers were often left to mete out their own forms of bush justice.[15] A special kind of Edwardian mateship was said to characterise relationships among the unmarried settlers who took up land holdings in Warlpiri and neighbouring Anmatyerre country. They were steadfast in their support of each other and of one voice when it came to the view that Aborigines should be kept in their place.[16]

The ground of these attitudes in governmental terms had been formalised in legislation decades earlier. A Northern Territory Aboriginals Act of 1910, passed by South Australian parliament in preparation for Commonwealth administration, placed an emphasis on 'rigid protection', with control of individuals defined in racial categories and legislated for as passive recipients of special treatment, much in the manner of prospective inmates of institutions — minors, mentally ill persons, the sick, the aged. Such legislation embalmed official assumptions about Aborigines for a long time.[17] In 1911 control of the Northern Territory passed from South Australia to the Commonwealth. Under an Ordinance of that same year a Chief Protector of Aborigines and sub-protectors were appointed. The Chief Protector had authority over the movement of Aboriginal people and could prevent others from entering their camps. He could take an Aboriginal person into custody and was deemed legal guardian of every Aboriginal child under 18 years of age.[18] Employment of Aboriginal people was subject to the approval of protectors. In the early 1920s the Commissioner of Police simultaneously held the position of Chief Protector of Aborigines. In 1927 the duty passed to the Government Health Officer.[19]

Through the 1920s as more people moved into Warlpiri territory pressure grew on the arid country's limited resources. A prolonged and severe drought increased the already tense competition between pastoralists and Aboriginal people for access to water and hunting grounds. As the situation grew increasingly desperate through this period there were many reports of attacks on cattle and settlers across the Centre.[20] Pastoralists argued that 'bush' Aborigines made cattle 'wild and restless', fretful and, when they came upon their scent, panic-stricken.[21] Warlpiri in particular were feared as violent, cattle-killing nomads.[22]

Since the height of the drought in 1926 Walter Braitling had occupied important Warlpiri country at Pikilyi, which contained the only significant permanent water sources in Ngalia Warlpiri territory. To the east cattle were grazing all the 'good country' along the Lander River. Hartwig argues that there is 'plenty of evidence' that by 1928 Aboriginal people in the southern Warlpiri and Anmatyerre regions were starving.[23] As tensions grew, rumours circulated among Randall Stafford's 'working boys' that 'the people from the west were going to come in and oust the white man from the country'.[24]

Well-placed observers noted at the time that Aboriginal people were killing stock as retaliation for being driven away from water sources as well as to restore 'self-confidence and prestige'.[25] Through this period there were several well-publicised incidents of whites being acquitted over the deaths of Aboriginal persons across inland and north Australia. In one

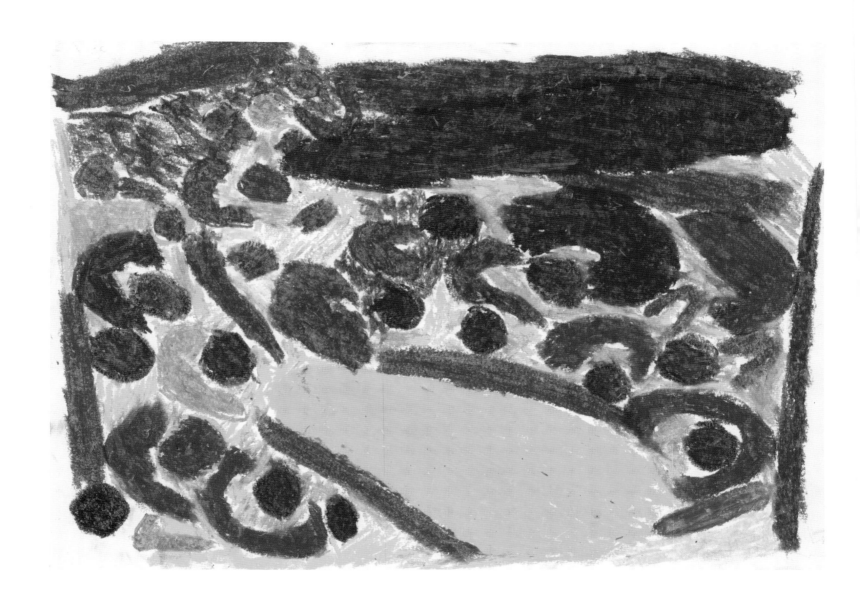

Figure 3:
Liddy Napanangka Walker:
*Remembering the scene of her
father's shooting*, Yuendumu 2011.

particularly horrific case Aboriginal man Lalili (or Lalliliki) died after having been dragged by a wire tied around his neck for 600 metres behind a station vehicle. The owner and head stockman of Mount Cavanagh Station were charged but later acquitted of the murder after the prosecution successfully argued that the skull tendered as evidence of the atrocity could not be conclusively identified.[26] Meanwhile in Warlpiri country, several Warlpiri were arrested at The Granites in association with the death by spearing of a miner. They were charged with murder and taken to Darwin to face court, but discharged for lack of evidence. With their case dismissed these men were turned loose on the outskirts of Darwin. Their families never heard from them again. Others were seized by miners on the goldfields and simply vanished.[27]

All of these tensions over access to resources and conflicting moral codes came to a head at Yurrkuru on the Lander River in August when Ngalia man Kamalyarrpa Japanangka, also know as Bullfrog, murdered dingo trapper Frederick Brooks in retaliation for Brooks' failure to act honourably in an exchange of the services of Japanangka's wife, Marungali Napurrurla. In the reprisals that followed, Constable George Murray teamed up with local pastoralists and black trackers and led a mounted and armed assault through Anmatyerre and Warlpiri country, killing an unknown number of men, women and children. Warlpiri people figure many scores were killed, with suggestions that entire family groups were mown down. Petronella Vaarzon-Morel has recorded detailed memories of survivors, including the recollections of Rosie Nungarrayi:

> ❝ The policemen came travelling this way, north, after the shooting time. They came from Pijaraparnta. That's where they came upon a lot of people and slaughtered them, our relatives. This happened when I was a young girl.
>
> After that, the policemen came to Liirlpari [Whitestone]. Again the policemen killed some people there. Then the policemen travelled west to Patirlirri [Rabbit Bore] looking for people. Again they killed a lot more of our people . . . For a whole day they went around shooting at people. They shot them just like bullocks. They shot the young men coming out from bush camp where

they'd been initiated. People were shot digging for rabbits in our country, Muranjayi. They were getting *yakajirri* berries, yams and *wanakiji* tomatoes. Those people they shot had nothing to do with it. The policemen shot them for nothing. Again they killed a lot of men there. No-one breathed. All were dead . . . [28] ❞

Liddy Napanangka Walker's drawing of her recollection of the scene of her father's shooting (figure 3) is as compelling and chilling as Rosie Nungarrayi's testimony. The setting is a protected area of well-treed country bordered by two large rocky outcrops. The large yellow and brown ovoid shapes in the foreground and along the top of the picture are rock formations, the roundels in pink, brown and blue are trees. Napanangka has drawn her father standing and then fallen to the ground after he was shot; he appears in the drawing as two figures, one curved and one straight in deep green in the mid-left of the picture. Napanangka herself appears as the small green arc on the furthest right hand side of the canvas, crouching with another child near a tree and being shielded by several adults depicted as larger pink and brown arcs. She did not see the man who shot her father, so he is not drawn.[29]

The initial court hearings into the killings, held in Alice Springs in September 1928, were conducted by Constable Murray himself.[30] The Presiding Magistrate committed two Warlpiri men to stand trial under an Act that was no longer in force. Referred to Darwin, the matter was heard by a Judge who was outraged by proceedings to date and a jury promptly returned a not guilty verdict. A subsequent Board of Inquiry produced a whitewash, it found 14 of the 'twenty and a number of others' shootings that had occurred were 'justified'. The actions of police parties were found not to be punitive expeditions; there was no provocation that 'could reasonably account for the depredations of the aborigines and their attacks on white men'. The Inquiry went on to criticise the bad influence of 'unattached missionaries', referring to Annie Lock who had been particularly outspoken about the Coniston killings, as well as the influence of 'inexperienced settlers and semi-civilized natives on myalls'; the inadequate means to deal with Aboriginal crimes that often went unpunished; and 'escaped prisoners from Darwin' who 'wandered about causing unrest and preaching revolt against the whites'. Finally, the Inquiry found 'there was no starvation among the natives of Central Australia, there being ample food and water for them'.[31]

The most telling aspect of this Inquiry was that the *very question of whether the shootings were justified* could itself be posed and answered straightforwardly. Here was a clear-cut assumption that Aboriginal people were not subject to the same laws of justice as non-Aboriginal people, that they were lesser human beings. The Inquiry was clearly aimed not at delivering justice but in confirming the evolving social order of the outback.

Running through submissions to the Inquiry was the wider idea that regardless of the findings, 'pacification' of the 'natives' was required to achieve successful colonial settlement. In his representation the then Chief Protector of Aborigines, CH Noblett, who was also at that time the Chief of Police, made clear he saw a certain inevitability to the killings,

they were acts of violence undertaken in support of a greater good: colonial nation-making:

> I deplore the killing of the natives as much as anyone but, *at times, it cannot be avoided and the same thing has happened in the settling of all new countries.* Lessons must be taught to people who murder others . . . Settlers are very fair to the natives but stock and natives do not and will not thrive together . . . If this industry is to be settled with a healthy white population, we must give the pioneers every protection both for themselves and their stock *otherwise the country must be left to the natives who have not the slightest idea of development in any shape or form.*[32]

Tim Rowse suggests the official failure to censure violence had a profound consequence, it meant that the '*possibility* of violence underlay all transactions'. Others put this more strongly — the understanding of violence as a necessary and legitimate element of colonisation, articulated clearly by Noblett, is

Figure 4:
Ruth Napaljarri Oldfield:
Recalling the different directions in which people fled, following the killings, Yuendumu 2011.

analysed by Henry Reynolds as part of a pattern repeated across Australia that constituted nothing short of war.[33] Approving the kind of pacification Noblett described as unavoidable, Brian Bowman, who had run Glen Helen Station south of Alice Springs, told Hartwig in 1960 that 'good' relationships emerged after the Coniston shootings.[34] In the wake of the killings Warlpiri fled in many directions (figure 4). Some never returned.

While it is possible to distil a clear settler–colonial moral code at work in the shootings and subsequent inquiries, a more complex set of relationships existed on the ground. Not all pastoralists were hostile. A number of them gave shelter to Warlpiri people fleeing the terror of the killings. Nor can we overlook the unlikely friendships between men such as Darby Jampijinpa Ross and Jack Saxby that were sustained over decades. The banal normality of rough justice would become a familiar feature of life in the desert.

In subsequent decades Warlpiri would be exposed to the tough love of a number of significant authority figures known for their 'hard' ways who were nevertheless genuinely respected. In remembering these men, such as Baptist missionary Tom Fleming who oversaw the welfare of people residing at Yuendumu for twenty-five years from 1950, people often refer sympathetically to his experience as a prisoner of the Japanese on the Thai–Cambodia border as explanation for how a person could be capable of brutal treatment of others. The idea of a good man who was also a hard man took shape on the frontier.

From the 1920s Warlpiri people were in various ways 'looked after' by pastoral families and other *kardiya*. They in turn incorporated *kardiya* into their own social world, bestowing names on them, sharing significant experiences, in some cases forging long-lasting friendships. The children of pastoralist families often grew up among Aboriginal companions, speaking their language and learning their ways of interacting.

Displacing the Warlpiri

In the decade that followed the First World War, returned soldiers were prominent among the

applicants for crown leases in the Northern Territory. One successful applicant was Walter Braitling, who sought and was granted a lease over 2,500 square miles of land that centred on Pikilyi, an area containing the most precious places in Warlpiri country: valuable permanent sources of water, a network of natural springs and water holes, with surrounding country replenished by these waters sustaining rich hunting grounds and sources of other foods. Pikilyi was literally an oasis in the desert. In Warlpiri reckoning it was also home to Warnayarra rainbow serpents, ancestral beings with exceptional power and moral authority.

Braitling's arrival makes an unrivalled impact upon the Warlpiri to the present, and so is worth dwelling upon in some detail. As told through the collaborative research of Lisa Watts and Simon Japangardi Fisher,[35] William Walter (Bill) Braitling, born in rural Queensland, had served in the Australian Imperial Force during the First World War, had seen action in France as a driver and gunner and was decorated for meritorious service in 1919. On return from the war he went droving through north Australia and in 1921 acquired a lease on an area of land adjacent to the large stations of Victoria River Downs and Wave Hill.

In an act that indicates how heavily the weight of the war hung upon the shoulders of those men who returned, Braitling named his leasehold Passchendaele, after the site of the battle that killed many of his mates. The moral structures of the battleground would indeed be carried across to the frontier, and loomed large in the cultural attitude that men such as Braitling would foster for the outback — an 'us' versus 'them' mentality, a sense among the settlers of themselves as an embattled minority, besieged by savages who threatened the very underpinnings of civilised life as well as by the government that failed to provide the basic infrastructure, security and other forms of support they requested. This was a vital element of the heroic sentiment among settlers who saw themselves as either 'helping to build the British Empire or . . . pioneering Australia for the Australians'.[36] Yet there are suggestions that Braitling's moral compass indicated a narrow field of integrity — it is said that he was effectively forced to leave his Passchendaele holding by the managers of neighbouring properties as a result of his dishonest dealings with their stock.[37]

In the lead up to the Second World War the price of wolfram — a mineral widely used in the production of ammunition — was rising and Braitling had discovered rich wolfram deposits under his lease. Prospectors working his fields complained of being under-paid and under-fed.[38] From the late 1930s he commenced stocking the property with sheep, goats and cattle and from this time Warlpiri access to their precious reserves of water and sacred places was severely curtailed. Braitling lured people to the area of Luurnpa-kurlangu proximate to the Mt Doreen homestead, establishing a ration depot from whence he could draw them to work in the wolfram mines. To enforce his prohibition on Warlpiri access to the water holes he enlisted his two 'half-caste' offsiders, Wilson and Cusack, to act as wardens of Pikilyi and chase away any persons who ventured near the springs. Rations were withheld and on a number of occasions people were flogged for transgressing this directive.[39]

Meanwhile cattle were allowed to roam freely, drinking directly from the large waterhole as if it were a trough, polluting the source and causing irreparable damage to the series of water holes and soakages. For this Braitling was criticised not only by Warlpiri people, but also by the 1935 Pastoral Investigation committee, which was unimpressed by his approach to water management.[40] From the 1940s he established a series of irrigation systems that took water from the spring and redirected it to watering points for cattle. And in an action Warlpiri would have found astonishing, Braitling placed a tank directly on top of Yapuwariji spring. It was subsequently blown away in a violent storm. In Warlpiri explanation the wrath of the 'cheeky' Warnayarra from the Eva Spring had been ignited. Infuriated, the spirit being 'hurled the tank away from the water'. This were subsequently replaced on the northern side well away from the spring itself.[41]

Now dependent on European supplies, Warlpiri moved sporadically between the goldfields and Mt Doreen, often leaving hostile circumstances for those that were only marginally better. Through the 1920s and 1930s the campaign to establish Aboriginal reserves in the region progressively built on the back of missionaries' and patrol officers' observation of the distress Warlpiri were suffering as a result of poor living conditions and maltreatment at the hands of pastoralists and miners, and growing hostilities over access to water in the midst of a severe and deepening drought.

After the brief rush petered out by late 1932, only a small number of prospectors remained working on The Granites goldfields. Fleeing Braitling's brutal regime, Warlpiri had been progressively moving into the area to take advantage of the permanent water supplies the miners had established and the promise of food. As the rush subsided prospectors wandered off through Warlpiri country in search of places that might yield greater promise. As they went they disturbed numerous Warlpiri places and precious water sources.[42] The two prospecting families that remained at The Granites had an increasing need for Warlpiri labour as the population of white itinerant workers moved on. It was in the decade after the rush that Warlpiri congregating in this area emerged as a significant problem for government and missionaries alike.[43]

In 1936 Cleland estimated approximately 150 people were regularly moving around in the vicinity of The Granites and Tanami mines. In patrols made in 1943 and 1944 Sweeney saw approximately 100 people in the area.[44] By this time the situation for Warlpiri at The Granites was close to desperate with 'almost everyone ill from pneumonia, gonorrhoea and related diseases'. Working men received rations that were insufficient for themselves and provided nothing for their families. Desperation was leading to fights over food. Police Constable Vic Hall visited and found the condition of people living there shocking. People were starving and naked, with no clothes or blankets provided.[45] Further south Patrol Officer Sweeney reported meeting a group of people near Ethel Creek with extreme cases of venereal disease, yaws, malnutrition and wounds from physical assault.[46]

It was sometime in this period that Abe Jangala (figure 5) recalled having first visited The Granites:

Figure 5:
Left to right: George Jampijinpa Cook, unidentified man carrying emu, Abe Jangala holding rifle, Hooker Creek c. 1953. (Photograph: Mervyn Meggitt, Meggitt Collection, AIATSIS, N390.128.)

Some of my people were working in the mine and they were given food for that . . . For about one and a half years I worked in the mine in Granites, and then I went back east, to the bush again to see my father, going off on my own, coming back again. I learned more about our business and then I was a real man, around 21 years old. Again I went to the Granites to work in the mine and I had a look in Tanami too. But I didn't like Tanami, after a few days I was back in Granites again where I worked for another few weeks before returning to the bush'.[47]

Abe Jangala's narrative reveals nothing of the distress observed by patrol officers but indicates the contrasting imperatives of the time — as Derek Elias observes, while some Warlpiri gave themselves over to the hard work in the mines, others kept away, with curious persons such as Jangala moving consciously between the two settings, with periods of hard work digging ore, carting water and gathering wood alleviated by long sojourns spent with family in the bush, subsisting on bush foods and immersed in ceremonial life.[48] Yet gradually but surely through this period the Tanami Desert, which Warlpiri began to refer to as 'hungry country', was being emptied out.

Driven to the mines and ration depots on the southern and northern edges of their country by drought and increasing dependence on *kardiya* supplies, Warlpiri were leaving the Tanami.

In 1940 missionary Laurie Reece observed Warlpiri working in dangerous circumstances in the mine at Mt Doreen and 'wondered what the reaction of a body such as the Antislavery League in London would be'.[49] Harry Jakamarra Nelson told of a team of Warlpiri men pushing a wheelbarrow of wolfram from Mt Singleton mines to the depot at Luurnpa-kurlangu, a distance more than 70 kilometres. There were accounts of women having sex in exchange for food. Braitling was notorious for chasing off men and boys, so he could gain access to girls. Patrol officers were struck by the absence of girls at some of the places they visited. There was a desperate mood among those who remained.[50]

In 1944 Sweeney was told of people 'being forbidden to wander about or camp on the natural waters in the country used by cattle', especially at Vaughan Springs. He was also told of three occasions when Braitling tied up and flogged Aboriginal men following transgression of his orders.[51] The following year Braitling was charged but found not guilty of causing grievous bodily harm to Jimija Jungarrayi, who he had helped raise from a child. At the conclusion of these hearings Braitling's lawyer made sweeping allegations against the Administrator, patrol officers, police, Baptists and Lutherans, even Doc Evatt for conspiring to drive him off his lease.[52]

Meanwhile Warlpiri were heading south to Haasts Bluff, where rationing had commenced in 1941. By 1945 Battarbee reported there were more than 400 people camping in the vicinity of Haasts Bluff, including 'Ngalias from the north'. Many of these people were suffering trachoma and yaws. Patrol officers continued to track the harsh treatment of Aboriginal people in the region, including one incident in which police investigating the death of an Aboriginal man chained seventeen prisoners and witnesses including women and children and forced them to walk more than 300 kilometres to Alice Springs to face court.[53]

The mounting pressure for reserves

Braitling's story conveys the worst excesses of the settler attitude — his disregard for the needs and concerns of Warlpiri people mirrors his disregard for the country and its vital resources.

If the attitude of settlers such as Braitling and chroniclers such as Baume stands for one kind of attitude to Central Australian Aboriginal people, camped with Warlpiri people in Ngalia country at Yunmaji in 1932 and 1934 and a decade later just a short journey from The Granites at Pirdipirdi, was amateur anthropologist Olive Pink, who could not have seen the situation through more different eyes. Pink was forthright in her protests against incidents of Warlpiri exploitation and suffering. She campaigned not only in favour of a reserve that would centre on Pikilyi, but also for Aboriginal rights in minerals to be recognised. Braitling and Pink spent considerable time exchanging their equally passionately held views regarding the future of the Warlpiri. Their correspondence tracks the steady demise of initial friendship into outright hostility. Braitling had a vision for a 'movable reserve' on which Warlpiri people would essentially follow the seasonal cycle of food supply and cattle could then follow them into the areas they vacated.[54] Pink meanwhile campaigned for a secular reserve. In her view, 'the Warlpiri needed good, well-watered land from which doggers, prospectors, pastoralists, missionaries and police would be excluded and over which they should hold mining rights'.[55]

Pink was interested to make a study of Warlpiri ritual life but her time in the desert was also marked by her cross-cultural aesthetic attitude. In making her home at Pirdipirdi in 1943 Pink did more than pitch a tent and set about studying the ways of her hosts. She brought with her seeds of favourite flowers that she planted and tended, maintaining a meagre garden in the searing arid conditions. She also bestowed names of her beloved homeland Tasmania on newborn children — Tasman, Risdon, Hobart, Derwent, for boys and the names of flowers for girls, Poppy, Rose, Iris, Marguerite, surrounding herself with 'echoes of the English cottage gardens of Tasmania and

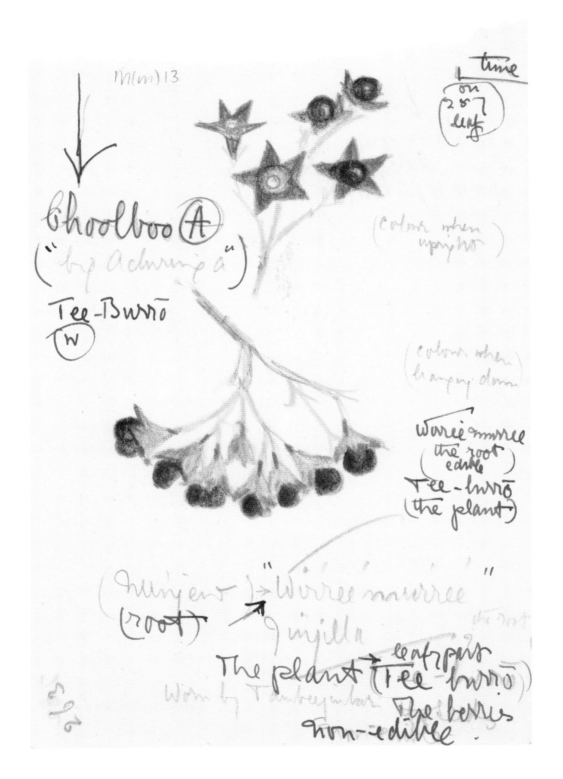

Figure 6:
Olive Pink made many drawings
of native flora during her time in
the desert (Olive Pink collection,
AIATSIS.)

her greatly respected teacher, Miss Poppy'.[56] Pink's Warlpiri hosts in turn named her Talkinjiya. She drew (figure 6) and cultivated native plants and in later life established the botanical gardens in Alice Springs that are maintained in her name. Notwithstanding her obstinacy and accounts of her rudeness to persons black and white, from Pink's time among the Warlpiri emerges the idea that different forms of beauty might coexist rather then settle in an antagonistic or hierarchical relationship.[57] She is remembered by Warlpiri today as the first campaigner for land rights and as a person who 'truly loved' Warlpiri people.

Pink's autonomy and uncompromising views were unusual. The work of other anthropologists in Central Australia from the turn of the century until the 1950s reveals the extent to which research, governmental activity, development agendas and ways of seeing were often entwined — albeit in diverse and sometimes discordant ways. Both Herbert Basedow and Baldwin Spencer were willing appointees to the role of Aboriginal Protector in 1911, but both resigned very soon after taking up these positions following disagreements with administrators.[58] In the decades that followed anthropologists were employed as government patrol officers (TGH Strehlow was the first for Central Australia),[59] less often they were contracted commercially. In 1946 Ronald and Catherine Berndt were employed by the Australian Investment Agency (Vesteys) to advise the company that operated cattle properties across the Northern Territory on how best to capitalise on Aboriginal labour. Deep tensions and incompatible aims characterised that relationship.[60] Marginalised from the academy Pink perhaps never found herself in a position to contemplate compromising her autonomy.

The campaign to ensure that the interests of pastoralists prevailed continued apace, with advocates voicing their claims loudly in the lead-up to the establishment of an Aboriginal reserve for Warlpiri. In January 1946 Braitling wrote to the NT Administrator, objecting to a native settlement in the vicinity of a stock route on the grounds that it would pollute stock water supplies and pose a threat to the safety of the travelling public en route to The Granites. He urged that no further land be granted to Aboriginals, and that, rather, land grants be dedicated

to the 'urgent needs by [sic] returned soldiers and others who intend to settle in the Northern Territory'.[61] Braitling's letter was followed promptly by an application by an ex-serviceman for a grazing licence over Block 1150, the area earmarked for the Aboriginal Reserve that would ultimately become Yuendumu settlement.[62] It was rejected. In March 1946 the solicitor acting on behalf of the Bokhara Pastoral Company wrote to the Administrator, protesting against the planned Aboriginal Reserve on the grounds that the block was too close to land intended for the breeding of imported and 'exceptionally costly' Karakul sheep. He complained to the Administrator that proximity to an Aboriginal Reserve would be 'disastrous' and the future of a 'valuable Australian industry' would be put at risk.[63]

Others argued that the establishment of an Aboriginal reserve close to stock routes and a major public road would constitute a 'distinct set back to the development of this area'.[64] The voice of the Chief Veterinary Officer was particularly loud — 'I am not prepared to have an arbitrary piece of land deducted for this purpose and cannot agree to a decision in regard to a reserve unless the country has been examined and suitable ground found'. He argued that the stock route from which Aboriginal people should be excluded should be one-and-a-half miles wide. The Director of Lands agreed.[65] Government files reveal much interdepartmental jostling over the allocation of land and its resourcing, and a sense of clear hierarchies in which the interests of pastoralists and livestock took precedence over the needs of Warlpiri people.

The steady move towards the establishment of a reserve and settlements for Warlpiri went hand in hand with this wider agenda for development of the interior. Both government and pastoralists saw reserves as achieving two related outcomes, the control of Aboriginal people and placement of them in close proximity to stations whereby their labour could be drawn upon as required. By 1945, just prior to his appointment of Ronald and Catherine Berndt, AS Bingle, the manager of Vesteys, wrote to the NT Administrator proposing that the agency could

Figure 7:
Mervyn Meggitt and
unidentified men
looking out to Warlpiri
country from Ngama.
(Photographer unknown,
Meggitt Collection,
AIATSIS N390.07.)

❛ co-operate with the Native Affairs Department in controlling and educating the blacks in the settlement to be of some commercial use . . . it will be necessary to have the natives in this settlement well under control, otherwise they are likely to roam about in the cattle area on the Wave Hill boundary and seriously interfere with the station working of the cattle.[66] ❜

In 1945 a temporary ration depot was established at Tanami in an attempt to deal with the deepening distress of people in that area — but poor water supply necessitated its relocation to The Granites. In anticipation of increased mining activity, the depot and Warlpiri were relocated again in May 1946 to a new site east of Mt Doreen at Rock Hill Bore, soon to be Yuendumu settlement. As it became clear that a second depot was required in the northern Tanami area plans progressed towards the establishment of a reserve on a soon-to-expire pastoral lease about forty miles south of Wave Hill.

At a distance removed politicians and bureaucrats grappled through this period with proposals for dealing with 'the half-caste problem' and the 'drift of natives into towns'.[67] By 1940 the ideas of protection were giving way to a new vision for Aborigines: social advancement, assimilation. In Central Australia government settlements would provide the setting for this new project of improvement. The Warlpiri themselves would be enlisted in the building of these settlements as part of the process of crafting new subjects. It was a vision that government and pastoral companies competed to articulate and realise, not always with shared interests in mind. In early 1946 AS Bingle wrote again to the Director of Native Affairs on the matter of improving the living conditions of natives on stations:

> We have decided we will erect a building at each of our station properties which can be used by those natives who are fed at the station kitchen as a dining room and general shelter when they are working and waiting about the station. We will also endeavour to improve the sanitation and further, we will try and organise the natives into building some better type of dwelling, we providing them with material . . .

There was never any question of the intended goal of such provisioning:

> We have pointed out to you that on many of our stations we are very short of native labour. We have had our anthropologists, Mr and Mrs Berndt, making a survey on the possibility of picking up the right class of native labour and generally settling native families on those stations encouraging the natives to breed and generally content themselves. We, of course, know that the nomadic habits of many of the tribes, are somewhat against them settling for long in one place. We feel that with proper treatment we can expect to encourage the natives to settle down somewhere in a convenient place with the existing natives that are now on our station properties.[68]

The reply from the Acting Director of Native Affairs urged the Agency to apply their proposed arrangements to all residents, not only workers — in the interests of nutrition, camp hygiene and cultivating improvement; 'it would teach them to use plates, cutlery, etc and would go a great way towards improving their future way of life — particularly the children'.[69] He discouraged the idea of providing building materials to the natives to erect their own shelters; 'very few have experience in building and the final result will probably be unsightly buildings and ruined material'. Bingle wrote back, miffed at the government's presumption to know better:

> I am certain that there is a limitation to what can be done in civilising aboriginals and putting them on the same level as a white man. We have illustrations from the troubles which have occurred in America and Africa. There the natives are intellectually of a much higher standard that [sic] the aboriginal. I repeat that the aboriginal is very adapted and satisfied in the environment of the cattle industry and it is for the benefit of that industry that they be encouraged to remain in it. We have very definite ideas as to satisfying our natives and we know that the Minister on his recent trip to the Territory considered the natives on the stations appeared to be very happy in their surroundings.[70]

In October 1946, the Director of Native Affairs wrote to the Administrator recommending the establishment of a new Aboriginal Reserve at Catfish.

In this new formation, there was a
gap between things and words, a
gap that could be crossed by seeing,
a form of seeing that would dictate
what it was possible to say.

Nicholas Mirzoeff, *The right to look*

Chapter 3
The superintendent's window

In mid-July 2013 I receive a phone call from a friend at Yuendumu, a woman in her early fifties, seeking my financial assistance to purchase food. Such calls are not uncommon, but have become more frequent in recent years as cost of living pressures have intensified. My friend tells me she has been forced to move from her house and is now living in an old 'tin house' on the edge of town, with no power, no running water, no toilet or shower. She has to walk some 200 metres along the road to use the bathroom in an overcrowded house occupied by relatives. Staying with this woman are three grandchildren under the age of eight whom she currently cares for. It is mid-winter, temperatures these past days have been unseasonally cold for Central Australia and it is raining. The tin house leaks. Housing availability at this time is worse than ever as, finally, after years of conflict between the Yuendumu community and the federal government, traditional owners have signed a forty-year lease, triggering a release of funds that will enable thirty new houses to be built and a further sixty to be renovated. In order that this work commence people whose houses are listed for demolition or renovation have been instructed to move out and establish humpies for themselves for the duration.

✳ ✳ ✳

If drought and conflict over access to water figured as crucial factors in Warlpiri being forced off their lands, the problem of water was not resolved with their relocation to settlements. Warlpiri would have marvelled at the technologies brought by Europeans to extract water from the ground; Larry Jungarrayi's drawing of the windmill and water tanks at Hooker Creek attests to this watchfulness (figure 1). Yet the

Figure 1:
Larry Jungarrayi: *The windmill and water tanks at Hooker Creek*, Hooker Creek 1953–4.
(Drawing #61, Meggitt Collection, AIATSIS.)

windmill's reliance on wind and batteries, both of which were often in short supply, meant the problem of water remained constant. In early February 1952 the situation was grim. A senior Gurinji man from Wave Hill arrived at Hooker Creek and presented himself to the superintendent as a rainmaker. He explained that he needed to stay in the area in order to make rain. The superintendent directed the man to return to Wave Hill as soon as possible.[1] In this place being newly carved out of the desert only one approach to the environment would find legitimacy.

Larry Jungarrayi made his drawing of the windmill and water tanks for Mervyn Meggitt less than a year after he and 130 of his countrymen were trucked into the new settlement. Twenty-five people had first been brought to Catfish ration depot in 1948. They were soon moved to the better-watered site at Hooker Creek. In return for rations these people were required to work, to help construct the settlement that the government decreed would be their new home. At the place of *Kiwinyi Jukurrpa*, Mosquito Dreaming, this meant gruelling physical work in a tough environment.

The settlement daily journal diligently kept by the superintendent provides glimpses of the challenging conditions under which people toiled — the climate was characterised by hot winds, lack of rain and extreme heat, followed by nerve-wracking periods of stillness which brought the settlement's windmill-powered water supply to a halt. Bitterly cold winds whipped through the settlement through the winter

months. Flies and mosquitoes were often thick in the air. The ground to be cultivated was rock-hard. In October 1952, six months before the Meggitts arrived, Superintendent Petherick reported a 'sour and unwilling' attitude of Warlpiri residents in the seasonal build-up. Reluctantly he allowed a group of 'eleven boys and lubras' who had been working without break for more than twelve months to 'go on holiday'. Two months later, four more workers who had been labouring for more than two years were permitted to follow.[2]

In carving out of the arid northern Tanami Desert a new settlement that would meet the needs of hundreds of Aboriginal people a raft of urgent tasks required attention — constructing houses, shelters and stores; securing water supply; digging lavatories; clearing and maintaining an airstrip; establishing vegetable gardens; carting fire wood; planting trees; servicing vehicles and bores; cooking meals; tending the sick and injured; cutting posts and digging holes for fence posts; and mustering, branding, killing and butchering cattle. Hard labour lay at the heart of the new settlement regime with its two interrelated goals — to construct a viable place for Warlpiri to live and produce a newly disciplined and work-ready Warlpiri subject. Essential to this process were not only methods of work but elaborate reporting practices. The superintendent was required to report daily on all the work done, the movements of people, incidents of illness and injury, status of infrastructure and levels of supplies, and on any other issues of significance. These reports were read, summarised, commented upon and filed by patrol officers and bureaucrats in Alice Springs and Darwin. The twinned practices of labour and print-literate surveillance were lodged at the heart of the post-war governance of Aboriginal people.

Larry Jungarrayi's picture *The malaka's house* (figure 2) makes clear that Warlpiri were watching the evolution of this new regime with heightened attention. As Tess Napaljarri, the adopted daughter of Larry Jungarrayi's brother, observed astutely as she looked carefully at this picture, the window Larry Jungarrayi drew is not an empty window, but a window with light shining behind it — light that is perceptible to those outside the house, light

Figure 2:
Larry Jungarrayi:
The malaka's house,
Hooker Creek 1953–4.
(Drawing #63, Meggitt
Collection, AIATSIS.)

created by kerosene lamp, light that signals night-time activity. 'He used to see this window close up from where he was staying, or maybe walking around. Maybe every morning he walked past this house?', she speculates. The window separates the space and nightlife of the superintendent and those in his company from the lives of Warlpiri people. What to make of this curious new structure? Meggitt reports that Larry Jungarrayi was most taken by the fly screen that surrounded the verandah of the house, but the drawing also hones in on the grid-like structure of windows as well as the interior space beyond. What went on behind that well-lit window? Napaljarri implies that we should interpret this drawing as a marker of Larry Jungarrayi's curiosity with white man's ways. While government authorities went about implementing new forms of surveillance and accounting, Warlpiri people returned the gaze, watching the ways these new strangers did things, with intensity.

In *The right to look: A counterhistory of visuality*, Nicholas Mirzoeff shows distinctive visual regimes, or ways of seeing, to be integral to the precise ways in which forms of authority have historically been enabled and legitimised. 'Visuality', he writes, 'sought to present authority as self-evident', it 'supplemented the violence of authority and its separations, forming a complex that came to seem natural by virtue of its investment in "history"'. Mirzoeff stresses that visuality is not confined to processes of perception, but rather 'is formed by a set of relations combining information, imagination and insight into a rendition of physical and psychic space'.[3] In the governance of Central Australian Aboriginal people, the remote settlement was the ground where this constellation of practices came together.

In pursuing the story of how post-settlement life unfolded for the Warlpiri, Larry Jungarrayi's drawing of *The malaka's house* guides our enquiry. This drawing, I will suggest, comments on *the act of picturing itself* at a time when the very shape and parameters of the Warlpiri world were in turmoil. It bespeaks the quiet watchfulness of an acute observer; it invites meditation on the weight and scale of change that Warlpiri people were experiencing at multiple intersecting levels. Perhaps most

surprisingly, given the weight of Warlpiri experience of the previous decades, this drawing withholds judgement on what these processes would amount to. Larry Jungarrayi's drawing, I will argue, is a potent enactment of what Mirzoeff terms 'the right to look', a way of seeing that stands outside of and refuses the categorising terms of the dominant visual regime, a way of seeing characterised by openness, a way of seeing that might give rise to a new attitude.[4]

Visuality, for Mirzoeff, is a *complex* of practices that involves classifying by naming, categorising and defining. A visual regime separates and segregates groups of people so classified to present them from cohering as political subjects, and it makes this separated classification seem right and hence aesthetic. Here Mirzoeff draws upon the work of Franz Fanon, who observed that this process generates an aesthetic of respect for the status quo, the aesthetics of the proper, of what is felt to be right and hence pleasing.[5] Mirzoeff highlights the intersection of modes of governance, forms of surveillance and the production of particular kinds of subjects. Such a conceptualisation is compelling for our enquiry as it allows for attention to be drawn to both governmental and Warlpiri regimes of visuality. It also provides a compelling prism through which to analyse the archive that details the practices by which the Warlpiri were made visible and governed in the mid-twentieth century. But a close reading of this material also reveals countless instances of bureaucratic failure and brings the stark certitude of 'regimes' into more murky and circumspect terrain.

Of humpies and houses — desert dwellings and the clash of ontologies

As the previous chapter made clear, many of the Warlpiri men and women transported to Hooker Creek would not have been strangers to European-style work regimes. Through the 1920s and 1930s growing numbers of Warlpiri were enlisted in stock work, domestic labour and mining. But the development of settlements involved productive work of a new kind: the construction of a new built environment, new structures that Warlpiri themselves would erect and occupy. In an earlier era the idea

Figure 3:
Bessie Nakamarra Sims: *Dreaming and 'might be houses'*, Yuendumu 2011.

Nakamarra described the central elements of this drawing as 'Dreamings' in unspecified country. The rectangular blocks around the top and bottom sections of the drawing, she suggested, 'might be houses'.

of Aboriginal people being 'savages' was marked by them having 'no idea of permanent abodes, no clothing, no knowledge of any implements save those fashioned out of wood, bone and stone . . . '[6] From 1946 onwards at Yuendumu they constructed houses, ration depots, hospitals, cleared roads and airstrips, made and tended vegetable gardens, cooked and cleaned.

Asked to draw something recalling experiences of her early life, an elderly woman since deceased, Bessie Nakamarra Sims, seems to envisage the world-making significance of housing being brought to Warlpiri country; she places Dreamings at the centre of her picture (figure 3) and surrounds them with block-like objects that she tells me, 'might be houses'. The composition of the picture conveys a sense of these objects fencing in the Dreamings.

In Warlpiri reckoning the house is the architectural structure that stands symbolically for the coming of *kardiya* and the new world order of settlement

that followed. Warlpiri were bewildered when they first encountered houses, complete with solid walls, roofs, windows, flyscreen. The windbreaks, shade trees, bough shelters and other temporary forms these desert-dwelling hunter-gathers erected could not have been more different. Purpose-built to cater to the needs of a highly nomadic existence, Warlpiri architecture supported life on the ground, as well as frequent and spontaneous movement from place to place.[7]

The predominantly flat spinifex plains of the Tanami Desert are characterised by open spaces with uninterrupted vistas across great distance. A need for clear perceptual access to the environment went hand in hand with a nomadic life in the desert; indeed, it was a matter of life and death. The primary requirement of Warlpiri structures, as observed by architect Catherine Keys,[8] was to maximise the capacity to see what was going on around them. Wind breaks and shelters were erected with short walls that provided necessary protection while enabling occupants of a camp to sense changing weather patterns, monitor children playing, register the approach and departure of people and other species, and observe myriad changes that occurred with the passing of time. Traditional shelters were not lived *in*, in the manner of a house, but rather *around*.[9] Camps were neither closed off nor separate from the immediate surrounding environment.[10]

The flexibility of shelters, which could be erected in a period of hours, met a wide range of needs, allowing people to move with ease into or out of shade, catch or escape breezes, position fires, control sanitation, find privacy and get close to or distant from others, responding to both social proscription and personal need.[11] From such a disposition, to move into a house, Joseph Reser observes, is to lose control over one's surroundings and circumstances. A roof gives protection from rain but cuts out morning sun and the view of the night sky; walls prevent breezes and impede a clear view of the environment around the house. Concrete, unlike earth and sand, leaves no clear trace of visitors, human or otherwise.

Beyond these elements of bodily experience, to move into a house is to put oneself at the behest of an entire new regime of utility and service provision; control over the most basic necessities, of water and light, comes to rest in the hands of others, the new kinds of entities established and authorised to deliver such resources — government agents, power and water authorities, local or regional councils. In the present this loss of control is signified by the entity of the Power and Water Authority card. In Warlpiri townships the setting sun gives rise to a flurried rush around town, as members of households whose cards have expired attempt to garner the funds to purchase a replacement before shops close and darkness descends. Failure to do so means no light, no electric stove, no hot water, no television, no electrified forms of entertainment.

The movement of people from humpies to houses was a central pillar of government policy and aimed to draw Aboriginal people into new kinds of living arrangements more closely resembling the nuclear family. Housing aimed to make Warlpiri sedentary subjects, increasing their visibility to government

Figure 4:
A *yujuku* shelter with Kingstrand huts in the background, Hooker Creek c. 1953–4. (Photograph: Mervyn Meggitt, Meggitt Collection, AIATSIS, N390.131.)

authorities, while curtailing their own requirements for visibility. At Yuendumu and other places the superintendent's house was the only house in the township erected on stilts. Still standing at Yuendumu today, now occupied by the manager of the art centre, the 'step house', as it has become known over the years, indicated the power of its inhabitant, who had a crucial vantage point from where to observe the movement of people and many of the goings on through the central areas of the town.

As Warlpiri became increasingly accustomed to making their camps in relatively close proximity to station homesteads and later alongside ration depots and government settlements, they drew European materials they found to be useful into their dwellings, combining these with tree branches, spinifex, broken-up termite mounds and other natural resources that were to hand. Corrugated iron and canvas tarpaulins were particularly highly valued for their capacity to keep out rain and rebuff winds.

The first generation of houses constructed at Yuendumu and Hooker Creek were Kingstrand corrugated iron houses, minimal iron shells nailed onto wooden frames. Erected as a material cornerstone of the first stage of the civilising process, these small one-room houses came without floors, insulation, running water or ablution facilities, internal structures or furniture. At Hooker Creek

Figure 5:
Ormay Nangala
Gallagher: *Different
ways of life*, Yuendumu
2011.

Nangala described this
picture as incorporating
two ways of life: orange
desert with humpy and
waterhole, how her
family used to live; and
nowadays, living in a
house and watering the
grass around the house
so it is green.

Warlpiri 'boys' were enlisted to erect the 'tin houses'. As part of this work they were also instructed to demolish and remove the 'old huts in the native camp' that Warlpiri occupied, to make way for the new housing. A dozen or more young men were involved in this construction in early 1953 while others dug holes for lavatories, cut posts for fencing, tended the vegetable garden and mustered stock. By February 1953 fifteen huts had been erected with another fifteen frames assembled.[12]

These 'hot little tin houses', 'rubbish houses', or 'toy houses' as Warlpiri derisively refer to them today, were built with little regard for the provision of basic comfort in the searing, arid environment of the Tanami Desert. They are remembered as being unbearable, oven-like on hot days and for their tendency to blow over in high winds. During Meggitt's time at Hooker Creek and to the bemusement of the superintendent, they remained unoccupied, with their 'residents' using them as storage rather than shelter. Warlpiri did however enthusiastically incorporate the new building

materials into the construction of their humpies — when an excess supply of iron was taken up for these purposes the superintendent was most unhappy and promptly instructed workers to reclaim 'all good iron' from the Warlpiri camp.[13] By April 1954 the superintendent reported that still 'only a few' huts were being used. That same year a dramatic whirlwind had toppled one of the huts, buckling it into 'a tarnished mess of iron and steel'.[14] Following Pholeros and Lea's compelling critical history of housing construction in the Northern Territory[15] we might identify the Kingstrands as 'non-houses', copies or simulations of houses that lack the material elements required to make real the qualities usually associated with a house — provision of shelter, safety, wellbeing.

For several years after the settlements at Yuendumu and Hooker Creek were established, Warlpiri camped at a distance from the town's central area. Two men in their sixties recall this early, mutually sustained, separation of domains at Yuendumu:

❝ . . . in those days, the houses were just a few
and only *kardiya* were living in houses. But us,
we used to live out in the camps or humpies. We
never used to sleep close to the houses or the
settlement at that time. We used to be a couple of
miles, or at least a fair way from the settlement
and the houses.

    . . . *kardiya* doesn't want *yapa* to come in close up
because they might steal something. And *yapa*
doesn't want to come in . . . [16] ❞

These reflections convey a sense of the mistrust that
pervaded relations between Warlpiri and government
authorities during this early period of settlement.
Note that this separation was also crucial to Warlpiri
maintaining social and physical space for the meting
out of their own forms of authority and modes of
interaction, beyond the gaze of the superintendant
and settlement authorities. The first people to occupy
European-style houses were seen as courageously
embracing not simply new architectural structures,
but a new and emerging world, with unknown
consequences.

From the 1960s the majority of Warlpiri people
followed their forebears out of camps and into the
subsequent generations of housing government
introduced. Yet what transpired over the next forty
years was by no means a seamless accommodation
of European-style living practices. Associations with
country, place of birth and the residential locations of
other kin continue to influence the ways people reside
across the township — North Camp, West Camp,
East Camp and South Camp identify not simply
geographic locations around the settlement, but often
various forms of dynamic orientation of those who
reside there.[17]

The 'problem' of housing stands in the present as
an intractable, vexed issue in Warlpiri townships as
it does across remote Australia. Metaphorically, the
house and all of the issues that attend to it marks
the conundrum of remote Aboriginal people's place
in Australian society. At one level the dilemma can
be expressed in deceptively simple terms: Warlpiri
want houses, yet they also want to continue to
live in ways that follow their own imperatives.
Anthropologist Yasmine Musharbash has written

about the divergent cultural logics associated with
European houses and Warlpiri camps. Drawing on
the writings of philosophers Gaston Bachelard and
Martin Heidegger, she suggests the camp and the
house stand for two different ways of figuring the
ontologically determining series building–dwelling–
thinking. In her ethnography of Warlpiri camps at
Yuendumu, Musharbash contrasts the ontological
salience of the house in European terms with the
Warlpiri concept *ngurra*. This term, often translated
as camp, conveys multiple ways of denoting place
and a people's relationship place. *Ngurra* carries
sentiments that contrast profoundly with mainstream
Australian values and aspirations — in the elegant
words of WEH Stanner:

❝ No English words are good enough to give a
sense of the links between an Aboriginal group
and its homeland. Our word 'home', warm and
suggestive though it might be, does not match the
Aboriginal word that may mean 'camp', 'hearth',
'country', 'everlasting home', 'totem place', 'life
source', 'spirit centre' and much else all in one.
Our word 'land' is too spare and meagre. We can
scarcely use it except with economic overtones
unless we happen to be poets.[18] ❞

Ngurra also indicates a high level of mobility between
places regarded as 'home', and mobility itself as a
crucial element of place-making. As a number of
the drawings made for Meggitt illustrate, creation
of ancestral places and mobility are intertwined
processes (see for example figure 6). Places are often
indicated by the movement of ancestral figures,
marked by the tracks left as they passed through
an area. Places were created by the actions and
interactions of ancestral beings who in a final act
would sediment themselves in the environment,
take themselves into the ground or sky, or proceed
elsewhere on further world-making journeys. In
the arid environment of the Tanami, the people
descended from these energetic ancestors are
similarly constantly on the move, looking to where
the next best source of sustenance or adventure might
be found.

In a compelling collaboration for the 1994 Adelaide
Festival, the late Warlpiri artist and senior law woman

Figure 6:
Alecky II Japaljarri:
Wampana (Wallaby Dreaming)
coming into Chilla Well area from the
south, Hooker Creek 1953–4.
(Drawing #97, Meggitt Collection,
AIATSIS.)

Dolly Nampijinpa Daniels and artist and Yuendumu Women's Centre coordinator, Anne Mosey, produced an installation *Ngurra (camp/home/country)*. The work consisted of two living spaces placed side by side — the exterior of a *yujuku* humpy and an interior sitting room of a European house. Each woman assembled her living space from materials brought from home — Nampijinpa brought *kurrkara* desert oak and *wajarnpi* ironwood branches from her country Warlukurlangu, Mosey populated her space with precious objects made and inherited. In her interview for the exhibition catalogue Nampijinpa spoke with Petronella Vaarzon-Morel about the complex distance between *yapa* and *kardiya* living arrangements; while the *yujuku* humpy indicates the specific places and ways in which *yapa* have historically lived, it also indicates a *lack* of many things: furniture, cupboards, telephones, cleanliness:

We Aborigines have nothing. We have a few things like branches, blankets and a small swag. A white person has plenty of things, everything. White people only know about reading papers to get news from faraway places. They have a lot of books and papers for themselves. They don't have Dreamings. They haven't got them, nothing. Aborigines have sacred things. In that way they are rich. They know their Dreamings. Now, today, they've got paper, and they know about liquor. Well Aborigines got that from the White people.[19]

However, the installation showed such disjunctures need not mark the limits or possibilities of cross-cultural relations. In a creative friendship deepened over many years, Mosey and Nampijinpa came to know each other through the material objects and domestic spaces each maintained and inhabited and through journeys made together. In so doing, as Vaarzon-Morel has observed, they produced an enlarged intercultural kinship.[20]

In the post-settlement era Warlpiri have deployed *ngurra* to flexibly respond to changing circumstances. Musharbash writes that by the late 1990s *ngurra* was articulated in eight distinct yet related ways; to denote shelter, a place where one sleeps, the idea of home (which usually invokes township of residence), ancestral place, ritual divisions, time, country and

Figure 7:
A photograph of Warlpiri in Adelaide parkland that circulated in online news reports, from *Adelaide Advertiser*, 9 March 2011, courtesy Newspix.

Figure 8:
Wendy Nungarrayi Brown: *My house at Yuendumu*, Yuendumu 2011.

Nungarrayi pointed out that, in making this picture, she has 'borrowed' the tree to the left of the house from her neighbour's garden — it improves the picture and makes a shaded place where she can imagine her family will sit.

all the elements of the world that pertain to country. At one level the suggestion is that this concept is elastic enough to incorporate the various forms of association — from persons who camp together on any particular occasion, to the co-residents (including non-Aboriginal people) of a town. But as Warlpiri have embraced elements of European styles of living they have also expanded their repertoire of possible living arrangements that might be strategically made under pressure. In the wake of the Northern Territory Intervention public debate over the crisis of housing in remote communities moved onto new ground, as the federal government sought to stimulate aspirations for private home ownership among people living on land held under inalienable communal title. In some places the new emergent policy program of normalisation was interpreted as a direct threat to Aboriginal ways of living. As one man from Yuendumu put it at that time:

> We don't know anything about mortgages . . . if I don't pay off my mortgage I might as well go and build a humpy, *yujuku*, where I don't have to pay mortgage . . . [21]

This way of identifying *alternate* forms of shelter as able to sustain fundamental needs pointedly communicates an imagined ability to sidestep government attempts to force Warlpiri people to change the way they live. In the face of perceived threats to those aspects of life Warlpiri value highly, this man suggests people may choose to move to a humpy, to an outstation, to places and forms of residence that are imagined to exist beyond the reach of the state. In certain circumstances, as Pincher Jampijinpa told anthropologist Michael Jackson at Lajamanu in the early 1990s, 'a house is just like a big jail'.[22]

As people move from place to place they carry their ways of dwelling with them. When more than 100 members of an extended family fled to Adelaide in late 2010 following the death that sparked the feud at Yuendumu, they stayed more than a month, moving between different forms of state-sponsored accommodation. After several weeks of mobile accommodation one group set up camp in a suburban park. Media attention to Warlpiri 'refugees' reported Adelaide residents' alarm at the perceived risk to hygiene and security posed by this group camping on public land. Affronted by the public ways in which Warlpiri conduct their daily and nightly affairs, local politicians instigated the eviction of the group and their return to Yuendumu. Warlpiri remained largely oblivious to these complaints and the short-lived media frenzy. Returning to Yuendumu they spoke of how well they had been 'looked after' by the people of Adelaide. On arriving home the exiled group occupied three adjacent houses on the south-eastern edge of Yuendumu, as physically distant from the 'other family' as possible. The many small sleeping camps established each evening at nightfall circled the three houses, creating security in numbers for those alert to the possible signs of violent retribution that might occur at any moment. Coexisting with the heightened tensions was a pervasive sense of pride; if nothing else these troubles had stimulated an intensification of family interaction and rejuvenated sense of honour.

As this episode suggests, in the present, houses and camps are rarely distinct options and more likely coexist and permeate each other[23] — people erect camps in the vicinity of houses, they sleep, cook and eat outside houses, using rooms designed as bedrooms predominantly for storage and safekeeping, while living areas are given over to accommodating large numbers of sleepers with mattresses laid out in rows. People move between and abandon houses in favour of temporary camps, especially in the wake of the death of a resident, but also for myriad other reasons. Nevertheless, the business of prioritising and attending to the community waiting list for new houses is a high order interest. Housing meetings in the township attract high attendance and highly charged debate.

Technologies of settlement

One of the ways in which senior people mark the distinction between *kardiya* and *yapa* ways of dwelling is that while *yapa* live on the ground — *walyangka* — *kardiya* live above it. Some exceptional *kardiya*, including anthropologist Nancy Munn, are remembered for having lived on the ground, in camps, 'like *yapa*'. This reference to bodily proximity and engagement with the earth has wider interpretive application than just to modes of dwelling — for Warlpiri people to 'sit down' invokes a foundational ontological principle, a way of being, a form of engagement between persons and environments. At a practical level to sit down is to make a camp, to break a journey. Pertinently, people who sit down together are regarded as related in varied but important ways. And the importance of sitting down together as a moral disposition, a framework for interaction, exchange, learning, is reinforced in cross-cultural situations. In matters of conflict and miscommunication between Warlpiri people and governments it is common to hear people appeal to ministers or bureaucrats to come and 'sit down' with them. To sit down involves bringing self and other into a situation of sustained mutual presence. This is the spatial requirement for engendering trust. In such contexts one hears with one's own ears, *purda-nyanyi*, a term which translates as *to know* as well as *to hear*. One sees with one's eyes, one recognises something, *milya-pinyi*. As is the case for all people who place revelation at the centre of their visual culture, whether the object of attention is a ceremonial object, a place, a bodily action, or a public event — to be physically proximate, to hear or to see, is to know.

Thus a deep constitutive relationship exists between the physical structures of dwelling, the bodily practices of interaction and visual regimes or ways of seeing. Bachelard saw the house as it figures in human imagination as 'one of the greatest powers of integration for the thoughts, memories and dreams of mankind', and a body of images that 'give mankind proofs or illusions of stability'.[24] While such a statement might be seen as shot through with Eurocentric assumptions, if 'house' is substituted for 'living arrangements' it becomes a compelling proposition. Several researchers attuned to the

Figure 9:
A scene from Hooker
Creek, 1953–4.
(Photograph: Mervyn
Meggitt, Meggitt
Collection, AIATSIS,
N390.583.)

intimate links between emotional and psychological wellbeing and ways of inhabiting environments have observed the deep trauma or chronic insecurity that follows when people are forced to move from familiar living arrangements to an alien situation that fails to fulfil basic needs for shelter and security.[25] While Warlpiri were moved into settlements in a concentrated period, the move to inhabit European housing has occurred over a much longer period and with considerable ambiguity. While housing may stand as a powerful symbol of Aboriginal people's successful assimilation, notably, it may also fail to transcend its status as more than symbol.[26]

So what circumstances did Warlpiri people find themselves in, having been transported over a gruelling five-day journey on the back of two trucks to Hooker Creek in early September 1952? It is important to hold in mind the situation as sketched in Chapter 2: the grim exploitative conditions of the gold and wolfram fields, the hostilities with hard pastoralists, and the overcrowded situation at the recently established settlement of Yuendumu. In late 1950 violent feuding erupted at Yuendumu, resulting in a number of people being killed in what archival documents describe as cases of 'tribal murder'. In selecting people to transfer to Hooker Creek care was taken by patrol officers and local authorities to remove from Yuendumu 'those who were instigators or likely instigators of trouble on the settlement'.[27] In the transfer of these 'trouble makers' to Hooker Creek, the under-staffed personnel at the new settlement would inherit a series of unanticipated challenges.

In August 1952 patrol officer Greenfield oversaw selection and transportation of 130 people to Hooker Creek on the back of two specially prepared transport vehicles driven from Darwin. About thirty Warnayaka, northern Warlpiri people, were collected from The Granites, a similar number of people from Mt Doreen, seventy people from Yuendumu and the remainder from Phillip Creek. Jack Newham, assistant superintendent at Yuendumu, travelled with Greenfield and following their arrival the two men spent a month at Hooker Creek, helping meet the needs of the population that had swollen overnight to 170.[28]

Months before their arrival, the superintendent had reported that all the Warlpiri people residing at Hooker Creek with the capacity for physical labour were 'fully occupied' and said to display 'a pleasing attitude'. But other entries in the settlement diary suggest such an attitude would have been precariously realised. In December 1951 the superintendent reported that he was 'having trouble making bread with wheatmeal flour'. The flour that had been supplied by Native Affairs was said to sour during the wet season and eating bread made from this flour had caused an outbreak of boils among the Warlpiri. Two days after this incident Superintendent Petherick wrote that a bad dust storm was causing many sore eyes. A horse died as a result of the dry conditions and hard feed. In January 1952 there was still 'no sign of rain, only wind and dust'.[29]

By March 1952 the place of Mosquito Dreaming was under siege from a plague of the creatures. Warlpiri were covered in bites, some turning septic. During the same month the superintendent reported that he had killed four native dogs on three separate occasions: 'for barking and making noise during night', for killing two fowl and for killing a goat. He would shoot more dogs in coming months, including two animals identified as having killed chickens owned by the Meggitts.[30]

The new Warlpiri residents had been transported to Hooker Creek before the settlement could accommodate them. The day after their arrival the superintendent reported that conditions were now 'very bad', with no wind and no water. Seventy people were promptly sent to camp out bush. In the weeks that followed many new arrivals required daily medical treatment. They were suffering serious sickness, with fever, vomiting and pneumonia-like symptoms, many of them unable to keep down liquids or food. An elderly woman and elderly man died within a fortnight of arriving. A baby died. The sick, it was reported, had either come from or been in contact with persons who had come from The Granites and Mt Doreen. By the end of the month the settlement was suffering from what appeared to be an epidemic. With no hospital yet constructed, and only limited medical supplies, very sick people were temporarily housed in the settlement 'garage'. Contact with the Royal Flying Doctor Service was maintained sporadically by unreliable radio. The settlement supply of precious kerosene, the only source of fuel for lights and refrigeration, was close to being exhausted, but the superintendent could not go in search of supplies with so many sick to tend.[31]

Three weeks after the trucks had delivered the new residents, Superintendent Petherick wrote to the Director of Native Affairs requesting the urgent issuing of handcuffs. Two of the new arrivals were suffering mental distress and there had been a series of violent outbursts. As the only permanent white authority on the ground, the superintendent appealed to Darwin to appreciate his situation and the need to have 'some way of holding a native in an extreme emergency'.[32] One man had other Warlpiri terrified. Five months passed and the same man was still in the settlement, still causing anxiety and distress. In March and again in April 1953 there were reports of this man being 'at his worst so far' with several

incidents of self-harm and of violent threats to others. The superintendent requested this man be removed from the settlement by medical staff. As his mental state deteriorated further, eight men were enlisted to handcuff the man's feet. He was then tied by his hands to a large hardwood frame in the saddle room for the night, which he soon 'tore to pieces'. A number of young men were instructed to watch the distressed man around the clock. He screamed all through the night. Finally, in early May he was removed by plane in the charge of a constable and a nurse and ultimately committed to a mental asylum in Adelaide.[33]

Through the first four months of 1953 conditions steadily worsened. In March, following the death of her baby, a distressed woman and eleven of her family walked the hundreds of miles back through the desert to Yuendumu. By May, when the Meggitts arrived, there was a 'ration crisis' at a time when the settlement was without a working vehicle and lacked a charger for the radio transceiver. It transpired that a total break down in communications between Hooker Creek and Native Affairs had occurred — a patrol officer had gone on six months leave and the supply orders and telegrams addressed to him fortnightly were simply piling high on his desk awaiting his return. Finally, the truck that brought Mervyn Meggitt into Hooker Creek in May came piled high with supplies. As Marie Mahood, wife of the Acting Superintendent Joe Mahood recalled:

> There were five tons of petrol, of which we still had plenty, seeing we had been one vehicle down on strength, but there was no kerosene. There were cartons and cartons of clothing. Some sugar, tea and jam, but no flour and no soap.[34]

Several weeks later, despite his lack of horsemanship, Mervyn Meggitt mounted a horse and rode the sixty miles to Wave Hill Station alongside Joe Mahood to seek an urgent loan of flour. A week later, a parliamentary party led by the Minister for Territories Paul Hasluck called at Wave Hill where the station manager took pleasure in advising him of the situation at Hooker Creek. The Minister promptly organised to visit the settlement. As luck would have

Figure 10:
Unidentified girls in
the grounds of the
superintendent's house,
Hooker Creek 1953–4.
(Photograph: Mervyn
Meggitt, Meggitt
Collection, AIATSIS,
N390.354.)

frustrations and situations of considerable stress —
tight departmental budgets; mismanagement and
politicking meant that while electrical wiring was
installed through the settlement in 1951, it would be
several years before electricity would be connected;
and fence posts were cut and holes dug by hard-
working Warlpiri men, but the supply of fencing
wire was postponed as a result of budget shortfalls,
to be considered again for possible funding in the
next financial year. Supply trucks arrived fortnightly,
heavily laden with large amounts of materials for
which the settlement had no use and often without
urgently needed basic food and medical supplies.

Like the settlers encountered in Chapter 2, the new
generation of people employed to run Aboriginal
settlements were deeply derisory of 'Head office' and
'Canberra'. Marie Mahood recalls the complete lack of
understanding of the social system and 'skin' names
that resulted in clerks and patrol officers recording
multiple versions of a name 'as they heard it from
its owner'. As a result one Tommy Djungarai was
referred to in official correspondence by six different
spellings, each newly spelled entry generating a
new identity for administration. In this process
pay cheques for workers proliferated, one for each
Chungaree, Joongerery, Tungary, Toongaree, Djangri
and Djungarai who appeared on government lists.[36]

Through the prism of the settlement diary, the
superintendent emerges as a different kind of
governmental agent to the slave overseer at the
centre of Mirzoeff's colonial regime of visuality,
a man poised at an appropriate vantage point
observing slaves at work. Here at Hooker Creek, as
was the case elsewhere in Australia, 'the *malaka*'
by necessity worked alongside his charges. The
diary, with its matter-of-fact tone and short-hand
reportage, conveys the superintendent, especially
Petherick who single-handedly oversaw the longest
phase of Hooker Creek's early development, as a
man of extraordinary, unabating energy, working
eleven-, twelve-, thirteen-hour days on the dizzying
array of tasks required of him. His visibility to
Warlpiri was distinctively embodied. He governed
with a firm hand — distributing rations and tending
the sick, but also shooting dogs, facilitating child
removals when directed to do so, and withholding

it, a supply truck drove into town just hours before
the Minister. Marie Mahood recalled the scene:

> ❝ Flour at last, more petrol but no kerosene, four
> enormous cartons of toilet paper and about
> twenty four-gallon tins of ex-army dried peas.
> The war had been over for eight years and the
> peas were feeling their age. I will never forget the
> expression on Paul Hasluck's face as he scooped
> up a handful, crumbled them and threw them
> down in disgust.[35] ❞

The tireless Superintendent Petherick who had
unsuccessfully sought a transfer from Hooker
Creek many months earlier, had finally gone on
leave in January 1953. The newly arrived assistant
Joe Mahood stepped into the position of acting
superintendent. His wife Marie Mahood's memoir
of the eleven months of 1953 the family spent in the
posting conveys with comic humour the bureaucratic
bungling that was a constant feature of governance
at a distance. But the humour only thinly veils deep

Figure 11:

Tess Napaljarri Ross: *Remembering a dust storm*, Yuendumu 2011.

Napaljarri recalls a violent dust storm at Yuendumu sometime in the early 1960s. At that time just one Warlpiri family occupied a brick house. People and dogs ran to that house to take cover.

rations to 'encourage' people to return to work from lengthy periods of ceremony. Embodying the state's contradictory attitude to remote Aboriginal people, through the figure of the superintendent's reign it is possible to glimpse something of how relations between Warlpiri and European Australians have evolved to take such complex ambiguous character.

At Hooker Creek the superintendant's house was the first building erected. Its construction was commenced under the oversight of the first superintendent, Bill Grimster, with each new arrival contributing to its upkeep and improvement. In early 1953 when the Mahoods arrived in the settlement Marie Mahood recalled the house:

> Consisted of one large bedroom, a large lounge-dining room, and a kitchen and pantry, with a wide fly-wired verandah all around with one corner partitioned off for a bathroom. It was built of cement-brick, cement floors and a small building adjacent to the kitchen end housed the toilet and the laundry, complete with copper and a pair of cement tubs.[37]

Warlpiri people came to know it as 'big house' — 'big house for a big man'. The work of constructing the flywire-covered verandah for this house was elaborate and time consuming. It absorbed the energies of Superintendent Petherick and 'three boys' over a three-week period in January 1952. Completion was delayed when the superintendent allowed his labourers to enjoy a long weekend of ceremonial activity in recognition that 'they have been working well'. By early February, a flywire door was added. Through this period there are regular mentions of the fly situation being 'very bad'.[38]

Across these periods of hot, dry, windy, dusty weather the superintendent and those he enlisted to work forged ahead, attempting to transform and tame the harsh environment, to cultivate it in the mirror of European expectation: planting trees, a lawn, vegetables, clearing an air strip. There were indications of the environment resisting. In February 1952, the superintendent wrote of the challenges of clearing the airstrip and the need to make a 'scraper' to clear grass rather than use the grader. The 'soft

Figure 12:
Edward Jungarrayi at
Hooker Creek, 1953–4.
(Photograph: Mervyn
Meggitt, Meggitt
Collection, AIATSIS,
N390.577.)

desert country', it seems, was bucking against attempts to remake its surface. The ground, the superintendent wrote, took 'too long to settle down after it [had] been graded.[39]

A year earlier a violent dust storm at Yuendumu (figure 11) spectacularly ripped the roof off the meat house and mission canteen and the walls of the teacher's residence. A teacher and her Warlpiri assistant were forced to take cover under a table while debris was tossed violently around them.[40]

While older people remember stark spatial separation of their camps from the settlement, weekday activities involved intense and intimate interactions of various kinds within the central settlement area. Larry Jungarrayi's attention to the window of the 'big house' invites conjecture that the interior of the house was unknown to him, yet women and no doubt some men were intimately familiar with these internal spaces where they worked as cleaners, cooks or laundry attendants. Larry Jungarrayi was employed as the baker in the 'Native Kitchen' at the time of Meggitt's fieldwork. Today, women who were the children of those women who worked for the superintendant recall being looked after inside the house by female relatives while their mothers worked. They remember attending pre-school classes inside the covered verandah and playing on the grass lawn (figure 10).

Men such as Larry Jungarrayi and Abe Jangala managed to balance their new work responsibilities with a robust ceremonial life, yet the settlement work regime discouraged 'working boys' from attending ritual events. The settlement diary records many instances when 'boys' were working while other settlement residents were elsewhere, engaged in initiation and other ceremonies. This was part and parcel of the government vision. By late March 1954, the Superintendent could claim success for the settlement's training regimes, as seventeen young men went off to be employed as stockmen on neighbouring stations.[41]

Flywire, windows, frames: new ways of seeing the desert

Considered alongside Meggitt's documentation, it seems reasonable to interpret Larry Jungarrayi's picture as a conjunction of window, flyscreen and house. As a functional component of European settlement houses, flywire plays a similar role to windows, keeping insects out, minimising the circulation of dust, allowing for visual and aural access to activity on the other side of the screen. As she looked at this picture with me Larry Jungarrayi's step-daughter identified it as a window. Windows fulfil a number of requirements in built structures. They establish relationships between and mark the separation of inside and outside spaces; they allow natural light into rooms that otherwise would be dark or reliant on other forms of illumination. Windows allow occupants of a dwelling to gaze upon an external scene, to have a clear view, while muting the stimulation of other senses. Windows also allow control over the degree to which inside spaces and activities can be viewed from outside.

Windows carry considerable symbolic weight in Warlpiri history, as they are introduced along with houses and other architectural structures, roads and vehicular transport with the coming of *kardiya*, people who live above the ground, shut off from the wider environment. In turn the introduction of windows heralds the beginning of a profound set of related shifts in experience — not just new things to look at and new ways of looking, but also a move to a relatively more sedentary life with newly regulated and routinised practices, new authority structures, new ways of ordering and marking time, new ways of fostering relationships. Seen in this way, windows stand for the settlement, a total institution.[42]

As a number of philosophers and anthropologists have observed, windows play a crucial part in instantiating a particular ontology of dwelling, a way of relating to environments distinguishing inside from outside, and a viewer who looks from those looked upon. For Robert Romanyshyn, the window:

> establishes as a condition of formal perception, a formal separation between a subject who sees the world and the world that is seen, and in so doing it sets the stage, as it were, for the retreat or withdrawal of the self from the world which characterises the dawn of the modern age.

> Ensconced behind the window the self becomes an observing subject, a spectator, as against a world which becomes the spectacle, an object of vision.[43]

The history of Cartesian perspective fills out the figure of the modern individual subject, one for whom vision is a heightened sense with the capacity to take a commanding view of a scene. Rarely do such accounts consider the perspective of people on the other side of the window beyond their status as *objects* of vision. What do those who are observed through the window *see when they look back*?

It is notable that Larry Jungarryi's picture draws attention not to the *view* through the window, not to the kind of perspective this newly encountered frame would enable, nor does it depict the activities imagined as occurring on the other side of the

Figure 13:
Willy Japangardi:
The superintendent's house, Hooker Creek 1953–4.
(Drawing #149, Meggitt Collection, AIATSIS.)

'The black is the house, the blue is the sky and the yellow is the spinifex' (Mervyn Meggitt.)

Figure 14:
Willy Japangardi:
The superintendent's house,
Hooker Creek 1953–4.
(Drawing #150, Meggitt Collection,
AIATSIS.)

'This is the house with trees at
Hooker Creek. You can see the
blue trees but . . . how that can
be a house I've no idea. The blue,
the black and the green just . . .
[its] post-impressionist' (Mervyn
Meggitt).

screen. His drawing forces the viewer to confront the structure itself: the flyscreen, the wooden frame, the window, the house, the light glowing within are all condensed.

Despite Meggitt's insistence that the men produced their pictures in isolation from each other, the existence of two further drawings of the house by Willy Japangardi suggest a more likely scenario, these structures were so new and compelling that the men explored the qualities of the house together. Indeed, some of them may have been involved in the hard labour of building the house or nailing that flywire onto its wooden frame. Did proximity to the practices of constructing the settlement and interacting with its authorities influence the way each man envisaged the structure? Significantly, Japangardi's vigorously executed works present the superintendant's house as an impenetrable black block.

There are significant differences between the drawings made by Willy Japangardi (figures 13 and 14) and Larry Jungarrayi's picture. Willy Japangardi, a man in his late twenties employed as a stockman, surveys the scene of the house from further distance than Larry Jungarrayi; he places the house in its surrounding environment, highlighting in exaggerated fashion that these strange new people lived very differently from Warlpiri, above the ground. To make his point, Willy Japangardi's picture places clear blue sky to separate the house from the yellow spinifex ground. In a way that seems continuous with the wider ways Warlpiri order relations between visible and invisible phenomena, Larry Jungarrayi presents us with the tangible structure of the house and the frame of the screen, but our focus is drawn to the spaces between the grid-like material structure. The vitality of his picture derives not from the structure itself but from the potency of the light shining within.

The window marks the limits of what can be seen, but Warlpiri people are wary of framing devices that fail to convey a full situation, an issue that emerges especially in their experience of photography. Nor do they find truth in the surface of images. Ancestral potency, a primary force in image making as well as the rhythms of the everyday, is in its essence invisible.

A dynamic interplay in social interaction insists on truthful representation but also careful seclusion of the most powerful image forms.

Fear and hope in an intercultural world

In drawing attention to the light shining inside the superintendent's house, Larry Jungarrayi attends to the place where power lies. Looked at from this perspective, his picture appears as a compelling assemblage of the ancestral, political and technological forms in which power was known to reside and circulate in the upheaval of 1952. Similarly to the way the revelation of ancestral power is carefully circumscribed in acrylic paintings, Larry Jungarrayi hints at, but does not reveal, and indeed may be unable to fathom, the illusive power of white men. The intangibility of this power is something Warlpiri people continue to wrestle with and court, stand in awe of and rally against.

By way of closing this chapter, let us contemplate the view from another window that would become familiar to Larry Jungarrayi two-and-a-half decades after he made his drawing for Meggitt — the view from the window of his 'tin house' at Yarripirlangu, Jungarrayi's paternal country and the site of an outstation established for him and his brothers in the wake of Warlpiri people being granted land rights. In this modest unlined tin shed, strikingly similar to the Stage One houses Warlpiri were encouraged to occupy at Hooker Creek, the window provides an unimpeded view of the mighty Yarripirlangu mountain range, the place of *Wardapi Jukurrpa*, Goanna Dreaming (figure 16).

A significant chapter in the policy history of Aboriginal affairs might be written via a consideration of these two differently framed views. Jungarrayi's picture of the superintendent's window takes on an added significance now it can be placed alongside his window at Yarripirlangu. But here we would do well to heed the guidance of Tess Napaljarri — as I entered the house at Yarripirlangu to contemplate this view in April 2011, she beckoned me outside and gestured to an area of spinifex-covered ground and the remnants of a camp-fire several metres away.

Figure 15:
Larry Jungarrayi:
The malaka's house,
Hooker Creek 1953–4.
(Drawing #63, Meggitt
Collection, AIATSIS.)

Figure 16:
The view from the
window of Larry
Jungarrayi's house, with
the mountain range
and his truck visible
in the background,
Yarripirlangu outstation,
2011. (Photograph:
Hannah Quinliven.)

'Anyway, Nangala', she told me, 'Jungarrayi and his wife slept out here'.

If we were to conclude this story with Larry Jungarrayi's return to Yarripirlangu we would be left with a deceptively simple tale of triumph. But another forty years have passed since that return. How do the pictures made in the 1950s resonate with Warlpiri sentiments at the end of the first decade of the twenty-first century? In Willy Japangardi's pictures of the house, the world of the white man is impenetrable, threatening, unreachable. Larry Jungarrayi's drawing is more circumspect. Glimpsed in close-up, the gaps between the weave of the flywire mesh appear as significant as the mesh itself, allowing splintered light to refract and dominate the picture. The viewer has no access to the kind of activity occurring in the glow of this light, but is presented with an image of unmistakable warmth.

In the *Poetics of space* Bachelard contemplates the psychological significance of a lighted window in human imagination. The 'lamp in the window', he suggests, 'is the house's eye'. He quotes a poem from Henry Bosco's novel *Hyacinthe,* lines that conjure well the contradictory states of hope and fear that the house embodies in Warlpiri reckoning.

> ❛ *Emmire*
> Walled In
>
> *Une lampe allumée derrière la fenêtre/ Veille au coeur secret de la nuit.*
> A lighted lamp in the window/ Watches in the secret heart of night.
>
> *Du regard emprisonné/ Entre ses quatre murs de pierre.*
> Of a gaze imprisoned/ Between its four stone walls.[44] ❜

If Larry Jungarrayi's picture ultimately seems to be a meditation on the power of the white man, does it also predict the implications of that power? The black geometric grid that structures the image might be read as witnessing the spatial, social, phenomenological transformations brought about by fences, brickwork, windows, flywire, roads. Similar to Bessie Nakamarra Sims' picture of *Jukurrpa* flanked by objects that 'might be houses' (figure 3) there is a strong sense here of new structuring constraints being brought to bear, and perhaps struggling to hold, a power coursing within. But the liveliness of the picture created by Larry Jungarrayi's blue-green shimmer works against reading these changes as straightforwardly negative in Warlpiri estimation. In Mirzoeff's terms this picture enacts Larry Jungarrayi's 'right to look', and significantly this look presents something more ambiguous than defiance.

Hope appears to radiate in the light of Larry Jungarrayi's drawing. Optimism and openness towards the new and the Other seem to be the moral sensibilities of this work. Willy Japangardi's black block presents a darker response to the coming of the white man. And so it is to the present. Among Warlpiri the house continues to stimulate imaginings of both hope and fear. Hope for the better life promised by government; fear that the same promise hides a more sinister agenda — to cleave Warlpiri from those things they continue to value, to force them to live like white people. Circling around this clash of images is a pervasive fear of losing the vestiges of control Warlpiri have over their lives.

INTERLUDE III
The road to Hooker Creek

by Elizabeth Nungarrayi Ross,
translated by Jeannie Nungarrayi Herbert[1]

Figure 1:
Jeannie Nungarrayi
Herbert (left) and Elizabeth
Nungarrayi Ross, on
the bank of Hooker
Creek, Lajamanu 2011.
(Photograph: Melinda
Hinkson.)

My name is Elizabeth Ross Herbert, from Lajamanu community.

My name is Jeannie Nungarrayi Herbert, I was born here in 1953, the same year as all these drawings were done.

Elizabeth Nungarrayi: My father, he was working at Yuendumu. He used to work in the garden, he used to water the garden. And a long time ago during welfare days he used to chop the wood and all that. My mother used to work in the hospital, washing sheets and all that for our people. They used coppers and their hands to wash those sheets. When they used to lie on those beds, when they were sick from fights, they used to sleep there. I had two mothers. The other mother used to look after me and she used to look after me and my brother Edward, at home.

My father had two wives. One of them was Lydia Nakamarra, the other was Beryl Nakamarra. Junjulurlu is my father's name, Dreaming name. Sugarbag Dreaming. They called him *Ngarlu pakarnu*. Japaljarris used to live there. In the afternoon they used to go back home.

They came from Alice Springs a long time ago. With two big trucks. They came with two big trucks and said to my father, the white men said, 'today we are going to take some of you to Hooker Creek'. Then after that, Japaljarri went and spoke to all his people. 'We are going to Hooker Creek, to another place, a strange place. We'll be going there. They are taking us there.' They were going around, getting their swags and everything they owned. And packing everything in those two big trucks. In one they put all the swags and whatever. And the second truck, they were putting everything on.

They felt really sad. Other people were really happy. Looking forward to moving to another place. We went with those two trucks. I was five years old when they took us there, to Hooker Creek. And my little brother, he was in the coolamon.

We started our journey and we drove towards Napperby, where the big river is. And all the people at Napperby, they ran everywhere, frightened, when they saw those big trucks coming. They thought they were coming for them. But anyway we went right through with those two big trucks, we went through Aileron.

They went Stuart Highway. We stopped there at the windmill, on the highway, other side of Aileron. We stopped there and had lunch there. Got off and went everywhere. They made lunch for us. They were cooking it. We had to line up in the old days. Men and women in lines. With billy cans, no plates. And after that, after they finished eating their food, they got on those trucks again and went to Phillip Creek, other side of Tennant Creek. We got more Warlpiri people there. More people jumped on the big truck. Our families were there. We were travelling through Pussycat Bore. We got off there, on that Buntine Highway, in the afternoon. They cooked us more food. We had lunch again and we all stood up in lines again. Same procedure as at Aileron. Men in one line, women in another line, children in front. Regiment style [laughter]. *Kardiya* like lines. They camped there, at Pussycat Bore.

Early in the morning they started cooking breakfast for us. Tea and porridge. Porridge was a very important one for us in those days. Children were first to be fed, as usual, always. The big ones [laughter], men and women, in the lines again.

After having breakfast and all that, people packed their bags and put them on top of the two trucks. They were putting all the children on top, and all the big people were jumping on. After that we all started coming. We came with those two vehicles to old Top Springs. Not the new one, the old one with the creek. Old Ma was there, she had quite a reputation. Then we went on. There were three tanks. We know the name of that place but we've forgotten. Might be King Bore. That's where we had lunch. We stopped there. Had our food again. Then we went to Wave Hill. At Wave Hill we picked up some other Warlpiri people who were living there. They got on the truck with us. We came through the old road, where the old Wave Hill Station is. There was a road through there. They drove through there, through Gordy Springs and through Catfish. They turned through Sunshine Bore and went that way, through Catfish. We came through Catfish, through that big billabong, other side of the power station there, through the billabong on the other side. A big yard was standing there. For cattle and horses. That's where they told us to get off. We were staying there. We slept there for a long time. We slept maybe a few nights or a week maybe. Maybe a month. They brought us here to Hooker Creek. Our camp was over there, near the power station.

You know where the CLC [Central Land Council] building is standing there? That building was there, workshop was there. A storeroom on the other side. There were only a few buildings there. They put a garden there. Grew some food and vegies. Tanks there, high ones and windmills. And a big yard, for horses and cattle. There was a trough where the animals used to drink. They had little houses, tiny houses. They built them for all the people.

Pawarrinji Jakamarra and Pulyuka Nungarrayi. They were the first ones here. Only a few people — Jakamarra, Napaljarri, two other Nampijinpas. They were here already. They were here when we came here, only a few people were living here. The CLC office building was standing — they used to work there, the superintendent's house, big house we called it. Big house for a big man, who ran the community, boss. They called it Big House. Some of us called it Superintendent's House. Mr Grenville was the superintendent we knew. Before him was Patrick [Petherick]. Our two mothers used to work there, in the garden. My father and two mothers, Beryl and Liddy, and my father Junjulurlu . . . Biddy and Liddy worked in the house, did the laundry. Looked after Mr Grenville's two daughters. And they used to let us sleep there.

Where the art centre is, there was a kitchen and dining room, there was no school. Other men used to go and chop wood all around the community. They used to go and chop firewood. There was a big camp oven. They used to cut the meat up and cook it in there for the

Figure 2: Hooker Creek settlement as seen from the windmill, c. 1953. (Photograph: Mervyn Meggitt, Meggitt Collection, AIATSIS, N390.58.)

Figure 3:
Joan Meggitt (left) holding baby Jeannie Nungarrayi, with Lydia Nakamarra holding baby Susan Nungarrayi. (Photograph: Mervyn Meggitt, Meggitt Collection, AIATSIS, N390.147.)

them names. Jeannie's name was Punayi, Susan's name was Lajayi, they were very happy for those two little Nungarrayis born at Lajamanu. The names were from the Kalkarinji people, the owners of this land. That old Jangala he was married to two Nungarrayis, our sisters. One Jungarrayi gave my other brother the name Pirriyarri, after that place called Yarrayi, 28 Mile Bore. They were giving those names to the children who were the same skin groups who were born on their land, but they didn't give the names to other children, only Nungarrayis and Jungarrayis.

When we broke up from school they used to always send us out, like 30 kilometres out of here on the Tanami Track. We used to camp there, all the family. At Christmas time from there, they took us another time to Yarrayi. They were doing ceremony there. Our brother Hector was born at this time. They were grabbing all the young boys for ceremony. They were dancing for those young men. Some of them went by foot to Gordon Downs, about 150 kilometres over the NT border. They took them there. Some of them, they went and got them with vehicles.

When we finished up they brought us back and those people they came walking back. They were very fit people. They used to walk everywhere. They were very strong. They used to come and work here. And sometimes they would send them to other cattle stations. Working as drovers. To Queensland, to other places, to Collarney Station, all around the western region. They used to come back after, Christmas time.

When they put the garden here one old man named Waringarri was working here by himself. We used to grow watermelon, corn. He used to keep it really healthy, really good. He used to cut all those vegetables, when they were grown he would take it to the kitchen, local mess, and they would make food for us.

A long time again when we used to go to school we used to go and stay one week at 19 Mile, 14 Mile, and a Fire Dreaming place Warlungalinpa. They used to go camping, used to take us out camping, Jungarrayi, Nungarrayi, Nangala, Jangala, they used to take us out camping for one week at a time.

We used to be OK long time ago. All the girls used to make little billy cans and we used to go and pick yellow bush currants, bush tomatoes, bush raisins, all the young girls used to go. And we used to bring back all those

people. In the boiler. A really big pot. They used to ring the bell all the time for people to come for lunch, dinner. Three times a day. Mothers and fathers used to bring their billy can and fill it up with food and take it back to camp. Children used to come and eat their meals on plates at the table. Then they would go to school. They used to scrub us in a big pot. With a scrubbing brush. When we mucked up, [the teacher] had a cane, a big stick. He used to hit the children on the hand, on their legs, on their bum, until they were black and blue. They were cruel in those days, those teachers.

They took our mothers and fathers out to Windham to watch the horse races. Our grandparents were looking after us. We were left behind with our grandparents.

In 1953 my two little sisters were born, Susan Nungarrayi Herbert and Jeannie Nungarrayi Herbert. When they were born here, a long time ago, in 1953, or 1954, 1955, they came from Wave Hill to Lajamanu, they brought the two little girls a coolamon, one each, and they gave presents for those two little girls who were born here. They gave foods we collected. We used to play around behind all these trees here. We used to climb trees. We used to cut those poison-ivy flowers, those purples ones, we used to eat them; they were delicacies for us. We used to dig those little bulbs, *janmarda*, bush onions, little small ones like *yarla*, they were delicious to eat. We used to eat well. And we used to exercise everyday. Everyday we would walk somewhere.

When I grew up, a white man took me to Cattle Creek to meet up with my promised husband. He said to me, 'come on, come here. Jump on'. We went to Wave Hill. He dropped us off. Another truck came from Cattle Creek Station. They came and got me and took me to Cattle Creek. My promised husband was waiting for me. At holiday time we went back to Wave Hill.

Jeannie Nungarrayi: Before they put her on, my sister and I saw what was happening. We saw her on the truck, with her auntie. We didn't want her to go. We cried for her. We protested. We ran along the road, crying out.

Elizabeth Nungarrayi: From here I stayed at Wave Hill. Then we walked from Wave Hill. We went to the hill to the top to the soakage. We slept there. Lay down and had a rest. We walked, a lot of us. Japaljarri, Jakamarra, all the families were walking. When we woke up in the morning we rolled our swags and started walking again. We walked along the creek, carrying the swags. We sat down and had a rest under the shade, because we were so tired. Some of our men went to get meat, goanna, turkey. They used to bring it back and we would cook it. We went and slept at the billabong, half-way. Then we went to the big creek. We had lunch. We slept again, on the road. We went to 19 Mile, the bore 19 miles from Lajamanu. We were walking back home. Another lot of people went through the road up there. We stayed at Jump Yard. We were getting a lot of bush game, goanna, turkeys. Some people went on the western side of the river; some people went on the eastern side. Some people slept on the eastern side, some slept on the western side. In the morning we woke up, it was a long, long way. Then I went to 19 Mile. Then we got happy. We were coming close. We woke up in the morning and went to the hill, on the eastern side. We made humpies out of leaves and grass. There was a big rain. We woke up again and we started walking to 7 Mile. We got up and we were sitting under the shade. We saw those people. They ran to us

from here. Without knowing we were there. They seen us. They were chopping wood. They seen us and they were surprised. They said, 'come on, jump on this truck!' And they brought us back to this place.

Melinda Hinkson: How did those people feel about being moved to Hooker Creek?

Elizabeth Nungarrayi: When they came and brought us back from Yuendumu, some of those people felt sad that they were in a strange area, strange country, and they felt out of place here. They walked all the way back. Tanami first, they knew where all the water holes were. To Granites, from Granites to Mt Doreen, from Mt Doreen to Yuendumu. They were homesick for their country . . . White men brought more people in. They were all right then, they got used to this country. Third lot of people.

They tried to settle at Catfish, but water wasn't good enough. No water underground, they didn't find it when they were digging for a bore. They found all the water here at Hooker Creek. People lived at Yarrayi for months and months, they couldn't find them, at ceremony time.

He was looking at those trees,
but thinking about his own country.

Tess Napaljarri Ross

Chapter 4
Back to Yarripirlangu

The year 2011 was one of considerable stress for Warlpiri people who call Yuendumu home. The return of copies of the Hooker Creek drawings coincided with protracted feuding that came hard on the heels of several years of shifting policy and public attitude to remote Aboriginal communities, culminating in the 2007 Northern Territory 'Emergency Response' Intervention. The Intervention was launched in dramatic fashion with a prime ministerial announcement, the declaration of a 'national emergency' following the release of a major investigative report that identified child sexual abuse as an issue widely afflicting remote Aboriginal communities. In a striking move, the Commonwealth seized legislative control of these jurisdictions, deployed the army to 'stabilise' them, and introduced a raft of complex legislation that would formally redirect Aboriginal affairs policy from a broad commitment to the principles of self-determination to those of normalisation.[1]

The campaign in support of this change in policy was aided by a stark politics of representation — the image of the suffering child emerged as a potently distressing new icon, circulating pervasively across mainstream media and wider reportage.[2] Large blue signs (figure 1) were erected near the entrance to 'prescribed communities', declaring these to be prohibited areas where alcohol and pornographic material were banned. Many Warlpiri people looked on in horror as public sentiment towards them noticeably shifted. Whereas in the era of self-determination Aboriginal 'culture' had been widely hailed in positive terms, some commentators were now indicting 'traditional Aboriginal culture' as the source of much that was wrong in remote Aboriginal life.

Figure 1:
The sign on the road to Yuendumu, June 2009. The graffiti identifies the then Prime Minister as an 'arsehole'. (Photograph: Jon Altman.)

A series of significant changes followed at the Territory level. Firstly, community government councils were replaced with regional shires, which took responsibility for local governance and delivery of many utilities and services out of the hands of local Aboriginal people and relocated such power to offices in regional centres such as Alice Springs. Secondly, the Northern Territory government announced the end of bilingual education as the broad framework for school-based learning. At Yuendumu, the conjunction of these governmental changes and the perception of a wider shift in public attitude to Aboriginal people combined with the effects of the local feud to produce a deeply demoralised sentiment. As I commenced this research Warlpiri people were experiencing many issues affecting them as significantly beyond their control. As well as an intensified critical attitude towards government and *kardiya* perceived as 'racist', across this period there was a noticeable rise in accusations and attributions of sorcery. Travel, especially to Alice Springs, brought with it intensified anxieties and very real risks.[3]

This was a highly volatile environment in which to instigate research dealing with Warlpiri cultural production of an earlier era. In the mid-1990s I had observed some of the ways in which the circulation of photographs and films made decades earlier had stimulated passionate debates about contemporary concerns. How would people respond to the drawings under circumstances of heightened stress and wariness?

One kind of response was relief — relief at having something engaging and positive to distract attention from the unrelenting tensions of the feud and its associated miseries. For some, my enquiries about the drawings presented a much needed opportunity to remind each other of the great collective pride vested in Warlpiri cultural heritage. Others were more questioning — what were these drawings and what were the circumstances under which they were produced? Where had they been all of these years? Was bringing them back here yet another reminder of the unequal power relations between *yapa* and *kardiya*, and of the potential trickiness at work in our interactions with each other? What was I going to do with them? Japangardi's wrestling with the status of the drawings explored in Chapter 1 brings some of these issues to the fore.

Such provocations were followed by another interpretive dilemma posed as I introduced Larry Jungarrayi's drawings to his brother's adopted daughter, Tess Napaljarri, who had lived with Larry for a period of her childhood. Meggitt had recorded the subject matter of a series of Larry Jungarrayi's drawings as 'trees at Hooker Creek'. When I put this proposition to Napaljarri she looked bewildered. How could he have painted trees at Hooker Creek? 'That's not his country. His country is Yarripirlangu. Maybe the old man was looking at those trees but he was really thinking about his own country', she put with some conviction. 'Here, see this one here', she said, picking up a laminated print of one of Larry Jungarrayi's drawings lying on the ground close by — 'you can see, that's the water tank at the outstation' (figure 2). Napaljarri's explanation pragmatically transcended questions of time; some twenty years had passed between the making of the drawing she perused and the installation of the water tank.

Figure 2:
(Top) Larry Jungarrayi, *Kirrirdi Creek*, Hooker Creek 1953–4. (Drawing #60, Meggitt Collection, AIATSIS.)

(Bottom) The water tank at Yarripirlangu outstation, Yarripirlangu 2011. (Photograph: Hannah Quinliven.)

In late April 2011, motivated by Tess Napaljarri's insistence that the 'trees at Hooker Creek' pictures were actually a scene from her father's beloved country, a small group of us make an overnight trip to the deceased artist's outstation. Our group included Napaljarri, two of her sisters, an adult daughter of one of those women, research assistant Hannah Quinliven and me, travelling in two four-wheel-drive vehicles. I was bewildered by the size of our entourage. Years earlier I was accustomed to vigorous competition for places in cars for any excursion out of the community, and especially out into the bush. This small group was a sure sign that people were thoroughly caught up with town issues.

The outstation is located approximately 70 kilometres to the west of Yuendumu. While there are good roads all the way, they have been little used in recent times and our drive was slow on account of the very long grass and small shrubs that grew in abundance in the wake of recent drenching rains, in some places making it difficult to distinguish between road and surrounding desert. On arrival at the outstation, which Napaljarri had not visited for several years, she was overcome with emotion. As she wandered around the tin huts, looking for signs of recent visitation, Napaljarri cried out and addressed the spirits of her ancestors, her deceased fathers and 'god fathers', expressing grief for their passing, for the passing of other relatives, and for many other unspoken griefs that had occurred since she was last at this place. 'We are only three sisters now', she declared, 'no brothers'. She announced our presence and asked the ancestors to look after us during our stay. Napaljarri then plonked herself down on the concrete porch of one of the huts and had a good hard cry.

The outstation village comprises eight corrugated iron huts that were erected in two stages — the first-stage houses have one room, the second-stage two rooms. These structures differ little from the Kingstrand huts erected at settlements thirty years earlier and explored in Chapter 3. The floors are concrete and the walls unlined and uninsulated, simple push open glassless 'windows' bring in light and ventilation. Wide verandahs provide shade and shelter from rain. Nearby the remnants of a fenced vegetable garden remain visible. Two hundred metres away on the verge of the long sand dune sits the outstation's water tank. A windmill lies prostrate on the ground nearby. Strewn around the edges of the village are four rusted car bodies, including Larry Jungarrayi's green Dodge truck that once transported people between the outstation and Yuendumu, now gradually being claimed by vegetation. A second rusted truck is parked in the skeletal wooden structure Napaljarri calls the 'garage'. She walks around with me, pointing out the houses that were used as single boys' and single girls' quarters, showing which family lived where.

The outer walls of several houses are decorated with pictures made recently by young people during country visits sponsored by the Yuendumu school. The wider vista is spectacular. The outstation sits above the spinifex plain that skirts the foot of the long Yarri Yarri mountain range. Mulga, desert oaks and grevillea trees dot the landscape, attracting many species of birds. In mythological terms this is the place where *Yanjilypiri* Night Sky and *Wardapi* Goanna converge. But Yarripirlangu women only paint goanna; they tell me they will not paint the night sky in the style that some other artists are now painting it, a style that breaks with the tradition of 'proper' Warlpiri iconography. They tell me it is dangerous to do so. Someone who made paintings like that got sick.

As night falls and we settle around a campfire, with meat sizzling on a griller plate, I bring out a selection of Larry Jungarrayi's drawings. While Napaljarri has seen these before, her sisters have not. She takes up a picture and explains that Meggitt the anthropologist thought this was 'trees at Hooker Creek' but she reckons their relative was thinking of this place when he made it. Her sisters murmur in agreement. Napaljarri goes on to recount the main Dreaming, the primary mythical account for the country on which we are camped, which centres on the illicit sexual liaison between a beautiful young Nungarrayi woman with hair like the sun and a Japangardi man from a distant country, her classificatory son-in-law. They had sex at several locations on and around the mountain range, where they left signs of their lovemaking. One of those sites is a potent source

Figure 3:
Tin house at
Yarripirlangu outstation
2011. (Photograph:
Hannah Quinliven.)

of love magic. On facing the wrath of the young woman's relatives the lovers turned themselves into sedimented forms in the landscape. Nungarrayi took herself into the ground, not far from where we are camping, where she remains in the form of a long sand dune. Japangardi flew back to Puyurru, Mt Theo. Napaljarri's telling is perfunctory; it has the feel of going through the motions. She tells me her daughter once took photographs of some of the Dreaming places deep in the mountain range, but they didn't develop — 'they didn't let those photos come out, those spirits'.

Our discussion moves on to other themes — places and events evoked by discussions of the pictures we pass around, snatches of memory of how this outstation once teemed with activity when the women lived here as children. Grapes and oranges were grown, chickens were kept — but only until someone left the gate to the chicken coop open and dogs got in. The women recall swimming as children in the water tank on hot days and being 'growled' for cooling themselves in the community's only supply of fresh water. They remember hunting for goanna, bush banana, honey ants, witchetty grubs, bush potatoes. The women and children would stay close to the outstation to harvest food while men walked off to more distant hunting grounds. They remember the friendly neighbouring pastoralist (rare in this part of the world), who every now and then would

bring freshly killed beef for Warlpiri families. When Mr Coppock got old he allowed the cattle station to be sold to Birds Australia as a conservation reserve, where Warlpiri now work as paid rangers. Larry Jungarrayi's brother Jimmy Jungarrayi was buried on the Newhaven Station lease at the pastoralist's invitation — the two men were good friends. The women laugh as they remember having come through the outstation a couple of years ago after the ceremony to hand over the station to its Warlpiri owners; kangaroos looked back at them from inside the tin houses.

There is talk of the windmill that once pumped water but now lies prostrate on the ground; it fell down after 'something' happened. One of the women suggests their sons should come out here and fix it up so people can come camping regularly here once more. Napaljarri says the 'ranger mob' should come and burn the long grass so the road can be seen. Her sister speaks of her son who is in Sydney studying for a Law degree and a daughter living in Adelaide. There is humorous talk of a neighbour who has gone mad as a result of drug use, the other day she was walking around without pants on. The women reflect emotionally on the 'beautiful young girl' who they had farewelled at a funeral yesterday, which had been attended by hundreds of people. She was fifteen years old and had committed suicide several weeks earlier in a neighbouring town.

Amidst the talk Napaljarri pulls out her mobile phone. 'No service, *lawa* [no]'. I laugh in amazement — could she really expect otherwise? But then why not. The magical power of mobile phones is uncanny in its ability to carry so much of significance through time and space. Napaljarri shows me a series of photographs on her small screen, one I have seen on the phones of other friends, a photo of a young man I have known since he was a child, my close friend's son and Napaljarri's grandson. Jakamarra is currently in Alice Springs prison along with two other related men of the same age — all awaiting trial on charges arising from the death that has sparked the protracted family feud that currently occupies the energies and attention of so many at Yuendumu.

Napaljarri searches the menu of her phone and plays a song by the man in question, a song celebrating the power of God, Wapirra.

👆 *Wapirra nyuntu kanpa nyinami wiri-nyayirni*
Father, you are existing, so big

Nyanyi kanpaju kankarlarra-nguru
You can see him, up in the sky

Wardinyi kanpaju nyinami
I'm so happy you exist for me

Parrangka manu mungangka
day and night

Tarnngangku karnangku
Forever, you are there for me

Warlkirni nyuntuyu
I am calling on you to help me be good

Wapirra, nyuntu junpa wiri oh ohh, jukujangu, wiri nyayirni
Father, you are so immense, you are so immensely powerful

Wapirra, nyuntu junpa wiri oh ohh, jukujangu, wiri nyayirni
Father, you are so immense, you are so immensely powerful

Wapirra . . . pulka pinyi
Father, I praise you

Karnangku
you are there for me

Nyuntu junpa wiri-nyayirni
you are so immense

Ohhh ohhh ohhhh Wapirra.
ohhh Father. 👈

Figure 4:
Tess Napaljarri Ross:
*Remembering a kangaroo
drive at Yarripirlangu*,
Yuendumu 2011.

The song's soaring chord sequence is given force by the raw and deeply melodic tenor of the young man's singing. Against the sobering knowledge of his current circumstances Jakamarra's voice acquires further weight. Looking into the orange coals of the fire and up to the wide star-smothered sky we are all caught up in the intensity of this moment. Napaljarri sings along, her voice catching a number of times. She was tired before we came away this afternoon. The trip had almost been aborted when word came to us as we were fuelling up our vehicles that fighting had broken out, yet again, in one of the camps and that relatives of the women were involved. Napaljarri insisted she was keen to come away, but the stresses

Figure 5:
Larry Jungarrayi's truck,
Yarripirlangu outstation
2011. (Photograph:
Hannah Quinliven.)

of the ongoing tensions and fighting in town and the emotional impact of coming 'home' to the outstation after such a long absence are taking their toll. She replays the song several times that night and again in the car the next day as we make the return journey back to Yuendumu.

At a certain point after we have eaten, Napaljarri announces she will give us a Bible reading. The reading is one she gave in Church earlier in the day. So, as the cool of night settles over us we take to our swags, arranged close to each other and to the fire. She commences reading in Warlpiri, translating each short passage into English for the benefit of the two *kardiya* who are present. It is a long reading, lasting a good 40 minutes. Lying in my swag I grow resigned to the strange melancholy that is descending over me. Napaljarri is, I observe, willing the Bible reading to fill the night's remaining social space, preferring to absorb herself in this exercise than leave herself open to the questions and discussions that would undoubtedly be pursued by the anthropologist. One by one I hear the sounds of our party falling asleep.

Bush trips I had taken fifteen years earlier had conditioned me to expect a deep transformation to occur on a journey like this one — the experience of being away from Yuendumu and out in country reordered people's preoccupations and noticeably lifted the mood and sentiment of a travelling group. In journeying out to country people left behind the intense pressures of the township. The pace of interactions slowed. Out in the bush there was a possibility of getting close to something that registered as little more than a chimerical presence in town. I was accustomed to lying under the stars with Warlpiri women, immersed in stories about the Beings that became those stars, sharing memories of times past, of different kinds of lives lived, whispered tales of sexual encounters, jokes, gossip. Trips to country stimulated the spirit, enlivened human interchange, generated new discussions and took interactions to a different register. Not so this time.[4]

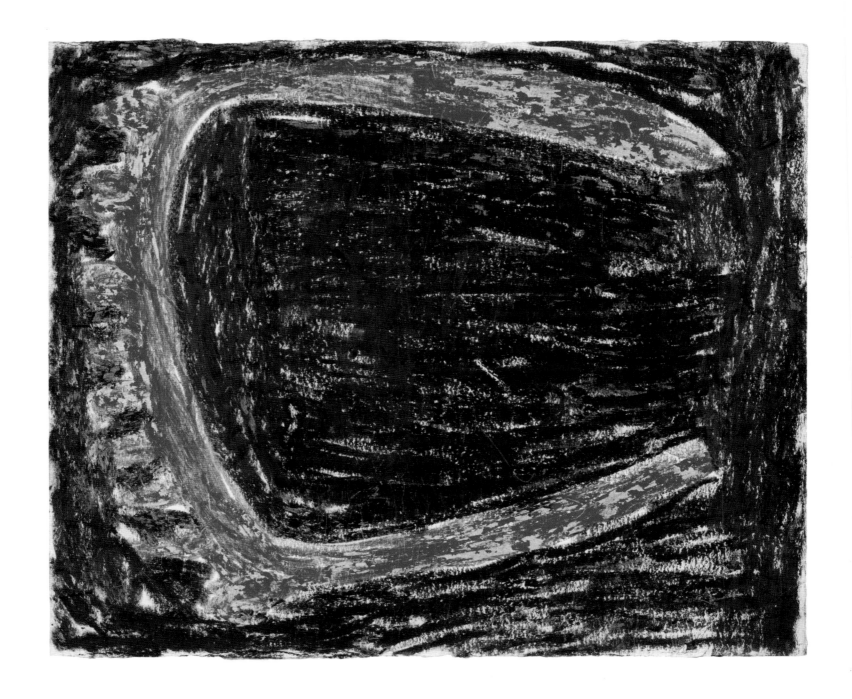

Figure 6:
Larry Jungarrayi:
Yarripirlangu, Hooker Creek 1953–4.
(Drawing #81, Meggitt Collection,
AIATSIS.)

'Back to Yarripirlangu hill country
again . . . This is the place where
Pitjuri grows, the narcotic that
people smoke. Here you have a
semi-circular hill in red with trees on
it and black representing the rest of
the country' (Mervyn Meggitt).

Technologies of place making

As I struggled to make sense of the experience of this bush trip, the work of Walter Benjamin came to mind. Recall that, for Benjamin, in ancient societies the mimetic faculty was a 'life-determining force';[5] a perceptual order that established proximate, empathetic relations between subjects and objects and lay at the heart of acts of creative production. The enactment of Warlpiri ancestral power through dance, song and painting — through a distinctive attitude to images — is exactly the kind of attitude Benjamin had in mind.

Benjamin locates the dissolution or transformation of the mimetic faculty in the rise of mechanical reproduction and codified forms of language and literacy, two processes crucially involved in introducing a plethora of new kinds of images which act to distance persons from more concrete and mystical ways of relating to their environments. As a result of taking up a scientific attitude with its abstract principles of rationality, modern societies are said to lack a mode of perception that 'made it possible to speak of a similarity which might exist between a constellation of stars and a human being'.[6] We live by a more abstracted engagement with the world around us and our ways of seeing, experiencing, making are transformed accordingly. This is not to suggest that we do not bestow magical power upon images. As Mitchell observes, our attitudes to images are marked by a double consciousness that privileges the rational but nevertheless enacts the magical.[7] Yet without doubt, abstract processes of modernity refigure relationships between human beings and their environments in decisive ways.

Napaljarri's withdrawal from the possible reading of the night sky, with its dynamic and vital forms of ancestral activity, in favour of the reading of the Warlpiri Bible might be interpreted as precisely the process of disenchantment and disengagement Benjamin was getting at. As I reflected upon the experience of this trip I recalled some of the fears that had been articulated by senior Warlpiri people prior to the introduction of broadcast television to their townships in the early 1980s. Foreseeing the imagined dangers of such an alarmingly powerful communicative system, one senior man, an outspoken critic of the federal government plan to launch the national satellite, told an inquiry, 'Aboriginal people got our land back to stop whitefellas chasing them . . . to stop whitefellas chasing them with things like satellites'.[8]

Yet, contrary to the impression given by my melancholy response to Napaljarri's Bible reading, Warlpiri do not identify Christianity as an alternative or challenging set of beliefs to *Jukurrpa*, the Warlpiri Law. Indeed, the old man cited here, Darby Jampijinpa Ross, was not only a man of great ritual authority, but also a committed churchman. Warlpiri religious philosophy allows for Wapirra, the all-powerful Father, to be granted primacy in their stories of creation as the all-mighty force who gave first life to the ancestors.[9] As one senior man put it to me, 'Captain Cook brought the Bible, but he didn't bring God. God was always here'. In the present, where the pressure bearing down upon the Warlpiri community is at times experienced as immense, where demographic changes mean that senior men do not command sufficient authority to enable them to resolve troubles of the magnitude and complexity that regularly arise, and where younger people are drawn to many different kinds of influences and aspirations than their parents and grandparents, Christians will appeal to the power of God as the only power strong enough to deal with such challenges.

At midnight our camp was awoken by Napaljarri calling out — 'Wapirra, we don't want those lights, keep us safe from those lights . . . .' I sat up and looked around. Napaljarri was shaken; two radiant lights shining close by had woken her from her sleep. I pointed out that the lights were being projected by the full moon reflecting off the silver bumper of a wrecked truck parked just over the way. We stoked the fire and went back to sleep.

As we drove back along the road to Yuendumu the following day, I reflected that this had been a trip on which the place Yarripirlangu, with its myriad sites, stories and histories, remained largely beyond reach. Curtailed by a combination of the women's more pressing concerns and the impassable long grass, we wandered around the outstation, gazed across the floodplain to the mighty mountain range, visited the soakage on the side of the road, dug unsuccessfully for *yarla* bush potatoes, exchanged snatches of memory, but got no closer than that. Was this short journey an endorsement of messages circulating in mainstream media and government policy papers — that the era of outstations, the era of self-determination, was over?[10] Our brief stop for lunch at the next outstation along the road, a larger village which had once flourished with its own school, only reinforced this uneasy sentiment. The classroom had been ransacked, school readers and other teaching materials were strewn across the floor. Birds and other small animals had been nesting among the piles of paper. Napaljarri, herself a teacher and teacher-linguist until her recent retirement, walked briskly through the mess. Referring nonchalantly to one of the traditional owners for this place she suggested, 'that [man] should come out here and clean this place up'.

Hidden transcripts and coercive authenticity

The women who made the trip to Yarripirlangu are all painters; one has travelled internationally to promote her art. Three decades after the instigation of the acrylic art movement at Yuendumu, canvas painting remains the only meaningful form of productive activity from which significant numbers of Warlpiri people at Yuendumu, and to a lesser extent Lajamanu, can earn an income. As acrylic art production has become a crucial carrier of certain codified understandings of Central Australian Aboriginality to wider Australia and the world beyond, paintings have come to carry particular ways of seeing 'country' as the seat of identity. Napaljarri's insistence that her relative would only have painted 'his own country' needs to be understood in the context of this codification.

The experience of our bush trip places such codification in stark relief. Here I am reminded of James Scott's distinction between hidden and public transcripts. 'With rare, but significant exceptions', Scott suggests, 'the public performance of the subordinate will, out of prudence, fear, and the desire to curry favour, be shaped to appeal to the

Figure 7: The road to Yarripirlangu, April 2011. (Photograph: Hannah Quinliven.)

expectations of the powerful'.[11] The public transcript in the current circumstances of Aboriginal Australia is one that subscribes to clear, unchanging criteria of authentic Aboriginality — clear and unchanging ways of understanding relationships between Aboriginal persons and place lie at the heart of this.[12] To paint anyone else's country is, in the eyes of legislative requirements and the expectations of non-Aboriginal observers, to undermine the accepted terms of cultural authenticity. Over time this discursive regime has impacted in numerous ways on the politics of Warlpiri representation, especially in the arena of painting. It is the sedimented influence of such expectations that I detect in Napaljarri's insistence that her stepfather would only have painted his own country, as well as in Japangardi's wrestling with the status of the drawings in Chapter 1 as either poor copies or 'truly dear' things. Where the politics of recognition are fraught and fragile and laced with suspicion, there is little prospect of a sympathetic consideration of forms of identity that reflect the complexity of post-settlement circumstances.

Figure 8:
Larry Jungarrayi,
Hooker Creek, 1953–4.
(Photograph: Mervyn
Meggitt, Meggitt
Collection, AIATSIS,
N390.35.)

The distracted attitude that characterised our trip to the outstation suggests an unspoken transcript of a different kind — here the status of country emerges as more complex and ambiguous, not pre-supposed as a primary constitutive element of self-identity, but rather one element in the wider field of Warlpiri concern and value. Here we are presented with two different modes of identity-projection, differently inflected by the concerns and consequences of history.

The public transcript for country emerged and was passionately honed in concert with the land rights movement that from the mid-1970s delivered inalienable title over large tracts of land to Warlpiri along with other Aboriginal people throughout the Northern Territory. It brought with it a wider political sentiment of acceptance of remote Aboriginal people's desires to pursue aspirations that differ from those found in metropolitan Australia. Outstations such as Yarripirlangu were born of these political circumstances. For women such as Tess Napaljarri the highpoint of that era marks a significant achievement in personal as well as collective terms; it was the period in which she completed her teacher training and helped put into practice the new movement in bilingual education. But much has changed since that time.

History has taught Warlpiri people that western law is untrustworthy — unlike Warlpiri law it is subject to constant change. Some live in fear of their land being taken from them, again. Hence the need to rigorously subscribe to codified modes of recognition. So it is that 'country' in its many mediated forms has become a matter to be dealt with carefully and conservatively.

Remembering Yarripirlangu

People who trace their ancestry to Yarripirlangu are descended from five brothers, of whom Larry Jungarrayi was the youngest, and four sisters, who in turn were the offspring of one Japaljarri man and his four Nakamarra wives. Both Japaljarri and his wives were all deceased by the late 1970s when members of the extended family re-established a base for themselves at Yarripirlangu. Jungarrayi men from Yarripirlangu married Nangala women from adjacent Nyirripi, Warlukurlangu and Watiyawanu countries; they acted reciprocally as *kirda* owner and *kurdungurlu* manager for each other's estates.

After Larry Jungarrayi died in 1990 people stopped living at Yarripirlangu. Of the brothers, only Jimmy Jungarrayi was still alive at that time, but he had relocated to Alice Springs some years earlier. A second outstation was subsequently established for one of the men's sons at Jungarrayi-warnu on the south-west side of the mountain range. By the mid-1990s both outstations were visited only infrequently, usually associated with an annual school-sponsored 'country visit'. I had attended one of these in 1995. My memory of that trip is coloured by the deeply emotional response of a now deceased Nakamarra, widow of one of Jimmy Jungarrayi's deceased sons. As we approached the expansive pool of water at Putaji-Putaji, Nakamarra's deep guttural wailing echoed off the walls of the surrounding rocky outcrops. She had not visited her husband's country for several years and the return to this place brought to the surface intense grief. In a more upbeat mood, one of her sons, himself by now a senior man, leapt to the peak above the rock pool where we were all gathered and in animated mood grasped the trunk of the knotty bloodwood tree growing on the cliff face, 'This is Japangardi, this is [that Japanangka's] father', he proclaimed.

Among the current generation of relatives who trace their ancestry to Yarripirlangu are several impressive men and woman who carry responsibilities across a wide field of activity. They include a noted police aide, a bureaucrat, translators and bi-cultural teachers, night patrollers, painters, media producers and broadcasters, board members of community organisations, sportsmen, musicians and one law student. Tess Napaljarri, recognised as *kirda*, an owner for Yarripirlangu, acquired her responsibilities not through birth but through being adopted in. Following the death of her father, a Jungarrayi man from a neighbouring country, Napaljarri's mother married Larry Jungarrayi's brother Mick Jungarrayi. She spent part of her childhood living at Yarripirlangu and grew up to be a highly regarded bilingual teacher, interpreter, night patroller, churchwoman and community leader.

While this extended family might be described as having achieved a high level of intercultural accomplishment there is a darker side to their post-settlement experience. One of Larry's brothers was removed by government authorities sometime in the 1940s. He was blind and light-skinned. It was five decades before Billy Panpa ('blind Billy') was reunited with Warlpiri relatives at Yuendumu, when he attended a family funeral. By this time all of his siblings were deceased. Another sister was understood to have been abducted by *jarnpa* malevolent beings while the family were living in the bush. In the two subsequent generations further children were removed on government orders — the son and daughter of two of Larry Jungarrayi's brothers sometime in the early 1960s, and one of Jimmy Jungarrayi's granddaughters was removed sometime in the 1970s. This most recent removal was resolved with the return of the child to her mother following the determined intervention of her older brother. In the early 1990s the family was further struck by tragedy when one of Jimmy Jungarrayi's sons and four members of his family died after their car broke down on an infrequently travelled road in the height of summer and they were stranded without drinking water.

How is such a litany of grief absorbed by a family over time? One way is by moving on and focussing on the present and future. The members of this extended family are spread across the continent — they live in Perth and Warakurna, Adelaide, Alice Springs, Hermannsburg, Walungurru and then across the Warlpiri townships of Nyirripi, Yuendumu, Willowra and Lajamanu. These traces of intergenerational experience through time and space give some compelling indications of how relationships to ancestral places — places that inevitably conjure up the persons with whom one shares inheritance, responsibility, pivotal life experiences — might be complexly felt and freighted in the present.

Stirring sentiments

In early 2013, two years after our overnight trip to Yarripirlangu, my research assistant Hannah Quinliven introduced Larry Jungarrayi's drawings to two of his brother's grandsons; one, a community leader based at the small Warlpiri community of Nyirripi, the other a busy bureaucrat based in Alice Springs. One brother was deeply moved by seeing the drawings and quietly took himself off to Yarripirlangu the following day. He visited a number of places and collected precious water from the mountain spring. Both brothers expressed considerable enthusiasm to undertake a trip to show us the places depicted by Larry Jungarrayi, and we made plans to do so several weeks later. When the appointed time came around however, the trip did not go ahead; for different reasons both men were preoccupied with more pressing business in Alice Springs.

My pursuit of the descendants of the Yarripirlangu brothers was sparked by a desire to generate some trace of Larry Jungarrayi, a man who left an indelible impression with his drawings, but who is largely absent in all the places a researcher might conventionally look. At the time I commenced this research Larry Jungarrayi had been dead for twenty years. The challenges of conjuring up a sense of the man and his legacy are multiple. Warlpiri attitudes to death have historically worked against the kinds of traditions celebrated in European societies that work to keep the memory of a person alive. While Warlpiri practices concerning the deceased are transforming, at the time of Larry Jungarrayi's death it was conventional for all belongings of the deceased to be either destroyed or redistributed among certain relations. His name would not have been spoken in the presence of his close relatives for a period of years. Notwithstanding the intimate memories held and expressed by those who grieve the loss of a loved-one, Warlpiri deceased are enfolded in a family lineage of place-based associations that tend to disperse the character and life trajectory of any particular individual.

Further, while Larry Jungarrayi was a senior Warlpiri man he would not have acquired significant material assets. In place of the customary papers and possessions that deceased persons of print-literate cultures leave behind, Larry Jungarrayi's most tangible legacy, aside from his outstation, lies in his collaboration with other senior men on the painting of the Yuendumu school doors and other significant paintings in the early 1980s. A large canvas painted with Paddy Japaljarri Sims and Paddy Japaljarri Stewart prominently towers above visitors on a wall of the National Gallery of Australia in Canberra. The same work graces the cover of Wally Caruna's landmark survey *Aboriginal art,* and as I draft this chapter it is on display at the Royal Academy of the Arts in London, in a major survey of Australian art. Interestingly, in the history of Yuendumu's acrylic painting movement Larry Jungarrayi is known largely for his collaborations with other men rather than for solo productions.

The painting of the Yuendumu school doors by five senior men has come to stand as the potent embodiment of the two-way education program that was introduced across remote Aboriginal townships through the 1980s, symbolically marking recognition of and respect for Warlpiri knowledge and authority in a place of western learning. The painting of the doors also marks a significant moment in the origin myth of Central Australian Aboriginal art history — a moment at which painting for ceremonial purposes was refigured for the purpose of a new kind of community-making. Tess Napaljarri was scribe and translator for the book that documents this project by Warlukurlangu Artists, *Kuruwarri — Yuendumu Doors*. In 1995, worn by weather, daily use and graffiti, the doors were purchased by the South Australian Museum, restored and put on exhibition.

There are of course many kinds of inheritances that can be traced intergenerationally. Many of the descendants of Larry Jungarrayi have earned income as painters and his influence is particularly apparent in the work of his brother's grandson Jay Jay Jungarrayi Spencer. As custodian of a potent love magic site at Yarripirlangu, Larry Jungarrayi had a reputation as a ladies' man. One grandson tells of wrestling with an inherited urge to pursue girlfriends, while a granddaughter tells me of the reputation held by Yarripirlangu women as powerful seductresses. Larry's own marriage was childless. He is said to have fathered a daughter, but she was raised by another family and is now deceased. There is no 'direct' descendent of Larry Jungarrayi. Yet as suggested by our story so far, Warlpiri are less concerned with biological descent than they are with the social circumstances of 'growing up' and 'looking after' one another.[13] Several of his brother's children spent periods of time residing with him and his wife Ruby Nangala at the outstation. They recall a quiet, kind and knowledgeable man.

Old monsters newly seen

One morning in late May 2013 I am sitting with one of Jimmy Jungarrayi's daughters on the sparsely grassed ground beside her house in an Alice Springs town camp. A sign on the front fence of Napaljarri's dwelling with its neat yard declares it to be an alcohol-free zone. I had visited this house briefly the previous afternoon and introduced the copies of the drawings to this woman. She was visibly moved to see the pictures and upbeat at the prospect of me returning the following day to share her memories of her father and his brothers. However, this

morning I find Napaljarri more reserved, deferring to the superior knowledge and memory of her absent brother, the man I had hoped to meet at this house, but who had left for the distant township of Walungurru the previous day. Another sister who resides in the house next door, who I had also hoped to see, had similarly departed the previous day for Yuendumu.

Among his more explicitly anthropomorphic pictures Larry Jungarrayi produced a series of drawings of *jarnpa*, malevolent beings. These *jarnpa* pictures, two by Larry Jungarrayi and two by Abe Jangala, are distinguished as the only drawings Meggitt directly referred to in any published writings.[14] Meggitt's account of *jarnpa* tracks the appearance of these figures in *Jukurrpa* narratives and songs. He reports having attended *jarnpa*-related ceremonies in December 1953 where Larry Jungarrayi and Abe Jangala danced together.

Meggitt describes *jarnpa* as malicious beings 'who on occasion seem to be wholly immaterial and to possess miraculous powers, yet have many human qualities and frailties'.[15] He lists the specific countries in which *jarnpa* are said to reside and reports that not all of the places named by his informants could be located.[16] *Jarnpa* were known to prefer sandhill country, to make their camps near rock holes surrounded by trees and dense vegetation. Warlpiri men told Meggitt *jarnpa* were capable of moving at extraordinary speed, through the air. Warlpiri could not see *jarnpa* yet had a clear sense of their physical characteristics — they were black, very black, blacker than Warlpiri people, with course hair that stood straight up, or headdresses that created the same effect. Their eyes were bright red and their mouths similarly a terrifying blood-red. They had huge penises that were always partially erect. They were left-handed, whistled like birds (although they could speak if they wished), wore emu-feathered boots and were invisible to all but dogs, *ngangkari* (medicine men), ancestral heroes and *kardiya*. Their invisibility meant they could enter a camp and steal anything they liked. In the dark of night people would extinguish fires if there was concern that *jarnpa* were close by.[17]

Jarnpa were known to take human wives. These women as well as small children were abducted when out hunting alone. Women were said to remain with their abductors because the sexual prowess of *jarnpa* kept them satisfied.[18] Those who were not taken as wives were raped and killed. *Jarnpa* left tell tale signs of their crimes, they snapped the necks of their victims by twisting the head back over the shoulder. Another signature method involved killing a victim by fatally damaging an internal organ; the afflicted person was killed but brought back to life for two to three days before they would fall down dead.[19] What Meggitt did not report and perhaps was not told, was that Larry Jungarrayi's family held that one of his sisters had been abducted by *jarnpa*.

Looking at these *jarnpa* drawings with Napaljarri in Alice Springs I am struck once again by the way the drawings get taken up to animate the pressing concerns of the present. Meggitt describes one figure not as *jarnpa* but more ambiguously as a 'man walking around in the night going to urinate . . .' (figure 10). As I hand this picture to Napaljarri and read its description she grimaces with recognition — '*jarnpa*', she says. I ask her to tell me about *jarnpa*. Pointing across the town camp she says she sometimes sees them silhouetted against the lamppost in the distance at nightfall. They come out at sunset, 'that's the real time for *jarnpa*'. In the long shadows that form at that time of day you can see them. They live 'in every country, in the *yuwurrku*', scrub. In the bush they are often close to *kurrkara* desert oak trees. They look like *kurrkara*, 'hairy trees, hairy men, *kurdaitcha*'. They do not talk. In earlier times, she emphasises, '*jarnpa* were not people, but *really jarnpa*'. They tried to 'get good-looking girls', were particularly attracted to nice-looking girls with combed and oiled hair and skin. They used to hang around the big dam at Yuendumu (a favoured drinking spot just outside the ten mile radius that marks the boundary of community-enforced alcohol prohibition), Napaljarri tells me.

Today, Napaljarri tells me, people are trying to turn themselves into *jarnpa*. 'They make themselves invisible. They've seen things on movies that they copy. They learn skills like ninja out in the bush.' These new *jarnpa*-people come into houses, they look at the layout of sleeping positions so they can come back in the dark and kill a person. There are lots of these *jarnpa*-people now and 'lots of people are getting killed'. I have heard similar stories from Warlpiri friends, accounting in part for the high levels of anxiety that currently pervade the community. Whereas in an earlier time Meggitt reported that fires were extinguished to ward off *jarnpa*, in the present Napaljarri leaves the lights on around the perimeter of her house all night to ward off these devils; she calls these lights 'angels'. Most important, however, is the presence of God. 'Wapirra looks out for us', she tells me.

> He's the big one; he stops them. Like a shield. You see them coming along that road [she nods in the direction of the highway], as the sun is going down. They can't come to this house. I don't drink. I pray to *Wapirra*.

'That trouble is over now at Yuendumu', Napaljarri observes. 'Only here in town we have these problems. They shouldn't come around here looking for fights. If they want to fight they should go to Afghanistan.' Napaljarri is slight of frame and as we sit on the ground she intermittently rubs a section of puckered skin on her neck and a long shiny scar on her right calf — there is a metal plate in there. She survived a horrific car accident three years ago in Adelaide in which the driver died. Her recovery was long and difficult. She used to drink, she tells me, but not since that accident. That's when she found God.

Napaljarri tells me that in recent times another kind of *jarnpa* has also started appearing, *jarnpa* who are not dangerous, just hungry. They enter houses in the night and take food. In the morning when people wake up they find their cupboards and refrigerators empty. But they know it wasn't people who ate that food, 'it was *jarnpa*'.

Picturing power

Larry Jungarrayi demonstrated a remarkable openness to European ways when, as a man in his early twenties, he willingly made the journey on the back of a truck from Yuendumu to the unknown destination of Hooker Creek. Several of his relatives boarded the truck alongside him, but changed their minds at the last minute and jumped off. Larry continued on. He stayed on at Hooker Creek,

Figure 9:
Larry Jungarrayi,
Jarnpa, Hooker Creek 1953–4.
(Drawing #53, Meggitt Collection,
AIATSIS.)

'This is his version of a demon, a *jarnpa* demon.
You'll notice a black demon with red eyes, a
huge penis, red footprints and a red cursing bag
in his hands. A very different interpretation from
Abe Jangala's and this is fair enough because
demons are invisible' (Mervyn Meggitt).

Figure 10:
Larry Jungarrayi:
A man in the night, Hooker Creek
1953–4.
(Drawing #54, Meggitt Collection,
AIATSIS.)

'A representational figure. A red figure. This is a man
who wanted to urinate in the middle of the night.
Got up, felt thirsty, got his billy can (which you see
in his hand) and is walking down to the red creek
with the red trees to get some water. The night
time is represented by the blue all round him. A
straightforward representation' (Mervyn Meggitt).

being employed as the community's baker among other things, until sometime in the 1970s when he returned to Yuendumu. Tess Napaljarri remembers the family gathering to meet Jungarrayi and his wife Nangala when they disembarked from the airplane. From Yuendumu he would ultimately relocate to his ancestral country Yarripirlangu as outstation infrastructure was established. Yet, as is the Warlpiri way, relocation did not signal an end to Jungarrayi's mobility. He frequently journeyed between Yarripirlangu and Yuendumu and throughout the region as social and other imperatives took him. Larry Jungarrayi died one night in 1990, drunk and asleep, on the open tray-back of a vehicle returning from Alice Springs to Yuendumu.

The knowledge that one of Larry Jungarrayi's siblings was thought to have been taken and killed by *jarnpa* and that three generations of this family suffered government-directed child removals lends heavy weight to Larry's drawings of devil figures and to his descendants' responses to them. It also makes his openness to taking the journey to the then unknown destination of Hooker Creek on the back of a government truck all the more remarkable.

At the time Larry Jungarrayi made his *jarnpa* pictures, Meggitt suggests these Evil Beings were conceived as a distinct class, not people, nor their ancestors. In the post-settlement period Warlpiri have had good reason to re-attribute evil monster-like activity to the realm of human agency. Questions of power loom large here. In 1955 Meggitt noted that white people were immune to *jarnpa* attack, and the presence in camp of a white man with a gun could be invoked to ward off *jarnpa*. He observed somewhat drily that the spectre of *jarnpa* served a particular purpose of social control — control asserted by senior men over women, over young men and over the orderly conduct of ceremonies. In the present *kardiya* continue to be regarded as having enhanced powers to see and ward off *jarnpa*; on one occasion in 1995 after I described an incident to friends it was put to me that I and I alone had seen a 'man' who was 'not *yapa*'.

Is there a relationship between the perceived expanding reach of white power in Warlpiri lives, the ricocheting effects of intergenerational structural violence[20] and a rise in reports of demon and sorcery activity? Against a background in which the experience of evil acts of many kinds is pervasively a part of life, the attribution of *jarnpa*-like capacities to living persons makes sense. In the circumstances considered here we find resonances with the 'occult economy' anthropologists Jean Comaroff and John Comaroff describe for South Africa.[21] Pursuing our preoccupation with *visual* culture, we might identify these Warlpiri narratives as conjuring traces of an occult *visual* economy, one in which pictures of cyclone monsters circulate on mobile phones, rain snakes are observed circling the sky above the Alice Springs prison and passing judgment on incarcerated inmates, dramatic news reports announce army deployments to remote communities sparking fears that soldiers are coming to take children away, a government 'emergency response' implicates Aboriginal men as child-abusing monsters, and an escalation of increasingly brutal attacks in Alice Springs, reported and real, all converge.

The economic base of this visual economy is marked by increasing levels of unemployment and few opportunities for sustained meaningful activity, the tightening of government regulation of many aspects of Warlpiri people's lives, including mandatory income management for welfare recipients, the outlawing of customary law practices and alarming rates of imprisonment. This set of circumstances calls for new magic,[22] new means by which Warlpiri might — in the face of every indication to the contrary — reclaim some power, if only the power to explain these circumstances to themselves.

The simultaneous pursuit of power in two directions — through shoring up the explanatory power of *Jukurrpa* and in attempting to secure positive recognition from *kardiya* — carries its own transformative force. Nancy Munn observed that the force of country as a set of moral dispositions resulted from the relative closure of the social and geographical life space.[23] It was in this context that the material world provided Warlpiri persons 'with images or fragments' of the self. More recently Munn has written of the 'transposibility' that enables the power of Aboriginal Law to move dynamically with persons and objects across space.[24] Six decades

Figure 11:
Abe Jangala:
Jarnpa, Hooker Creek 1953–4.
(Drawing #28, Meggitt Collection,
AIATSIS.)

'Naturalistic representations of spotted demons in human form fighting with boomerangs . . . Demon footprints all over the place. One demon with a huge circle between his legs — that's demon testicles, the significance of which I don't know. Here, sand hills and you can see Abe is now looking/trying to handle perspective again or starting to handle it. [There are] sand hill flowers on top of the sand hills and a very sparse kind of pattern . . . I must say this one looks like an Easter Island statue. No, he hasn't seen those. This is simply demons fighting with boomerangs in the sand hill country. That's all he has to say about it' (Mervyn Meggitt).

after the first Warlpiri settlements were established, country is clearly much less contained, as is the workings of power. In such contexts images provide potent vehicles for the remaking of power. Images, as Mitchell observes, are 'active players in the game of establishing and changing values'.[25] But it is not only new images that furnish change. So it is that at a time when Warlpiri feel intensely the pressures brought to bear upon them from many directions, old pictures of *jarnpa* are re-imagined for new circumstances.

INTERLUDE IV
Remembering Mervyn Meggitt (1924–2004)

Figure 1:
Mervyn Meggitt with
Freddy Jangala (left) and
two unidentified men,
Hooker Creek 1953–4.
(Photograph: Joan Meggitt,
Meggitt Collection, AIATSIS,
N390.142.)

Mervyn Meggitt's Warlpiri ethnography *Desert people* is widely considered a classic in the Australian anthropological literature. His achievements are all the more impressive given that his research in Central Australia involved just ten months at Hooker Creek in 1953 and 1954 for a Masters thesis, plus two brief return visits to Warlpiri country in 1955 and 1960. Meggitt was trained at Sydney University from 1948, after the foundation chair of anthropology AR Radcliffe-Brown had departed and AP Elkin had assumed this position, the only chair in the discipline in an Australian university at that time. Meggitt studied psychology, philosophy and ancient history in first year and then took up anthropology when it was possible to do so in second year. A committed and energetic student, Meggitt completed honours in psychology before submitting a second thesis in anthropology. His widow Joan recalls that he received the university medal for one degree and topped his class for the other. There was a moment of uncertainty when he was torn between pursuing higher research in both disciplines.

The making of an anthropologist

Elkin supervised Meggitt's Masters thesis and dictated his choice of field sites. He subsequently had a hand in securing Meggitt's early academic positions. But Meggitt's approach to fieldwork showed the influence of Ian Hogbin, who had studied under Malinowski at the London School of Economics.[1] Joan Meggitt describes her husband as 'very curious', a man of great intellectual interest and energy, with a good disposition for fieldwork. Mervyn had injured his knee badly in a bicycle accident as a child. He was not mechanically minded, did not drive a car and was a poor horse rider. Joan brought a range of practical support to the partnership. Both single children of Queensland country-town families, Joan and Mervyn travelled well and were at ease in the bush and in any sort of company. Mervyn adopted attire close to that of his informants in the field: shorts, sandals and a hat. Warlpiri addressed him by the adoptive skin name of Jupurrurla or 'Nugget' — Joan recalls 'Nugget' was the closest approximation to 'Meggitt' Warlpiri could enunciate. It was also a nickname Europeans commonly bestowed on relatively short Aboriginal men. Standing at approximately five foot eight inches, Meggitt was relatively short in comparison to his Warlpiri interlocutors.

Mervyn was born in the rural Queensland town of Warwick. His father worked as a salesman of household goods. He grew up in Roma until his parents sent him to board at the Church of England Grammar School in Brisbane. On turning seventeen he joined the navy and saw active service as a signalman. Interactions with locals in Biak, Papua New Guinea, were said to have stirred his interest in studying anthropology. Mervyn and Joan met in 1946 as Mervyn was in the process of being discharged. Mervyn completed matriculation in 1947 and enrolled in a Bachelor of Arts at Sydney University the following year with the support of a Commonwealth Reconstruction and Training Scheme scholarship offered to returned servicemen. Mervyn and Joan were married in January 1949.

While Joan earned the substantial wage needed to cover their cost of living, during term breaks Mervyn took various jobs, working short stints as a gravedigger, an attendant at a glassworks factory, a night-shift worker in a post office, a production-line worker in a cordial factory and a jackaroo on a sheep station. In this latter position he earned the approval of the station manager who was keen for him to stay on, despite his lack of horsemanship. No doubt Meggitt's fastidiousness impressed employers; this had been cultivated by his mother and then enforced in four years attending boarding school and during his time in the navy.

After completing his Masters degree Meggitt was convinced by Elkin to go on to a PhD (which was now possible at Sydney), with a new study of the Enga in the Papua New Guinea Highlands. Jeremy Beckett recalls that this suggestion was particularly appealing as it offered the chance to work with people who were still primarily self-sufficient and as yet little influenced by colonisation.[2] Mervyn and Joan would continue to make return visits to Papua New Guinea every three years until the early 1980s. They left Australia with Mervyn taking up a research fellowship at Manchester in 1963, and then relocated to the United States the following year for a position at Ann Arbour, Michigan. Neither of these positions proved to be particularly congenial and two years later Meggitt secured a post at City University of New York where he remained until his retirement.

Enga research dominated Meggitt's anthropological attention across his career, but sporadically from 1968 to 1986 he also undertook work in an Andalucian fishing village in Spain. He is said to have thrown himself into this research with characteristic gusto, learning the language and spending late nights in deep conversation with men in the town's bar. He never published any of this research. Beckett speculates that Meggitt's failure to write about Andalucia resulted from an inability to get sufficient distance; unlike the Warlpiri and Enga, the Spanish fishermen 'were too much like him'.[3] However, Joan recalls the intimidating presence of the secret police in the village who were watching everyone and had a close eye on Mervyn. Undertaking research in Franco's Spain was a risky endeavour and Mervyn was determined not to jeopardise the safety of his informants.[4]

Meggitt's research interests were not politically motivated, nor did he aspire to be a public intellectual. His career reveals more a commitment to the intellectual work of anthropology rather than to a particular community of people — notwithstanding that the Meggitts did return to the Enga every three years for more than two decades. But anthropology was a job. That he was able to walk away from it on retirement with such astounding finality signals this. Meggitt gave up anthropology in much in the same way as he earlier gave up driving and photography on deciding he lacked the arts of each.[5] Retiring from City University of New York as Distinguished Emeritus Professor in 1992, Meggitt didn't go to any meetings or give any seminars. He did not publish papers. Living directly behind the Metropolitan Museum of Art in New York, he then dedicated himself to the world of galleries and art history.

Looking back across Meggitt's career, his time at Hooker Creek emerges as a discrete and highly focused period. As with all of his substantial fieldwork expeditions, Mervyn was accompanied by the vivacious and energetic Joan (figure 2). Joan features in many of Mervyn's Hooker Creek photographs, often in the company of Warlpiri with a look of sparkling enjoyment across her face. It was Joan who collected the small number of drawings made by Warlpiri women and who furnished her husband with insights into women's experience in Warlpiri society. Such a husband-and-wife approach to fieldwork was conducive to efficient research.

Joan and others close to Mervyn recall he was 'very good at telling stories against himself'; he had a great, self-deprecating humour. He was said to be the life of the party as a young man, but got quieter with age. He had a strong degree of personal reserve. Joan recalls he didn't like asking personal questions of his informants and did not like having them asked of himself. In fact, Joan suggests that this reticence to pry into other people's business was an important factor in his turning away from anthropology.

Towards the end of Meggitt's working life there was, in fact, a confluence of forces at play. The pair stopped visiting the Enga in the early 1980s, dedicating that time to visiting aging parents in Brisbane who required their attention. By then an aggressive postcolonial politics had emerged in the Papua New Guinea Highlands, resulting in some confronting altercations between Mervyn and younger Enga. In the same period, American anthropology was on the cusp of a paradigm shift as structural-functionalism met its final challenge from a new approach that rejected anthropology as an exercise in the collection of facts and emphasised rather the work of interpretation. Beckett recalled that in the case of Meggitt this new anthropology influenced by the work of Clifford Geertz 'simply made him angry'.[6]

Beckett recalls his friend as a highly engaging presenter:

> He delivered his papers with verve, based in a command of the facts and an enviable incisiveness, enlivened by shafts of wit that in the right company might verge on the raunchy. I well remember a hilarious paper on Enga fantasies delivered at Sydney about what he called 'the cannibal cock' — humour which owed a good deal to his early days in country Queensland and the Australian navy. He never lost his Australian accent.'[7]

Mervyn was first diagnosed with lung cancer in 1984 when he was sixty. He had been a smoker since his time in the navy, but had quit a decade before the diagnosis. In August 2004 secondary cancers were discovered following a trip to Australia where he struggled to keep his usual energetic pace of travel. The grim prognosis gave him three months to live. He died in November 2004.

On anthropological attention

> As the mythical ancestors and culture heroes of the long past Dreamtime had defined the characteristics of the totality once and for all when they had participated in its creation and shaping, any subsequent change in any variable would inevitably affect the whole — and that for

the worse. Thus it was the duty of every man to ensure, mainly in magico-religious means, that the status quo be preserved, an obligation that obviously ruled out most possibilities of cultural innovation, whether in the sphere of technology or of law.[8]

Ethnographic work in the period of Meggitt's training and research at Hooker Creek was shaped by the circumstances of that time, in the shadow of the Second World War, emerging from a culture of efficiency, no-nonsense practicality and making-do. Fieldworkers were trained to go off to the field with eyes wide open, attentive to much that went on around them. Meggitt was exceptionally energetic and meticulous, but as the quote above suggests, his attention — like that of others of his generation — was honed to reading cultural situations in terms of continuity over change. In the field of mid-century anthropology, what mattered in culture was to be carved out of the day to day. Priority focus was given to what Stanner had dubbed 'high culture', the ceremonial realm and social organisation. Anthropologists of this period were eager to distil the rules and models by which Aboriginal people lived. The ideology of the Dreaming premised an unchanging world order; people were compelled to 'follow up the Dreaming'. In the Warlpiri case this was reinforced by an insistence that ritual occasions be conducted 'proper way'. Such attitudes as observed by anthropologists were taken as evidence that Aboriginal societies were overwhelmingly conservative.

Once such an analysis was grasped ethnographic attention was attuned accordingly, directed away from seeing activity in terms of innovation or change. The article in which Meggitt articulates these ideas is an exploration of Aboriginal 'forms of government'; he makes similar arguments about a Warlpiri tendency towards conservation of natural species in a paper on the relationship between Warlpiri and dingoes.[9] In Chapter 1 of this book I explored similar sentiments expressed by Meggitt's contemporaries in relation to Central Australian Aboriginal visual culture. Art was read as mirroring the shape and sentiment of the wider society.

Meggitt wrote careful and detailed structural-functionalist anthropology, despite his suggestion that 'true' structural-functionalist accounts of Aboriginal Australia were not achievable due to the degree of colonial disruption experienced.[10] Beckett observes that Meggitt would be regarded today as a positivist and 'probably wouldn't have objected to the label'.[11] *Desert people* is lively with

Figure 2:
From left, Lydia Nakamarra with baby Connie Nungarrayi, Joan Meggitt, Lucy Nakamarra, unidentified girl, Hooker Creek c. 1953–4. (Photograph: Mervyn Meggitt, Meggitt Collection, AIATSIS, N390.90.)

observational anecdote, but it is ultimately a methodical work constrained by the conceptual thinking within which it was framed.

Meggitt's lengthy papers on Warlpiri initiation and on *jarnpa* malevolent spirits are where his meticulous research gives rise to his most compelling writing. His 1966 paper, 'Gadjari among the Walbiri,' inspired by Stanner's *On Aboriginal religion*, reveals Meggitt's deep attentiveness to ceremonial activity. A celebration of the ritual at the heart of Warlpiri high culture, the paper deals with material that cannot be explored here. What this writing reveals beyond its descriptive content is not only an alert and scrupulous fieldworker, but also a man emotionally moved by Warlpiri cultural life. Conveyed in compelling fashion are the epic, world-making events of Warlpiri *Jukurrpa*, the journeys traversed over considerable distance, the dramas that unfold along the way, the tragedies and treacheries of human and spirit dealings, and the continual cycle of death and birth that are replayed again and again across this body

of cosmology. Meggitt also conjures well the energy, curiosity and pleasure that drives these vital tales and their re-enactment. This is no technical translation. Writing of a particular performance Meggitt observes, 'the stage-management is superb and the singing of haunting beauty'.[12]

Among Warlpiri people today there remain only the slimmest traces of memory of Mervyn Meggitt, unsurprising given that six decades have passed since his time at Hooker Creek and all of his close informants have died. Meggitt has become synonymous with *Desert people*, his book that circulates among interested men from time to time. Two responses to the book are common; the first is anger at Meggitt's publication of photographs and descriptive material regarded as either restricted or in other ways inappropriate for public circulation. The second response is more circumspect, seeing Meggitt's work as valuable for its contribution to recording important cultural material for future generations of Warlpiri.

Any drawn place is both a here
and an elsewhere.

John Berger, *Berger on drawing*

Chapter 5
Trees at Hooker Creek

In the journey tracked in the previous chapter Larry Jungarrayi's drawings of *jarnpa* prompted Napaljarri to talk of terrifying killers. But when Jerry Jangala looks at the *jarnpa* pictures made by his classificatory 'big brother', Abe Jangala, he speaks of countrymen.

On looking at these drawings as we sit together out the back of the Warnayaka Art Centre at Lajamanu in August 2013, Jerry Jangala becomes animated and tells me a series of stories in quick succession. The first story concerns Jerry Jangala's classificatory grandparents Jangala and Nungarrayi who lived in Kurlpulurnu country. One day the couple placed their baby boy Jampijinpa under a tree while they went to get water from a rockhole close by. On their return their baby had vanished. They knew straightaway, a *jarnpa* had taken him. The *jarnpa* transformed the baby boy into a *jarnpa* and took him to a place called Walangara. Many years later that Jampijinpa came back, as a grown man. Jerry Jangala saw him once. By that time the *jarnpa* had acquired a family. Jerry Jangala remembers seeing them all lined up, shadowed against the horizon, one night when his family were camped at Wardilka near Mt Theo. That's 'really *jarnpa* country', he tells me.

Another time, Jerry Jangala was camped in the same country with his family. He was about six years old. They all went to collect *marnakiji* bush sultana and *yuparli* bush banana. After they had collected a good amount of fruit everyone gathered round and made a camp at the base of a *ngapiri* river red gum tree. After they had eaten and rested a while, all the family dispersed to go hunting again, except Jerry Jangala. He stayed behind eating more of the freshly collected fruit. As they all walked away Jangala

Figure 1:
Abe Jangala,
Jarnpa in the sandhills,
Hooker Creek 1953–4.
(Drawing #29, Meggitt
Collection, AIATSIS.)

'Demons, hidden in the sand hills, spotted demons and you can see them with their peculiar headdresses on. The headdresses are supposed to make them invisible. The sand hills are represented and on top of the sand hills, red flowers which may be Sturt Desert Pea or something of that kind' (Mervyn Meggitt).

saw what looked to be a man and his family appear, walking towards him. When he saw that family he was no longer able to eat the fruit, his eyes began to sting and his body felt numb. The family were *jarnpa*. The *jarnpa*-man, who Jangala knew as Jampijinpa, his classificatory father, came close. He threw dust in front of Jerry Jangala and picked him up. He said, 'Jangala, I want to take you'. Then he took the boy south-west to mulga country, to a place called Mantarla. He kept Jangala there until late afternoon. Meanwhile his family were unaware that Jangala had been taken. They were hunting in another direction from the camp.

That *jarnpa* looked after Jerry Jangala, fed him goanna and kangaroo and then brought him back to his family. By then everyone was looking for him. His mother was crying. They thought Jangala had been taken by *jarnpa* or a snake. When he was brought back to his family Jangala had an unquenchable thirst and quickly threw himself down to drink water from a rockhole. Then he vomited very violently. Jangala's father was a *ngangkari*, a traditional healer, and he treated the boy to undo the affects of *jarnpa's* powers. Jangala recalls he was so exhausted by this episode he couldn't walk around for several weeks.

In another story Jerry Jangala tells of how the same *jarnpa* family came and took two dogs belonging to another family, took them to Winnecke Creek. Members of that family deduced that the dogs had been taken by *jarnpa* and called out to them at sunset, 'bring back those two dogs!' The next morning the dogs returned. The same thing happened to another family who had a problem with too much drinking; their dogs were similarly taken away by *jarnpa* overnight and returned the following morning. I ask Jangala why the *jarnpa* took these dogs. He tells me he is not sure, perhaps they thought they knew them.

In Jerry Jangala's story there is a sense of *jarnpa* ambiguously occupying human form and able to be seen by some Warlpiri such as himself, under certain circumstances. Emphasising their humanness, Jerry Jangala recalls that one Jangala man, the son of that Jampijinpa *jarnpa*, 'finished up' (died) at Wave Hill. Another Jangala man from Wave Hill, he tells me, is still called '*Jarnpa*'. *Jarnpa* visits are not unusual

occurrences for Jerry Jangala's family because they are regarded as *warlalja*, countrymen; they have rights to occupy and move through the same country. *Jarnpa* are tricky, the subject of curiosity, they are dangerous and mysterious, they abduct children and dogs, but they are not deadly. Jangala tells me he still sings ceremonies for *jarnpa* at *kurdiji* initiation time.

Jerry Jangala moves from sharing these stories of *jarnpa* deeds to describing the etiquette of how people should move through country:

> we can't just walk in like *kardiya*, [and say] 'ah this is nice country, I'm gonna take this country'. We got to talk to that country, apologise to that country. Otherwise we might have that goanna and we might get sick. Country might not have right feeling for me.

'Country and people feel', Jangala tells me; 'country gives back if you treat it properly. If you want to cut wood for a campfire, you got to treat that country properly.'

Such matters of moral attitude to country and its resources are crucial to older Warlpiri people and acquire heightened sensitivities where much movement of people has occurred. These sensitivities and the confrontation with settler–colonial attitudes have put new demands on Warlpiri principles, causing men like Jangala to find new ways to articulate them with clarity and force. In speaking of 'apologising' to country Jangala indicates the appropriate attitude of a man who has been introduced to, rather than directly inherited, ownership of a place.[1] In this chapter we take up these questions of moral attitude to country and the relations between persons they necessarily entail, returning for one last time to the conundrum raised by Larry Jungarrayi's series of drawings identified by Meggitt as 'trees at Hooker Creek'.

Depictions of trees, figures recognisable to the European eye as trees, are a strongly recurring feature through the drawings Meggitt collected. Fifty-five of 119 public drawings include what Meggitt describes as 'representational' depictions of trees, trees drawn in numerous ways by numerous picture makers. The questions posed by these trees are not

Figure 2:
(Left) Abe Jangala: *A landscape in the desert*, Hooker Creek 1953–4. (Drawing #37, Meggitt Collection, AIATSIS.)

'Note the stylized perspective and the massing of colours. The trees are a version of the silky oak. The drawing is intended to be purely decorative' (Mervyn Meggitt.)

(Right) Abe Jangala, *Landscape in the desert*, Hooker Creek 1953–4. (Drawing #38, Meggitt Collection, AIATSIS.)

'The same thing. These are the hills out in the desert. Again you have a waterhole (a black circle) and then the lines that give you the hills (the perspective in the background — red hills, yellow hills, black hills) and then a small tree done on one side. This is becoming very far removed from totemic drawing.' (Mervyn Meggitt.)

separate from those posed by Abe Jangala and Larry Jungarrayi's *jarnpa* drawings; indeed, in some cases, the drawings of trees and *jarnpa* appear to mark shared trajectories, conjuring up interacting elements of specific places and the Warlpiri world at large.

Recall Napaljarri's observation that *jarnpa* occupy *kurrkara*, desert oak tree country; she described *jarnpa* as hairy men who look like *kurrkara*. In figure 1 Abe Jangala depicts *jarnpa* in the sand dune country they are known to occupy, surrounded by a species of flowering plant that Meggitt speculates might be Sturt's Desert Pea. It is unclear whether this attribution came from Abe Jangala or Mervyn Meggitt. Jerry Jangala is perplexed by Meggitt's description of the tree as 'a desert version of the silky oak'. Desert walnuts, not oaks, Jerry Jangala insists, grow in the country of his fathers and grandfathers, the country Abe is likely to have pictured.

One confusion at work in this comparative picture is that Larry Jungarrayi, whose pictures April Napaljarri responded to was Ngalia, a southern Warlpiri man, while Abe Jangala was Warnayaka, northern Warlpiri. The country of the southern Tanami Desert is markedly different from the north and populated by different species of trees. Meggitt's non-specific attributions of species may pose no problem to a European reader, but they flummox Warlpiri as each species points to different country. What the quandary reveals is that species of trees matter enormously, they provide anchor points from which other things follow or can be deduced, they index

known places, particular ancestors, certain persons' right to tell, paint, sing.

The European tendency to deploy vague abstract categories sits at odds with such a Warlpiri attitude. In his essay 'The science of the concrete',[2] Claude Levi-Strauss rejected the idea that the abstract categories of European science indicated a higher level of intelligence in the working of human minds. Rather, he suggested more or less abstract ways of thinking indicated differences in interests and attention to the world at large. Levi-Strauss was particularly interested in the tendency of native societies to identify by name seemingly infinite varieties of natural species. He suggested a community might have dozens of names for a class of trees not for utilitarian or biological reasons, but to satisfy intellectual needs. Levi-Strauss showed classification to be part of a universal human need for order. An approach to classification in one sector of life mapped onto others, so that attitudes to the natural world were similarly enacted in the structure of kin relations, mythology, food and art.

Warlpiri would have provided rich data for Levi-Strauss' experiments in structural analysis, and Nancy Munn's work on Warlpiri image making is in many ways an exercise in exploring the efficacy of such an approach. But as this book has highlighted there are elements of picturing in the Hooker Creek drawings that do not easily seem to fit such schema, and these have led our enquiry in other directions.

Figure 3:
Larry Jungarrayi:
Trees at Hooker Creek, Hooker
Creek 1953–4.
(Drawing #57, Meggitt Collection,
AIATSIS.)

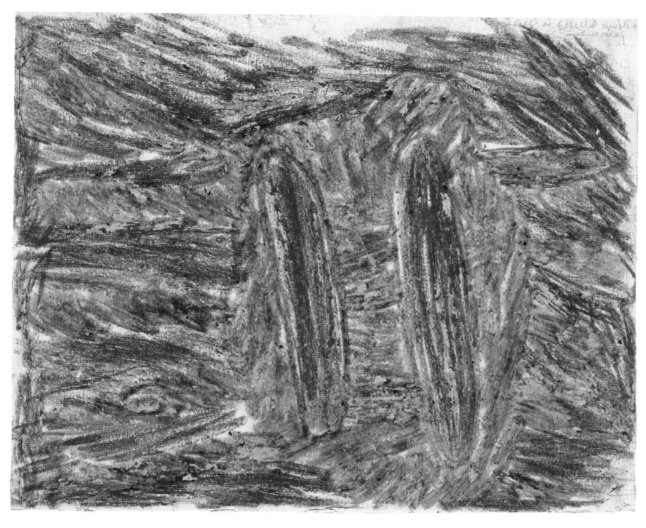

Figure 4:
Larry Jungarrayi:
Red country with blue trees, Hooker Creek 1953–4.
(Drawing #82, Meggitt Collection, AIATSIS.)

In a final attempt to grapple with the quandary posed by the drawings, in this chapter I pursue two avenues, one by way of John Berger, the other by way of Jerry Jangala, the younger classificatory brother of Abe Jangala, who has lived all of his adult life in and around Hooker Creek.

Looking at trees

In his treatise *Berger On drawing*, Berger distinguishes between three kinds of drawings. Firstly, those which study and question visible phenomena, an approach to drawing, he suggests, that carries traces of the artist's gaze, interrogating the strangeness of what is before him. A second class of drawings distil images or ideas in the mind's eye, things that are often closed to another person. And, in a third class, drawings are made from memory; drawings declare: 'I saw this'.[3]

Through this categorisation Berger seems to presume a clear demarcation of attention, that drawing involves an undistracted mode of engagement between drawing subject and drawn object. Yet does attention work in this way? Is it not the case that intense focus frees the mind to wander, to meditate upon things not being directly apprehended? Cannot all three aspects coalesce in the same drawing? Drawing in what we might refer to as the Warlpiri natural history mode — drawings that produce visual accounts of true happenings as recalled by the maker — by their very nature combine the action and authority of observation with the depiction of images taken from dreams. The demarcation between history and mythology is not easily made in Warlpiri reckoning, as others have noted in various contexts,[4] and indeed shall be seen below.

Figure 5:
Larry Jungarrayi:
Yarripirlangu, Hooker
Creek 1953-4.
(Drawing #49, Meggitt
Collection, AIATSIS.)

Recall that for Berger a picture of a tree depicts not a tree but *a tree being looked at*. So, how do Warlpiri people look at trees? One way to address this question (and keeping the work of Levi-Strauss close to mind) is through language. *Watiya* denotes a generic class of trees, shrubs, wood and also spears. But in most contexts Warlpiri will identify specifically named species for particular purposes. Trees have different densities and qualities of wood, bark, foliage and seeds suited to a wide variety of uses. Different species are favoured for making fire, for erecting humpies strong enough to withstand dramatic weather events, for shaping spears and carving boomerangs, digging sticks, dancing boards and other ritual paraphernalia. Branches of foliage from particular shrubs are utilised for smoking new babies and ritually cleansing domestic and public spaces following a death. Different species of tree are directly linked to the locations where they grow; such locatedness in turn confers authority and ownership

of species on particular persons and lineages of persons. Identified as *kurrkara* desert oak, *yinirnti* bean tree, *wapurnungku* ghost gum, *marrarnki* desert walnut, trees are significant actors in the ancestral order. Particular trees are identified as persons, deceased relatives incarnate. Trees acquire sacredness by virtue of becoming conception sites, the places where babies are conceived. Thus trees are *made into places* as a result of human action.[5]

While the tenets of this way of seeing are collectively held, the two perspectives on *jarnpa* canvassed in this and the previous chapter make clear that *shared ways of seeing do not equate with seeing the same thing.* Questions of social location, gender and life history bear down upon the way any particular person looks at a picture. Eric Michaels observed strong gendered differences in what men and women saw in video footage in the early 1980s.[6] Drawings made in response to the 1950s drawings suggest that the eyes of senior women are attracted to those elements that minimise risk of transgression; when Rosie Nangala took up Abe's *jarnpa* drawing (Interlude I) as a stimulation for her own picture making she was firmly focused on the 'flowers' surrounding the *jarnpa* figures. This approach appears to enact a wider attitude to *Jukurrpa* and country — one which is careful and conservative, avoiding places and stories that are other people's business. Such an attitude to drawing mimics the attitude one should take to foreign or unfamiliar country.[7]

People with authority to do so see other things, for example, Larry Jungarrayi's drawing #82, described by Meggitt as 'red country with blue trees' (figure 4), is interpreted by two senior men as depicting the figures of Japangardi and Nungarrayi lying down, that is, the central characters whose illicit sexual liaison lies at the heart of Yarripirlangu's creation. In short, people see — or at least declare publicly that they see — what they are entitled to see. This is why Larry's trees at Hooker Creek provoke such bewilderment. There is, I am told, no entitlement, no rational explanation for why that man would give those trees his attention, no understandable reason why he should reveal those trees as the subject of his desire. The apparently simple act of looking at a tree is no neutral or disinterested act, but one weighty with associations and consequences.

So, attitudes to trees and to pictures of trees enact wider Warlpiri ways of ordering relations between persons and the world at large. In the era of settlement, the assumptions underpinning such an order were upended in multiple ways. Men such as Larry Jungarrayi and Abe Jangala were enlisted in work gangs to cut trees down, clearing the way for new vehicular roads from The Granites to Hooker Creek, from Alice Springs to Tennant Creek. They cut poles from branches and erected fences to establish boundaries between the properties and reserves proclaimed under the new European law that had been rolled out across stolen Warlpiri lands.

While the cutting of trees in and of itself was not new — Warlpiri relied heavily on wood for the construction of their own shelters, for making fire, spears, carrying bowls and ritual objects — the settlement regime was brought into being with a radical new European vision of clearing and construction. At the centre of this vision was the premise that human beings (at least Europeans) were separate from and masters over their environment.

The drawings Larry Jungarrayi made for Meggitt reveal he was much taken with trees. His drawings enact many ways of looking at trees. Trees coloured red or surrounded by red — reading from other drawings where Meggitt says he made this explicit, Jungarrayi seems to have consciously chosen this colour to convey power. Trees resembling, as men have pointed out to me, ritual paraphernalia, indicating he intended these images of trees to stand for Warlpiri power, trees running in multiple directions and planes (figure 5). Larry's brother's daughter April Napaljarri sparkled with recognition when she took up this drawing — 'ah, yes, *mangamanga* mulga, spinifex and mulga tree country', she said with a smile. 'That's my country. You can see all that mulga to the north of the outstation, and then all that spinifex country. Those are men's places; women need to stay away from them.'

Jungarrayi's drawings of unidentified bush suggest other dimensions of looking that are not so easily conveyed — immersion and attention — especially to the ground, but also to colour. These pictures (eg. figure 6) are unusual for their exploration of the qualities of colour and texture and light, playing with the ways image making draws forth emotional affect. Here Larry Jungarrayi seems to be most closely engaged in the kind of personal work of drawing that Berger writes of. The drawings have a mesmerising and dispersed quality; they seem, as Meggitt observes, a great distance from the ritual images whose icons are painted on bodies, objects and the ground with stark coloration and clarity intended to communicate to all who look upon them. Warlpiri ceremonies, Dreaming narratives and songs are high on passion and emotion, but these 'bush' pictures convey their emotional affects more quietly, depicting movement and light, as well as a shimmering, radiant power.

Figure 6:
Larry Jungarrayi:
Bush, Hooker Creek
1953–4.
(Drawing #66, Meggitt
Collection, AIATSIS.)

'An impressionistic view
of the bush. A pattern
in green and yellow'
(Mervyn Meggitt).

In pursuit of possible explanations for why Larry Jungarrayi may have depicted trees at Hooker Creek as well as non-place specific pictures of 'bush' we must look to other instances of Warlpiri creative action that followed people's relocation to Hooker Creek. Consider Jerry Jangala's story told in response to my question of how he came to have an outstation on what is ostensibly Gurinji land, at Lulju, just a few kilometres from the settlement. He tells the story in two parts that operate at two levels. The first locates the personal circumstances of Jerry Jangala's own life in relation to national events; notably the 1967 Referendum, hailed symbolically for the spirit of inclusion it extended to Aboriginal people and for marking an historic shift that would follow to a less paternalistic governance regime.[8] In Jangala's telling the significance of the Referendum is marked very differently — as Warlpiri became 'free people' who could drink, his life cascaded out of control. He, like many other Warlpiri, hails the role of Christianity in helping him regain sobriety and steadiness in life purpose. The move by Jangala to occupy Lulju with permission of Gurinji owners is integral to the story he tells of how he managed to steer a path back to regain control of his life and the capacity to help

others. As we talk and walk around the block at Lulju in late 2011 he points out the hole in the water tank that means there is no water supply at present and thus no prospect of living here. And indeed on my next visit to Lajamanu two years later, I find Jangala residing in the township as the broken tank is yet to be repaired.

In the second part of the story Jangala enfolds his 'little station' firmly into his family's intergenerational trajectory and he does so by telling me about three trees. He starts with the identification of the large *wirrkali* bloodwood tree that stands prominently adjacent to the tin houses. This is a sacred tree, it has become so since Jangala's family came to occupy this place, it marks the conception site for the first generation of children born to Jangala's family who camped beneath that tree before any housing had been established. Jangala then points out a *yinirnti* bean tree now standing several metres high, planted he tells me from a seed brought from his mother's country. Finally he points out a *nurrku* snappy gum tree he transplanted from the banks of Hooker Creek. As Jangala's story and actions compellingly suggest, trees mark itineraries, journeys made by persons — in this case from ancestral country — to settlement, to outstation. In Jerry Jangala's telling the bringing of these trees to this place provided a special kind of ontological anchorage, quite literally marking the uprooting and re-embedding of people in a new place.[9]

Seeing new places

Ethnomusicologist Stephen Wild, who conducted research at Hooker Creek as a PhD student in 1969 and 1970, observed that after Warlpiri were trucked to the settlement ritual activity intensified as part of the process of adjustment to a new life. Perhaps paradoxically there was more time for ceremonial business in the new settlement with its regimented working hours and provision of rations. The intensification of ceremony was vital as the newly assembled community of people struggled to ground themselves. Yet as time passed these rituals 'were associated with country that an increasing proportion of the population had never seen'.[10] Unsurprisingly many Ngalia, southern Warlpiri, walked back to

Yuendumu to be closer to their ancestral places. Something further was required to deal with the profound experience of dislocation and to legitimise the occupation of new country; new acts of place making were urgently needed to help people stay. According to Wild vigorous and innovative ritual activity followed on two fronts — there was an intensification of ceremonies that focused beyond Warlpiri country proximate to the new settlement, and there was adoption of ceremonies from Aboriginal groups to the north and north-west.

In one example of this process of adjustment to life at Hooker Creek, Abe Jangala (who was also renowned as a great dancer, figure 8) told Wild of a rain *purlapa*, a ceremonial song he was given by a spirit agent who visited him during a period of illness (Dreamings commonly come to people in dreams or states of illness). In the account that follows, note the way personal history and cosmology become entwined in the recounting of this new Warlpiri song. To quote Wild:

❝ The song cycle [series] starts at Ngawantji near Linnekar Creek, a tributary of the Ord River, plain country where Abe has been. From there it goes to a place called Palangayi and then to Inverway (cattle station). From Inverway it goes to Nongra Lake, where the spirit agent looked at bloodwood trees and sang about them. From Nongra Lake Abe and the spirit agent travelled to Warlumaninpa, about 30 miles west of Hooker Creek [Lajamanu], and there **the spirit agent looked at a thick line of trees along the creek south of the settlement**, and sang about them as far as Tipitipul. They then travelled to the 19 Mile Bore and to Wakakara, a Whirlwind Dreaming site near the bore which belongs to Kurinji and Mudbara tribes. There the spirit agent looked at a dead spirit agent and sang about it. Abe had seen the dead spirit agent there himself when he was chasing a goanna — it just consisted of bones. It was because Abe had seen this that the spirit agent taught him the songs about it. They then travelled to Kuruja, a line of hills this side of Top Spring — it is a Rain Dreaming site belonging to Kurinji, Mudbara and Warlpiri, and its dreaming track comes from Kurlpulurnu . . . They then travelled to Top Spring, then north along the road to Katherine . . . The

Figure 7:
Larry Jungarrayi:
Red trees beside Hooker Creek, Hooker Creek 1953–4.
(Drawing #70, Meggitt Collection, AIATSIS.)

spirit agent stopped along the road about twenty miles north of Top Spring at a water hole called Kamanji, which he sang about. Then he stopped at King River to sing about that. After that they travelled north to the salt water at Darwin . . . All the places the spirit agent sang about Abe had seen, and that is why he taught them to Abe.[11] ❞

In recounting this song Abe Jangala, as Wild observes, marks no clear distinction between his own identity and that of the spirit being. The two interweave and merge; the focus is on the journey itself, on the places *seen* by both. The story of acquiring the song follows the song itself; the act of creation *is* the song's narrative.

Figure 8:
Abe Jangala (centre, dancing), Hooker Creek 1953–4. (Photograph: Mervyn Meggitt, Meggitt Collection AIATSIS, N390.125.)

Abe conveys a sense of energetic and searching movement; as a young man he sought out the strange new world of the mining camps at The Granites and Tanami, but only stayed for short periods, after which he would retreat into the desert to immerse himself in the teachings of his father. He learned much about his ancestral country.[12] It was during this period as a fully initiated man in his early twenties that Abe Jangala acquired the stories and knowledge of this country that he depicted in a series of water drawings for Meggitt (figures 9 and 10). Several decades later he would go on to achieve acclaim for the acrylic paintings he made of these places and Dreamings.

As the war broke out Abe Jangala and other men were taken by truck to Alice Springs to build army barracks, a picture theatre, landing strips and bitumen roads. Men such as Abe have fond memories of that time; they found themselves to be on more equal terms with white men, their fellow labourers, than had ever been the case before. Following war's end, Abe Jangala went to Yuendumu where his family were then living, and spent several years making roads, cutting trees, building the airstrip and cutting timber for shelters and sheds.[13] Abe was a hard worker and enlisted to accompany the grader driver to clear a track to Catfish in preparation for the new settlement. He and one of his brothers worked the road as far as Supplejack, about 450 kilometres north of Yuendumu. At that point the two men declared their homesickness and walked back across the desert. Despite his reluctance, Abe then found himself on the back of the first truck of twenty people transported to Catfish by patrol officers to commence construction of the new settlement in 1948. In the intervening years he continued to move between Hooker Creek and Yuendumu, finding himself yet again on the back of one of the trucks that transported people out of Yuendumu in 1952:

When old people recall the journey they made as children on the back of two trucks from Yuendumu to Hooker Creek they similarly tell of the itinerary of the journey, the names of places where they stopped for rest, the camps made, the food they were served and the manner of that serving — in billycans, the people 'all lined up'. They recall the corned beef portions cut from the largest can many had seen, the carrot, beans, wheat flour for making damper, a special kind of black tobacco. They recall the bush foods harvested during the brief respites (bush potato, goanna, witchetty grub, bush onion), the long distance walked at one point in the journey before the truck returned to collect them and bring them to their final destination. The manner of remembering these journeys mimics the narrative form and interests of Dreaming narratives; Dreamings and history interpenetrate, they blend together as vehicles for world making.

Jangala recorded aspects of his life story for an oral history project sponsored by the NT Department of Education in 1977. In this account of his early life

> . . . nobody was asked if they wanted to go, they were just told. I went with them back to Hooker Creek, where they had to start a new life.
>
> But after two months some people started to drift back. This was not our country, this was Gurinji country, we didn't have our dreaming sites here, and especially the old people were not happy. So they simply walked back, all the way,

Figure 9:
Abe Jangala: *Rain snakes*, Hooker
Creek 1953–4.
(Drawing #33, Meggitt Collection,
AIATSIS.)

'Abe's idea of two rain snakes with a young one in the
sandhill country. The snakes are travelling towards
a waterhole around which bushes grow' (Mervyn
Meggitt). Notice the shrub-like figure to the bottom left
of the picture, very similar in style to the foliage that
predominates across Abe's *jarnpa* picture (figure 1).

Figure 10:
Abe Jangala: *Papinya*, Hooker
Creek 1953–4.
(Drawing #34, Meggitt Collection,
AIATSIS.)

'This is an interesting one. This is Papinya, the place — a rock hole and soak where two rain snakes live and it's near The Granites. Here you have a very neat depiction of the rock hole and the two snakes going into the rock hole. Near the rock hole is a huge lizard, a goanna, that looks really like a crocodile the way it's been drawn. It's been bitten by one of the rain snakes. Also, an emu, overdrawn and then if you look from the rock hole to the right you have the hills running away into the distance. Abe . . . says as you look at the hills, they turn into clouds and you see the clouds at the top in black and again the hills underneath the clouds and an emu coming from behind the hills to join up with the tails of the rain snakes. You can see the whole thing is a very sensitive, sweeping, circular pattern. No matter where you start in the drawing, you end up going right around. I think it's one of Abe's better efforts' (Mervyn Meggitt).

to Yuendumu, Mt Doreen and Granites. Others stayed for about ten months and then walked back. But I stayed, with others, and we built an airstrip, on the place where the transmitter station and the old rubbish dump is now. It was hard work, we had to cut and clear away all the bushes and trees and the European overseers were tough on us, always shouting at us and pushing us around. We were never paid any wages, just given rations of food, like everywhere.[14] 🌂

As suggested by his own memoir, Abe Jangala was a man adept at moving between *yapa* and *kardiya* contexts. By the time the Meggitts arrived at Hooker Creek Abe Jangala had been installed as head worker. Yet this did not preclude him from an active ceremonial life and intensive work as an informant to Meggitt. Joan Meggitt recalls that the two men became close friends.

Yet Abe's picture making indicates nothing of the intense intercultural history his life traverses. Unlike the drawings of his classificatory brother-in-law Larry Jungarrayi, not a single one of Abe Jangala's drawings deal with settlement architecture or hint at the new kinds of landscapes he encountered as he moved around, either by choice or under order. Abe confined his focus to the depiction of the Dreamings and country he inherited from his father. But within that range of focus he was, as Meggitt observed, just as caught up in creative experimental picturing as was Larry Jungarrayi.

Looking at this drawing (figure 10) Jerry Jangala declares his classificatory elder brother put 'the right one for this area'. He points out the pencil figures of emu and goanna that he tells me reside in countries adjacent to Papinya. He tells of a kind of hawk, *kirrkirlanji*, who picked up a snake at Wanimpiji and brought him through Papinya to a soakage called Mungularri. The snake fell from the bird's mouth into the rockhole at Papinya and kept travelling to Kurlpulurnu. The rounded black elements across the top of the drawing 'might be' the deep rockholes atop Kurlpulurnu Hill. The rainbow Jerry Jangala identifies in Abe's picture travelled from Kurlpulurnu to Christmas Bore. He goes on to speak about the many lines of rain activity in the area, as well as the *Kunya Kunya* song his father knew, a song to slow the rain,

to make it more gentle if there were violent lightning storms around. Water, snake, emu — they were 'all friends', all countrymen, 'they travelled together a long way', says Jerry Jangala.

In separate conversations I learn that Kurlpulurnu, as well as the important rain site in the neighbouring country Lungkarra-jarra, are now lost places. So difficult to get to, they have not been visited for decades. Sometime in the 1970s there was a great storm that washed away the sacred tree and soakage at Lungkarra-jarra. A number of expeditions to find these places, the most recent to the Kurlpulurnu area about ten years ago sponsored by the Central Land Council, have been unsuccessful. As Abe Jangala's drawings suggest, this is deep sandhill country, inaccessible by car. When Warlpiri walked out of that country sometime in the mid-1940s, driven by curiosity to visit the cattle station at Willowra and the new settlement at Yuendumu, they were unknowingly leaving those places behind, quite possibly for the last time.

Just as the media of song, story and drawing become mechanisms for holding on to lost places, they also provide the means by which people can picture themselves in new places:

🌂 and there the spirit agent looked at a thick line of trees along the creek south of the settlement, and sang about them as far as Tipitipul. 🌂

Could it be that in Abe Jangala's tale of journeying and the claim to authority and legitimacy it stakes lie an explanation for Larry Jungarrayi's trees? Indeed, might the line of trees sung by Abe be the very same set of trees pictured by Larry? Read through the prism of these creative adjustments to new places, have we not found our explanation, namely that Larry Jungarrayi was coming to terms with this new place in a similar fashion to that which Wild has recorded for Abe Jangala, only in crayon on paper rather than song? It seems a compelling proposition, but one that is roundly rejected by Jerry Jangala and other senior Warlpiri men who remain deeply bewildered by these 'trees at Hooker Creek' pictures.

Why would Larry Jungarrayi put those trees? *Which trees did he put in these pictures?* Jerry Jangala works back from Warlpiri premises; there were three sacred trees here at the settlement when we arrived, he tells me. A *wapurnungku* ghost gum tree near the ceremonial ground east of the township associated with a *kakalyalya / nguumarra* bird. That Dreaming is for Jakamarra, Nakamarra, Jupurrurla and Napurrurla. Then there is that *wirrkali* bloodwood tree that got killed by fire. That tree 'squared himself'. That tree is for Japaljarri, Napaljarri, Jungarrayi and Nungarrayi. And thirdly, he tells me there is a white gum, an important place for the *wampana* Hare Wallaby Dreaming for Jampijinpa, Nampijinpa, Jangala and Nangala.

Whichever way he looks at it, Jerry Jangala proclaims, Larry Jungarrayi was not the right man to put those trees. He was not *kurdungurlu* manager. He was not Warnayaka, northern Warlpiri. That Jungarrayi, Jerry Jangala tells me, '*didn't look right for this place*'.

Figure 11:
Joan Meggitt with baby Jean Nungarrayi, Hooker Creek 1953. (Photograph: Mervyn Meggitt, Meggitt Collection, AIATSIS, N390.148.)

Naming the future

If the primary vehicles of dynamic place making are stories, Dreaming trajectories, images conveyed in songs and ceremonial action, practices of naming provide another front along which we can learn much about Warlpiri post-settlement realities.

The recording of names, misspelled and duplicated, was as we saw in Chapter 3 one feature of how government agents and patrol officers misheard and misrecognised Warlpiri. When Joan Meggitt took up the position of matron of the newly constructed 'hospital', she acquired the job of bestowing European names on newborn babies. While six decades later Warlpiri memories of Mervyn and Joan Meggitt exist as little more than shadowy traces, the couple left long-standing marks on the community in the form of these names bestowed, notwithstanding that Joan's involvement in naming babies is not recalled today.

Joan remembers naming perhaps half a dozen children (all those born) in that year. She remembers that she gave babies Mervyn's parents' names, Reginald and Susan, but not the names of her own parents, Margaret and William, as these were already common. Joan tried hard to come up with names that people could pronounce. Susan was not especially successful in this regard, with Warlpiri struggling to sound the hard 'S' as it does not appear as the first letter of Warlpiri words. Lydia Nakamarra referred to her child as 'Tuden'. Joan gave her own name, or the closest approximation she says Warlpiri could enunciate, Jean, to the daughter of Lydia's co-wife Beryl. Joan dubbed the same chubby baby 'Prog Prog', Pidgin English for frog. Some months later Joan was horrified to find the child had been registered by that name by the Department of Native Affairs, and wrote a stern letter demanding the register be corrected.

Sixty years on, this baby Jeannie Nungarrayi Herbert (figure 11) has grown to be a formidable intercultural community leader, interpreter and translator. She is also an authority on Warlpiri names. As I sit with her and her sister Elizabeth Nungarrayi Ross at Lajamanu in late 2011, looking through Meggitt's photographs, Jeannie patiently but persistently instructs me to list the Warlpiri names of individuals depicted in those photographs, persons who earlier in the day had been identified at a well-attended public meeting by their more recently acquired European names. Nungarrayi repeats this process again, patiently but firmly, as we speak on the telephone a number of times as I draft these pages. While her own mother became widely known as Beryl, Nungarrayi will have us remember her as Ngalyinpa and Tiyurrpa. Her father, named by Europeans Alecky I, was Junjulurlu or Wirlyirri. His brother Alecky II was Turnu jukurrpa. Jeannie's second mother and Joan's friend Lydia Nakamarra was Yijadurru.

This dynamic scene of naming and counter-naming reveals some of the intimate complexity of post-settlement relations. European naming is a core civilising practice, it is geared towards the creation of discrete autonomous individuals who can be addressed and administered accordingly. Across remote Australia the European names bestowed on Aboriginal people chart the attitudes of those vested with such power to name — Hitler, Mussolini, Plum Jam, Donkey, Topsy. But in the case of Joan Meggitt's naming practices, as with Olive Pink's bestowal of the names of her favourite flowers and beloved homeland on Warlpiri she camped with in the 1930s and 1940s, another kind of gesture is being made. Relationships of genuine care and affinity are established.

Warlpiri names and subsection or 'skin' names emplace people in a different form of relationship. Unlike the intercultural acts explored here Warlpiri names are chosen within strict frames of possibility, they are given without scope for arbitrariness. Warlpiri names locate persons socially and geographically; they mark a person as kin for others in ways that are publicly known and with significances that point beyond the settlement to other places and ways of knowing places.

European names were not the only names bestowed upon newborn Warlpiri babies at Hooker Creek in 1953. Jeannie Nungarrayi and her sister Susan were named by Joan Meggitt but they were also visited by a senior Gurinji man who came from Kalkarinji to bestow the names Punayi and Lajayi respectively on the baby girls, as well as gifts of *parrajas*, carved

wooden baby-carriers. The man in question was an old Jangala who was married to the girls' older sister. He named their brother Edward Pirriyarri, after a nearby place Yarrayi, 28 Mile Bore. These Gurinji gifts of names occurred as part of a wider exchange and a clear enactment of hospitality, a gesture to help anchor the newly arrived Ngalia family in this environment, an act crucial to those people's acquisition of a sense of rightful belonging.

When I ask Jerry Jangala to tell me something of his memories of Hooker Creek in its early days he starts haltingly, referring to the small number of buildings, but then quickly jumps back to his time walking around in the bush in the vicinity of his birthplace Pawa, near Willowra, as a small child. The tale he goes on to recount is epic in proportions, it takes an hour and a half to tell and covers several years involving much travel on foot and incorporating many dramatic events: Jerry Jangala's bewildered first encounter with a white person (Olive Pink), the retribution he witnessed being wielded out to one Warlpiri man for taking another man's promised wife, a graphically recalled incident of cattle duffing, the raiding of a stockman's supply camp, the loss of a beloved dog poisoned as a result of eating beef laced to kill wild dogs. Throughout, as this old man recalls the pivotal

Figure 12:
Trees at Hooker Creek, November 2011.
(Photograph: Melinda Hinkson.)

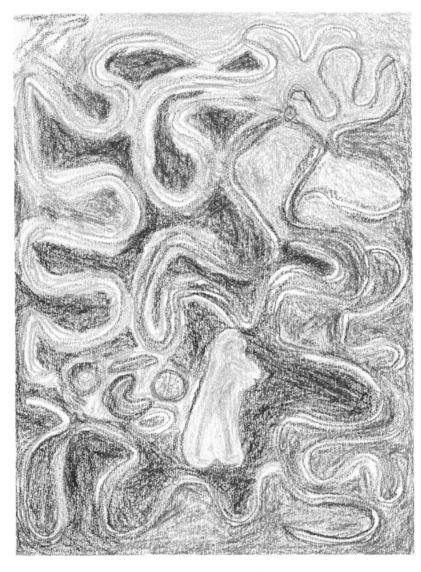

Figure 13:
Biddy Napaljarri Tims:
*Self-portrait with sister
and ngalyipi vine*,
Lajamanu 2013.

on, Warlpiri people's place at Hooker Creek is still tentatively held.

Prompted by my suggestion that it might be possible to do so, just for fun, one old woman reluctantly draws herself as a stick figure clothed in trousers and shirt (figure 13), having just shared with me memories of life as a young woman employed to wash dishes on Mt Doreen Station. She completes this figure then quickly adds another, her sister with hunting equipment, digging stick and carrying bowl, this time depicted in the classical iconography of arc and lines, and surrounds them all with her *Ngalyipi* Snake Vine Dreaming.

Her move seems similar to Jangala's polite deflection of my request that he talk to me about Hooker Creek; the ground of post-settlement experience is not the natural place of authorised storytelling. There are complicated and risky politics to be waded through in pitching oneself in this new kind of public territory. Tales of life, vernacular tales, both Jangala and Napaljarri indicate, must be framed by what Warlpiri commonly incite as 'proper ways' of talking for places, persons, events. No one can just speak about any place — history might be collectively held but talking for the circumstances of a place is an authorised activity. A similar rhythm guides the approach many people take to drawing — in the course of the research for this book, when invited to draw memories, events recalled from long ago, many would first draw the Dreamings and countries they commonly paint in acrylic, as if laying the ground of their publicly recognised identity, before making pictures of events witnessed or scenes from early life, and concluding with another 'Dreaming picture'.

The space between drawing and looking

Is there anything more to be said of Larry's drawings of trees? Is the conundrum a simple case of Meggitt wrongly attributing drawings that *looked like* those in the vicinity of Hooker Creek but were in fact of Yarripirlangu? Certainly several of the 'tree' drawings are ripe to be read in such a way. For example, a number of people have suggested that #69 (figure 14) *looks like* the sand dune at Yarripirlangu

events of his early life he adopts the perspective of that child.

Significantly, Jangala's tale ends where I had tried to instigate its commencement; arriving at Yuendumu as the settlement was being constructed, the family stayed a period of some months before Jerry Jangala and his family found themselves boarding the truck for the journey to Hooker Creek. There are many poignancies to this story, among them, one family's story of leaving behind life in the bush, and the fact that after such a long life this man of considerable authority still reaches for events and places from the deep past for the stories he can most confidently speak to, not the post-settlement period. Six decades with the mountain range hovering above it in the background.

If such drawings might be read as signs of homesickness, declarations of love for absent country, this would again seem to confirm Larry's trees as a creative response to the ontological challenge of forced migration — if one is to stay on foreign land it is crucial to find a way to creatively transform the experience of dislocation into accommodation. Homesickness was a strong factor in the multiple incidents of Warlpiri people leaving Hooker Creek and walking all the way back across the Tanami Desert to Yuendumu. Among these people who voted with their feet were Wally Japaljarri who also drew for Meggitt, who made the long walk south accompanied by his two wives and extended family. Wally Japaljarri, like Larry Jungarrayi, was southern Ngalia, his country was Ngarapalya, not far west of Jungarrayi's Yarripirlangu. Wally never returned to Lajamanu. But Larry Jungarrayi stayed on at the new settlement, not returning to Yuendumu until sometime in the 1970s. We cannot know whether the attitude seemingly enacted in his drawings helped Larry Jungarrayi during his years at Hooker Creek. The journey undertaken via this book has not resolved the quandary surrounding these drawings.[15]

With heightened perception renowned Australian anthropologist WEH Stanner wrote of the deep intergenerational shifts of allegiance and value he witnessed among Murrin-patha people in north Australia from the 1930s to the 1950s. He wrote in strongly unsentimental ways of the voluntary departure from ancestral country that had brought those people to the Mission at Port Keats and made the observation:

> Country is a high interest with a high value; rich sentiments cluster around it; but there are other interests; all are relative, and any can be displaced. If the bond between a person and clan-estate were always in all circumstances of the all absorbing kind it has sometimes been represented to be, then migrations of the kind I have described simply could not have occurred.[16]

The question with which Stanner was struggling in his consideration of Murrin-patha people's transforming attachments to ancestral country centred on what future they faced. He observed that as people left country behind they carried forward *ideas* of those places:

> Here the former territories have been given up long since, but each adult knows his clan country and that of his mother. They are still indispensible names for use as pointers and reckoners.[17]

It is notable that, aside from the one overnight excursion to Yarripirlangu described in Chapter 4, all the talk of Warlpiri countries explored in this book has occurred at a distance from those places, in conversations held at Yuendumu, Lajamanu, Nyirripi, Alice Springs and Canberra. The drawings have served as a new set of anchor points and stimuli for thinking and talking about places, some that continue to be visited, others which live on as names, as traces of memory that live on in individual minds and bodies, in stories shared, in canvases painted.

One of Berger's central propositions is that drawing is a form of sense-making of a private kind, with no concern for what Walter Benjamin identified as a picture's 'exhibition value'.[18] In other words, drawings of the kind Berger had in mind are not made to communicate, nor are they political acts in the sense that we have come to understand Aboriginal country paintings, staking a claim to recognition in the public domain. But this is not to suggest that these private acts of drawing are beyond politics — Berger stresses their *future focused* aspect: 'a line, an area of tone, is not really important because it records what you have seen, but because of what it will lead you on to see.'[19] He describes the process of coming to terms with something from the intimate perspective of the person who draws. What seems crucial to highlight here is not drawing as an act of *mastery* so much as *affinity*:

> Following up its logic in order to check its accuracy, you find confirmation or denial in the object itself or in your memory of it. Each confirmation or denial brings you closer to the object, until finally you are, as it were, inside it:

Figure 14:
Larry Jungarrayi: *Red trees, red creek and blue spinifex at Hooker Creek*, Hooker Creek 1953–4. (Drawing #69, Meggitt Collection, AIATSIS.)

'This drawing was a mental synthesis. The artist was not before the landscape at the time of the drawing' (Mervyn Meggitt).

the contours you have drawn no longer marking the edge of what you have seen, but the edge of what you have become.[20]

Finally Berger confirms that certain 'great drawings' collapse the distinct categories he has earlier established. Referring to a landscape drawn in 1553 by Dutch artist Pieter Brueghel, Berger suggests,

> everything appears to exist in space, the complexity of everything vibrates — yet what one is looking at is only a project on paper. Reality and project become inseparable. One finds oneself on the threshold before the creation of the world. Such drawings, using the future tense, *foresee*, forever.[21]

I resist the temptation to reproduce here, yet again, Larry Jungarrayi's drawing *The malaka's house*. It is the Warlpiri drawing that comes closest to enacting what Berger describes. If the Warlpiri drawings part company with Berger's analysis it is at the point he insists that specific classes of drawing enact distinct temporalities. Jerry Jangala's stories told in response to Abe Jangala's drawings make this clear, as do many of the responses explored throughout this book; for Warlpiri such separation of time into discrete units of past, present, future does not make sense. These drawings emerge from a temporal ordering that envelopes past, present, future. Berger does, however, provide us with one final beguiling proposition with which we shall leave Larry Jungarrayi's trees:

> Any drawn place is both a *here* and an *elsewhere*. There is nothing else like these places; they are to be found only in drawings . . . *Here* embodies necessity; *elsewhere* offers freedom. The human condition begins when the two are face to face.[22]

Figure 15:
Larry Jungarrayi:
Red trees at Hooker Creek,
Hooker Creek 1953–4.
(Drawing #76, Meggitt
Collection, AIATSIS.)

Mervyn Meggitt: 'The creek in red, the trees in red, the bush in black and blue.'

Peter Hamilton: 'It wasn't a night representation?'

Mervyn Meggitt: 'I don't think so; at least he didn't say so.'

An image comes back to me; and
I say in my heart: that's really him,
that's really her. I recognize him, I
recognize her.

Paul Ricoeur, *Memory, history, forgetting*

Chapter 6
Remembering the future

Meggitt's description of this mesmerising picture (figure 1) provokes a series of questions. Did Larry Jungarrayi witness a killing, as Meggitt suggests? Might this have been one of the 'tribal murders' reported by government authorities in 1950,[1] an incident that partly precipitated the transport of people to Hooker Creek? Or, is it possible that Meggitt's documentation blurs Larry Jungarrayi's description of events depicted in the drawing with his own extrapolation? In short, was Meggitt *told* or did he *deduce* that this spearing resulted in death? Jerry Jangala tells of another possible incident the drawing might refer to, given that the man throwing the spear is identified as a Japaljarri (Larry Jungarrayi's classificatory father). Jangala recalls an episode from his childhood where a Japaljarri in his extended family took the promised wife of another Japaljarri man. The union was not challenged until several weeks later when the travelling group arrived at Yuendumu where the aggrieved man was living. He took sanctioned action against the wife-stealer before an assembled gathering. In this case the man receiving the punishment dodged Japaljarri's spear and subsequently received a knife wound to the back of the shoulder. The man's assailant invited him to repay the injury to 'square' the situation. At the conclusion of this exchange of cuts, the dispute was said to be resolved.

This beguiling drawing may of course refer to neither event. On first glance the spearing picture might be interpreted as the kind of witnessing drawing that Berger writes of, a picture that declares 'I saw this'. Meggitt's description encourages us to look at the drawing in this way, to see the depiction of the victim of the spearing as having fallen back on the ground, spear lodged in his stomach. Yet the drawing itself does not easily settle for this description. The figure

Figure 1:
Larry Jungarrayi:
The spearing of a man at Yuendumu native settlement, Hooker Creek 1953–4.
(Drawing #48, Meggitt Collection, AIATSIS.)

'The man with a spear in his belly has fallen on the red sand. Nearby are trees and a creek. The killer is not depicted, but his spear thrower is shown. The reason for this is that the killer was Larry's classificatory 'father', and he thought it would be indelicate to draw his 'father' in the act of spearing somebody. Larry said he saw this killing take place' (Mervyn Meggitt).

of the man, arms and legs outstretched, appears taut and full of life, a long way from dead. The spear thrower, the elongated object 'facing' the man, Meggitt suggests, stands in for the person throwing the spear. The spear itself is drawn at an unusual right angle to the spear thrower, it does not mimic the action of spear throwing, and it hits the lower abdomen of its victim. Traditional punishment, or 'payback' spearings as they are often referred to today, would rarely if ever pierce a man's stomach, by accident or design.[2] Such spearings involve the tightly regulated punishment of a person as retribution for a transgression of public order. Spearings of men in accord with proper custom are aimed at the upper thigh. On occasion they would involve several injuries to the same region of the body, depending on the severity of the crime committed. In rare circumstances an artery would be punctured and the victim might bleed to death, but death by spearing in such contexts was unusual. Other forms of retribution resulted in death.[3]

Larry Jungarrayi's depiction of the spear making contact with the victim's stomach is suggestive of another interpretation. Rather than drawing an incident simply as he saw it, Larry Jungarrayi's picture appears to involve two layers of commentary — aiming the spear at the victim's stomach, *miyalu*, Jungarrayi draws attention to the part of the body where Warlpiri locate the vital spirit, the seat of emotions. While the act of spearing spills blood from the thigh of the transgressor, traditional punishment as a system of retributive justice bears down upon the person at the level of the spirit. In submitting to punishment a person who has effectively broken away from society presents himself as willing to be brought back within the fold. Traditional punishment is in this way a systematised set of practices that undergirds the moral order of the Warlpiri universe.

Interpreted thus, Larry Jungarrayi's drawing would appear to *record* a specific witnessed event *and present* that event as the enactment of a wider system of moral-spiritual justice. The vigorous red and yellow that radiates across the picture provides it with its electricity-like charge and seems to declare: here lies power. My proposition is speculative; it would be exceptional for Warlpiri to take such an abstract overarching approach to customary concerns. To grapple analytically like this is the purview of European epistemology, Warlpiri knowledge and Law tend to be expressed in much more concrete, located terms. Yet the composition of this picture and the work undertaken by Larry Jungarrayi to affect the charge that reverberates at its centre invites such speculation.

Pushing this line of argument to its logical conclusion, the picture seems to enact the 'Warlpiri world theory' Nancy Munn identified at work in classical iconographic drawings, presaged on the notion of 'coming out–going in'.[4] In this case that crucial dynamic is affected not through an arrangement of circles and lines, but in the dialectical engagement of the figure of the human body with the spear and spear thrower. The strong black line of trees that runs along the upper part of the drawing is, as we have seen, a signature element of Larry Jungarrayi's picture making — do these trees mark the specific place he witnessed these events? Meggitt suggests so. Might Jungarrayi also intend the line of emplaced trees to *stand for* Warlpiri law? Quite possibly, agrees the senior Warlpiri man, himself educated in abstract knowledge, with whom I discuss these matters. If my speculation is granted, we might take one further step and ask could this picture constitute a kind of pair for Jungarrayi's *The malaka's house*, each drawing an attempt to distil the respective powers of Warlpiri and European rules of law?

'That's the one we're worried about now', says one senior woman sternly, taking this picture from a pile we are looking through together at Lajamanu in August 2013. 'The government's trying to take away our law'. She is referring to legislative arrangements associated with the Northern Territory National Emergency Response that effectively outlawed the practice of Aboriginal customary law, and specifically forms of retribution involving physical violence. One Warlpiri explanation for the protracted interfamily feud at Yuendumu is that people have been prohibited from sorting out their own troubles; police move in to make arrests every time there is an attempt to resolve the feud according to Warlpiri principles. Through 2011 and 2012 the Warlpiri community at Yuendumu experienced astonishing levels of imprisonment, even by their own contemporary standards.

In the end the feud was resolved by peaceful means. In early 2013 Yuendumu hosted a 'jobs expo', a surreal event given the deeply entrenched high levels of Warlpiri unemployment. I am told that while no new jobs may have eventuated, the unusual spectacle and festival-like atmosphere of this occasion played an important role in dissolving hostilities, drawing reticent people from across the township into shared space. Not long after, Warlpiri mourned the death of a ritually senior woman who was grandmother to one of the young men imprisoned over the death that sparked the feud. The last words the deceased woman reportedly spoke to her children were to 'look to Wapirra' (God) and 'think about the future' for her great grandchildren. She appealed to her children to end the fighting. Some weeks later, three of her daughters took it upon themselves to walk across the town to make peace with the opposing family, who graciously accepted their offering.

✳ ✳ ✳

In this final chapter I briefly take up the question of how European technologies of picturing have influenced Warlpiri ways of seeing and remembering. Worthy of a much longer and more substantial exploration than this book allows, the limited materials that shape this discussion are a series of drawings made in the late 1960s in the Yuendumu school and more recently in the context of research for this book. Through the prism of these drawings and the discussions they have triggered it becomes possible to gauge something of the inextricable relationship between Warlpiri visions of the past and aspirations for the future. Implicit in these considerations is a hope that one day *kardiya* might come to deal with Warlpiri in terms other than the mirrored effects of their own expectations.

Remembering in the present

❝ If memory is in fact a capacity, the power of remembering, it is more fundamentally a figure of care, that basic anthropological structure of our historical condition ❞

(Paul Ricoeur, *Memory, History, Forgetting*).[5]

❝ It's about like a Port Arthur Massacre. And the Trade Centre in New York. A Bali bombing. That's the history, you know? This was going back, way back, in 1928. It didn't happen (just) anywhere. It just happened where we stand, on the river, the bank of the river. ❞

(W Jampijinpa Brown).[6]

Speaking in September 2013 to an SBS journalist on the occasion of the eighty-fifth anniversary of the Coniston Massacre, W Jampijinpa Brown, who would die just a month later, appealed to his listeners to accept this striking comparative picture. Notwithstanding the recent turn to postcolonial critique and federal and state government apologies to the Stolen Generations, Warlpiri people remain deeply aware of the selective nature of Australian memorial culture. Their appeals for recognition of the Coniston killings are thus filtered through observations of the public weight given to tragedies afflicting people other than themselves. What Jampijinpa subtly highlights is not simply the comparative scale of death and devastation, but the radical inequality of our attention and care to these momentous events. As Ricoeur intimates, memory is a process steeped in moral implications. Every act of remembering simultaneously involves one of forgetting. What we choose to remember and publicly mark reveals much about what and whom we care for.

Recall the first responses of senior women and men to the Hooker Creek drawings — '*Wiyarrpa*', dear one, dearly missed — the Hooker Creek drawings were greeted as traces of persons, places and a way of life long gone. These emotional responses give weight to Ricoeur's observation that intimate engagements between persons and images lie at the heart of acts of remembering. It is clear that Warlpiri in the present look at the 1950s drawings through veils of separation and transformation. These transformations can be traced through what people say and do, but also through forms of picturing themselves — whether these be the new ways of drawing introduced through the school, or the new ways of seeing country afforded by motor car, helicopter and plane, as well as photography, video, mobile phone and

Figure 2:
(Top) Madeleine Napangardi
Dixon: *Remembering fleeing
the brumbies at Hooker
Creek sometime in the 1970s*,
Yuendumu 2011.

Figure 3:
(Bottom) Madeleine
Napangardi Dixon: *Ranger
story*, Yuendumu 2011.

Google Earth. In the post-settlement era such ways
of seeing dynamically shape a framework for life that
bears down on how people remember and how they
see themselves. At a wider level the journey taken
via this book has revealed that Warlpiri responses to
images are filtered through expectations and desires
— acts of seeing reflect aspirations to be seen in
certain ways by others.

Madeleine Napangardi was born and grew up in
Lajamanu. Her father was head stockman and she
recalls a day when brumbies stampeded through the
township and she and other children ran to the tin
houses in terror (figure 2). Her picture visualises a
recalled event, but also her love and admiration for
her father. Napangardi moved to Yuendumu where
she completed school, and like her father went on to
confidently move across radically different kinds of
social space. An enthusiastic student and traveller,
Napangardi enjoys working alongside *kardiya*. She
secured a prestigious position as head women's
ranger on the eve of Warlpiri being granted the
largest Indigenous Protected Area in the country over
the South Tanami Desert (figure 3).

The shift from stock work to rangering is just one
of many recent changes in Warlpiri people's ways
of relating to country. In July 2013 Warlpiri were
granted non-exclusive native title rights over Pikilyi,
the Warlpiri heartland under leasehold to Mt Doreen
Station, the origins of which were discussed in
Chapter 2. Now managed by the grandson of Walter
Braitling, the property has been listed for sale for
several years, but at an asking price set to ensure
Warlpiri can never purchase it. One recently deceased
senior traditional owner for the area, Japangardi,
used to tell the manager straight up whenever their
paths crossed: 'you've stolen my land.' It was a
standing joke between the two of them, a joke that
relied for its dark humour on the directness and truth
of Japangardi's accusation.

For some, the Hooker Creek drawings sparked
questions about the motivation of those who made
them. One senior man saw particular significance in
the drawings having been made so long before the
acrylic painting movement started. The son of one of
Yuendumu's most renowned and well-renumerated

painters, this man was intrigued that the drawings were apparently made outside economic exchange. Did the men who made those drawings get paid? Not as far as I know, I told him. 'Those paintings now sell for a million dollars', he reflected, referring implicitly to the sale at auction in recent years of early Papunya paintings. 'What for they made those drawings?' I misinterpreted his line of enquiry as honing in on yet another perceived incident of *kardiya* exploitation, but found I was wrong. This man was genuinely consumed by the question of what motivated his forebears to produce this large pile of pictures we had looked through together. Two days later he put it to me thus: the drawings were a gift, 'those people were not thinking of money, they were thinking of us, they were thinking of the future'.

Our brief discussion on this second occasion occurs as this man pauses for a break from his labour; he is clearing ground upon which to build a humpy, 200 metres across the road from his house. Having stoically refused for five years to sign over the lease of township's housing blocks to the federal government — a move that would trigger the release of significant funding for housing and associated infrastructure — traditional owners had recently changed their minds. A mass construction and renovation project was about to commence. Dozens of construction staff and their portable village were due to arrive any day. Residents of houses to be demolished or renovated were advised to vacate their dwellings. No alternative accommodation was to be provided. In a move that echoed directives of an earlier era when missionaries and superintendents sent people 'out bush' when supplies were low, Warlpiri were simply expected to fend for themselves.

While this eviction on the cusp of winter exacerbated already stressful circumstances for some, especially women looking after young children, others were nonplussed. Some were even upbeat. After the resolution of the protracted feuding both within the community and between the community and government, there was a sense of relief and optimism in the air; finally something productive seemed to be happening. At Yuendumu in August 2013 a friend's family members were camped in their makeshift abode — a neatly built, robust shelter constructed of wooden branches, corrugated iron, tarpaulins and rope, erected snugly above a neat line of beds. The mood of this camp was particularly jovial; they told me this was much better than living in a house, they were warmed by a fire and stimulated by the unimpeded interaction with the sky and their surrounds. They were in hearing distance of the family next door who similarly had set up an outdoor camp. Jokes and other communications volleyed through the night air.

On the first weekend of August 2013 Yuendumu hosted the fiftieth-anniversary Yuendumu Sports Weekend. Following a two-year hiatus when the annual carnival was cancelled due to the ongoing feud, an unprecedented level of regional support saw 21 football teams and their supporters from across inland Australia assemble for the competition that was once dubbed the Black Olympics. This was entirely Aboriginal business. European residents who regularly voiced frustrations at the challenges of working alongside Warlpiri in the day-to-day business of community organisations looked on in amazement as the Warlpiri social body rose up to seamlessly orchestrate this massive event, with round-the-clock football, softball, basketball, battle of the bands competitions and the conclusion of 'sorry business' mortuary rights for Japangardi who had died weeks prior. In addition to all of this, the community mounted what some described as a 'parade' preceding the commencement of competitive activities, with hundreds of people sweeping through the township to grieve and honour the many prominent people who had died in the period since the last event was held. Visiting media billed this as a 'reconciliation march'.[7]

Sports weekend is the new regional ritual gathering, drawing large contingents of people from communities across vast distances. In the manner of managing more classical forms of ceremony, the hosts have authority to determine when the games will end. Commentators' celebration of this show of community cohesion, sporting prowess and pride quickly turned to criticism when it became clear that the sports weekend would run into a week and kids would not be turning up to school for the duration.[8]

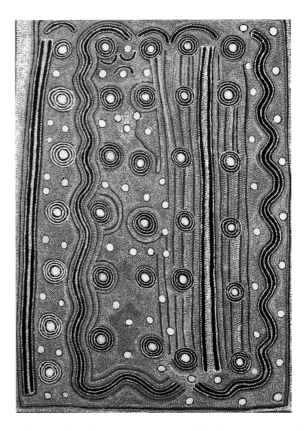

Figure 4: (Left) Alma Nungarrayi Granites: *Yanjilypiri or Napaljarri-warnu Jukurrpa* (Star or Seven Sisters Dreaming), 2010.

Figure 5: (Right) Paddy Japaljarri Sims: *Yanjilypiri Jukurrpa* (Night Sky Dreaming), 2003.

Both images courtesy Warlukurlangu Artists Association.

At the basketball court at 10pm on Sunday night, the senior woman overseeing both women's softball and basketball competitions made an appeal to participating teams on two fronts — she sternly told the assembled players there had been much time wasting earlier in the day as several teams failed to turn up to play as scheduled. Tomorrow was finals day; teams who fail to turn up on time will 'forfeit'. And another thing — young people need to come forward to train to be umpires for next year; all the women doing that work are now too old!

Art production is another kind of work that Warlpiri require no encouragement to undertake. At Lajamanu people turn up at the art centre from early morning, make breakfast and settle into painting. The atmosphere is upbeat; spirited greetings of 'good morning!' are hailed across the large workroom. A core group of 20 to 30 people circulate through the art centre on a daily basis. Here the stress is on social welfare, and on Warlpiri ownership and carriage of the enterprise. A rocky earlier history of mismanagement saw the Warnayaka Art Centre close twice for prolonged periods following fraudulent

dealings, first by an international dealer and second an art coordinator. In both cases stock worth thousands of dollars was taken from the community without payment. In the most dramatic case, in the early 1990s, a man serving as part-paid art centre coordinator left the community with a substantial number of paintings he had not paid for and promoted them as his private collection to a reputable commercial gallery in Melbourne, who agreed to put them on exhibition for sale. The exhibition was cancelled on legal advice just prior to opening. This man was later convicted and sentenced to nineteen years in prison for the brutal murder of his grandmother, an act committed several years before he arrived at Lajamanu.[9]

Today, under the steady watch of a committed manager with no background in arts management, the art centre is firmly of the community. People paint as they like and contribute to the full range of duties to keep the centre functioning on a day-to-day basis. It is a place of activity and social interaction, not driven by financial imperative. Some who come to spend time at the art centre do not themselves paint.

They come for the company, for the good feeling of being around people who are engaged in work that stimulates the spirit. The artists work among piles of paintings they have produced over many years that have failed to sell. No one seems fussed.

Down the road at Yuendumu the Warlukurlangu Artists Association is run by a high-calibre management team of two women with significant credentials in the art world. The director sees her job as generating income and the centre operates with the support of a steady stream of volunteers, many of them European backpackers looking for a short but significant immersion in a remote community. There are no Warlpiri art workers, a clear distinction is observed between the staff of the centre and the members who paint. The income generated by this art centre grew significantly and remained relatively strong over the last decade. At a time when community art centres are struggling, with Aboriginal art centre sales having halved in the wake of the 2008 global financial crisis, Warlukurlangu remains relatively robust.[10] The centre's ability to respond to the wider economic climate arises from a clear managerial vision that sees painting activity in terms of income generation for most members rather than fine art production. In recent years Warlukurlangu's revenue has been directed towards diverse community-based enterprise, contributing to the funding of the Yuendumu swimming pool, the community-based diabetes program and the establishment of a program to improve the nutrition and welfare of Yuendumu's dog population.[11]

The Warlpiri artist whose paintings currently attract the greatest interest from international galleries is a retired school teacher, Alma Nungarrayi Granites, who has taken to painting the *Yanjilypiri* Night Sky Dreaming inherited from her late father (figure 5) in a new guise — the sky as we see it. She works closely with an art-school trained art centre manager, exploring satellite imagery and experimenting with various effects in the making of her paintings. Nungarrayi is an enthusiastic participant in artists' workshops. Curious to learn from others, most recently in 2013 she attended a print workshop in New Mexico. After a trip to Singapore for the opening of an exhibition of her work in 2010, Nungarrayi painted *Yanjilypiri* above the Singaporean skyline (figure 4).

Learning to see interculturally

Drawn independently of each other, the two pictures, figures 6 and 7, recall two distinct scenes, a ceremonial gathering out in the bush near Willowra and the landscaped design of the Yuendumu 'park' as the artist recalls it from the early 1970s. The two drawings resemble each other in several ways; both convey scenes of cultivated sociality, meeting places of significant kinds. Lola Nampijinpa, a quiet woman in her fifties, surveys the scene of a large group congregated for a *kurdiji* initiation ceremony from a distant vantage point (figure 6). Her commanding view enables her to include the various camps of people: women seated painting up and singing in the foreground, men gathered together singing in relative seclusion to the top left of the picture, children playing at the top right, two hunters departing with spears in pursuit of meat with which to feed the crowd. Nampijinpa made this picture at the culmination of a week of deeply engaged drawing. Many of her earlier pictures were unpeopled landscapes, depicting places in the same area of country.

Ormay Nangala's drawing (figure 7) was made more quickly. Ormay, a teacher's aide employed at the school, adopts a similar vantage point from which to convey the scene of the Yuendumu town square. She recalls a period from her childhood on the cusp of the self-determination era when experimental town planning incorporated Aboriginal principles into the design of public spaces.[12] Here intersecting paths converge on a grassed centre. White rocks mark out recognisably Warlpiri symbols — a *wirlki* 'No. 7' boomerang, the arc of a windbreak and camp, curved lines denoting two human figures, the arrow-shaped track of an emu. While the composition of both drawings may well have been cultivated in the classroom, there is something distinctively Warlpiri in the focus and dynamism of each. Both drawings appear to enact a Warlpiri concern with locatedness and mobility. Both incorporate core sites, centres of intense activity and the human action that produces and enlivens those places.

The distinctive experience of growing up in the settlements of Yuendumu and Hooker Creek soon after their establishment gave rise to a generation of Warlpiri people insightfully engaged with the ways of Europeans. This disposition was cultivated in the school where English was the only language spoken and formalities between teacher and pupils were strictly enforced. School excursions provided young adults with their first experiences of distant places. Some went on to further deepen their European learning at teachers college and occasionally university, acquiring new ways to express themselves, gaining confidence in the procedures of *kardiya* and often a passion for further engagements with the wider world through travel, films and, to a lesser extent, reading.

Progressively over the eight-decade period traversed by this book, the parameters of the Warlpiri world have widened. Manual arts teacher David Tunley recalls huddling with several Warlpiri men around his radio at Yuendumu in 1969 to listen to the broadcast of the moon landing. Tunley explained to the men what was going on. They replied, 'yes', they had heard about this. 'Were they *kardiya* on the moon?', one old men asked. 'Yes', Tunley replied. 'What for those silly buggers up there?' the old man replied with some bemusement. Meanwhile, up the road at Hooker Creek, news of the moon landing sent deep fear and alarm through the community — now they were on the moon, it was said, *kardiya* could look down on *yapa* and aim at them with their rifles. Some recall watching the moon landing on black and white television. They interpreted the images as indicating the proximity of those astronauts to Warlpiri country. In short, the moon landing signified yet a further increase in white power.[13] Reflecting on events of that period, women at Lajamanu recall how distressed they were on learning of the death of JF Kennedy:

💬 Everybody cried but they didn't know him. Men, women and children and all the white people cried. Before television, we never even saw the man. That's why I'm laughing it seems so funny now. But he was an important man, and he had children . . . we heard it on the radio. They liked him because he helped people. Someone told us he worked with all the Negro people; he had a good heart.[14] 💬

Figure 6 (Top):
Lola Nampijinpa Brown:
Remembering kurdiji near Willowra, Yuendumu 2011.

Figure 7 (Bottom):
Ormay Nangala Gallagher:
Yuendumu park as it was in my childhood, Yuendumu 2011.

In the late 1960s Warlpiri communities were on the eve of another transformation, as the policy of assimilation was poised to end with the election of the Whitlam government in 1972. Heralding in a new period of bipartisan policy approach, self-determination would be the new catch-cry in Aboriginal politics. With this shift Warlpiri would be supported to pursue erstwhile discouraged cultural imperatives in new institutional forms — outstations, bilingual education programs, art centres, media associations. Classical Warlpiri forms of image making were encouraged. Much has been written of the visual cultural production fostered throughout remote Aboriginal Australia in this policy era.[15] Very little attention has been paid to the picture making that was occurring in the preceding era. As explored in Chapter 1, the disciplinary aims of the school led anthropologists and other scholars to dismiss the creative work produced in these settings as culturally inauthentic, *only for making white people happy*. However, my argument has been that pictures made where Warlpiri and other people come together have much to reveal about the way Warlpiri see their place in the world. Chapter 1 debunked the idea that a clear separation can be made between pure Warlpiri forms of picturing and those that are influenced by cross-cultural interchange.

Was the young man who made the picture, figure 9, drawing himself? His teacher? Another student at work, or an imagined subject? The features of the face are not recognisably Warlpiri, although black shading indicates an Aboriginal person. The content and composition of this drawing stand at odds with much of the visual work explored throughout this book. The drawing calls to mind one of the first broadcasts of Warlpiri news made after the launch of an unlicensed television station at Yuendumu in 1985. A video recording captures the scene in the broadcasting room, conversation between young men in Warlpiri, with much joking and playing around. On being advised that they are 'on air' two men seated side-by-side in front of the camera compose themselves and begin talking to each other in English. Their discussion takes a question–answer format, one asks the other, 'What's your name?', 'Where do you live?', 'What do you work?'[16] Like this scene in

Figure 8: Neville Japangardi Poulson's picture of the moon landing, Yuendumu c. 1969. Slide courtesy David Tunley (the drawing has been misplaced).

making television in the style that may well have been observed to be 'proper', this portrait seems to be an exercise in mimicking European conventions of the genre, that is, recognising the European face as *the face* that 'fits' the portrait frame.

However, there is more going on in this picture. Like Larry Jungarrayi's drawings that fill the page with colour and detail, this drawing not only depicts the face and torso of its subject: it is just as attentive to the environment in which the sitter is located as well as the mirror mechanism that enabled the making of the picture. The grey besser brick and barred window locate the activity of portraiture within the internal spaces of a built structure. Might this be interpreted as a kind of double movement on the part of the picture maker, conveying the Warlpiri imperative to identify persons in the specific landscapes with which they are associated, but also testifying to the drawing's own locational history, a drawing made at the direction of the teacher with the aid of this new technology of seeing?

Another drawing from the same class, figure 10, shows its subject looking straight out of the picture; this time the subject's face is depicted with Warlpiri features and a bright blue house in the background locates him in the settlement environment. What to make of the line of black that runs along the base

Figure 9 (Top):
Artist unknown:
Unidentified portrait, Yuendumu
school c. 1968–70.
(David Tunley Collection.)

Figure 10 (Bottom):
Artist unknown:
Unidentified portrait, Yuendumu
school c. 1968–70.
(David Tunley Colllection.)

of the drawing? It seems to break with the picture's otherwise diligent attention to depicting the features of a scene — could it be that the maker was marking the colour of his skin as a foundational element of his portrait?

The most accomplished Warlpiri portrait artist is the man whose thoughtful responses to the 1950s drawings have substantially framed parts of this book's enquiry. Japangardi died unexpectedly in July 2013, leaving many people grieving the loss of a significant man. Deeply philosophical in his observations of the European world and the peculiarities of *kardiya* ways, Japangardi also took great pleasure in the new 'freedoms' he had acquired through techniques and technologies *kardiya* brought into his community. He described himself as someone who loved reading history. Japangardi regarded schoolteacher David Tunley as a close friend and recalled learning new ways of seeing and picture making in his classroom.

While Tunley recalls that he did little in the way of 'teaching' his Warlpiri students to draw,[17] Japangardi credited his teacher with showing him the techniques of landscape watercolour painting. Japangardi remembered that Tunley instructed his students how to depict perspective, how to draw distance, highlighting the distinction between the appearance of objects at a distance in terms of haze and those close up in terms of clear lines. To achieve such affects, Japangardi learned to draw and paint distant country in watercolour (figure 12), in the tradition of Arrernte artist Albert Namatjira. Once he had perfected watercolour, Japangardi decided he wanted to make his 'own style', so he 'moved to portraits'. Again Tunley was his tutor, showing Japangardi how to approach portrait pictures (figure 11) using straight lines, grids and pencil lines to centre the image of the person. Another technique of this new approach to picture making involved taking the drawing surface from being flat, horizontal, to a 45-degree angle, 'otherwise the shapes would be wrong'. So drawing in this mode could no longer occur on the ground, it required new media and new material support, new bodily comportment of the artists — a new technology of drawing.

Figure 11: Neville Japangardi Poulson: *Portrait of Mitton Poulson*, Yuendumu school c. 1968–70. (David Tunley Collection.)

Figure 12: Neville Japangardi Poulson: *Landscape*, Yuendumu School c. 1968–70. (David Tunley Collection.)

This glimpse of Tunley's classroom reminds us that mastering the art of line making was a significant element of the settlement civilising process, simultaneously acquired along with the forms of manual labour people were inducted into to build the settlement — cutting trees and splitting wood to craft straight fence posts to be erected in straight lines along straight roads went hand in hand with the grid and the line cultivated in school-based teaching. In this late assimilation period there was no sense that Warlpiri people should be encouraged to pursue their own 'traditional' forms of image making. The classroom was strictly a place of European

Figure 13:
Felicity Nampijinpa Robertson:
Remembering school country visits,
Yuendumu 2011.

learning. Paternalism remained the dominant sentiment, Tunley recalls.

But Japangardi highlighted another side of this process: the pleasure to be gained in this new knowledge and method, the satisfaction in perfecting the skills, the creative freedom found in adopting these new ways of seeing and picturing. There seem to be echoes here of the pleasure Meggitt identified at work in Abe Jangala and Larry Jungarrayi's drawing for the sake of drawing.

As an enthusiastic maker of drawings Japangardi also had opportunities to use a camera and overhead projector. He aspired to own a camera, so that he might take photographs of people as he wished and use these as the basis for his portrait making. Photographs, he said, 'freed' him up to look at his subjects in a way that he could not look at living people. But, Japangardi told me, he was aware of heightened sensitivities around cameras, he knew he could not take a camera in the car if he was travelling with old people — they would fear him photographing sacred places. He conveyed well the tensions between a new kind of space for individual creativity and experimentation opened up by new technologies of seeing, and pre-existing social spaces threatened by such autonomous creative acts. Years earlier Japangardi had talked to me about the process of working towards achieving a state of being 'free to the world'; driven by curiosity, requiring studious commitment to European education and close attention to the ways *kardiya* do things, through mastery one secured freedom.

When he died Japangardi left behind a box of drawings, paintings and photographs. In a community of people often characterised by its lack of concern for material possession, for producing paintings that are sent out to the world and not retained, this man had a unique capacity to build and maintain his own personal archive of cultural production.

Japangardi's committed experimental picture making is one example of a related set of practices that followed the acquisition of relatively high levels of print literacy and the associated culture of the school. This set of practices was being laid

down at the time the Hooker Creek drawings were made. By the 1980s and 1990s education itself had become a site of focused political activism, with formidable school committees at both Lajamanu and Yuendumu regularly making demands on the Northern Territory government to cede some degree of control to Warlpiri people. As part of the strategy to 'fight fire with fire' as some at Yuendumu described these political battles, people schooled in the 1950s and 1960s became adept at deploying bureaucratic practices, with fine-tuned appreciation of the need for careful minute and note taking, formal decision-making processes in meetings and letters composed and addressed to ministers. On several occasions in the mid-1990s I observed community leaders successfully playing visiting bureaucrats on their own terms.

The recent radical dilution of a formal bilingual curriculum by the NT government has had multiple ramifications; teaching in Warlpiri language is now a marginalised component of the school day and many Warlpiri teaching aides have lost their jobs. Two generations of men and women achieved significant formal qualifications and newfound respect for their contributions as teachers in the school. The loss of these teaching positions has been deeply demoralising.

One woman drew attention to these issues when she produced a series of drawings recalling scenes from the school country visits she had helped organise as part of her duties as a teaching aide in the Yuendumu school. Her drawing activity culminated in a painted canvas (figure 13), made on a day when the drawing supplies I had provided were exhausted. Felicity Nampijinpa remembered these country visits with some pride as a time of great happiness, when she and her father co-hosted a school group at Puturru. In her canvas she depicts the black and white participants together, making their way by car, visiting soakages, sleeping in tents. These are memories tinged with bitterness — they take on heightened significance in the wake of Nampijinpa having recently lost her job at the school. Painting has in recent years become a pastime of retired and retrenched schoolteachers, providing a new form of meaningful activity, a creative medium through which to reflect upon life's circumstances and a means by which to supplement significantly reduced household income.

＊　　＊　　＊

Much writing about Central Australian painting characterises certain periods of intense activity in terms of spontaneous emergence. The Hooker Creek drawings along with the other drawings considered here make two interventions in this wider art history. At a simple level they plug a gap in the widely presumed trajectory of art practice, from ceremonial painting to painting for the market. More significantly they destabilise narratives of firstness — whether these be found in the writings of anthropologists keen to establish the value of their own experiments in fieldwork, or those of art historians wishing to inscribe the fine art significance of particular moments of cultural production. Our journey by way of the Warlpiri drawings has revealed intercultural forms of creative expression to be ubiquitous with colonial and post-settlement life.

There are many other backstories that might be recovered to fill out this rich and dynamic history of visual cultural production. One such story comes from Frank Baarda, long-time resident of Yuendumu and manager of the Yuendumu Mining Company, who recalls senior men's short-lived experiment with painting rocks several years prior to the painting of the school doors. The impetus for the rock-painting project was income generation. The 'rocks' in question were Yuendumu flatstone, a kind of sandstone sourced not far from the town and identified as of the Cambrian age, approximately four million years old. Men painted the stones with Dreaming designs and Frank then lugged the rocks to Melbourne in a suitcase. He recalls the cool response he received from gallery owners; it was pointed out that the weight of the rocks made them a highly unlikely prospect for international purchasers.[18] One specimen found its way in to the collections of the National Museum of Australia.

Seeing the future

The drawings considered throughout this book have provided compelling vantage points from which to consider the profound transformations of

Figure 14:
The giant hairy man rumoured to have been spotted near Yuendumu in August 2013. Image received via text message.

post-settlement Warlpiri life. While the drawings have consistently called out concerns of the present, the stories told through and in response to these drawings provide no single vision for the future, no clear collective view of Warlpiri aspirations. In responses to the drawings we have met diverse and contested interests, aspirations and pressures at play in people's lives. Yet certain shared trajectories are evident. One is an attitude that I have suggested can be identified in some of Larry Jungarrayi's pictures — an openness to the world and the new. Such an attitude manifests in myriad ways in contemporary life. For example, the newest additions to the extended family of one of Larry Jungarrayi's brothers are two young children with a Sudanese father, a man who came to live in Alice Springs after being granted political asylum in Australia. The children of this union are growing up in an Alice Springs town camp, speaking the languages of both parents, who have since separated but continue to share responsibility for the children. Other children in this extended family attend school in Alice Springs, pointedly not the designated Aboriginal school. Older children are boarding at secondary college in Brisbane. A woman in this extended family recently married an Indian taxi driver. Her Warlpiri family were not invited to the wedding, but with pride and some amusement carry the wedding photo on their mobile phones. It is said that the married couple plan to move to Brisbane.

Meanwhile at Yuendumu friends speak, among other things, of wanting high fences built around their houses to stop people looking at them. One speaks of the romance she is engaged in via Facebook with an Afro-American soldier who promises to come and take her away to a new life. Others speak of *yapa* still living in the desert, out beyond Mt Theo — people see their fires and tracks from time to time. In late August 2013 I receive an excited phone call from a friend — people have reported seeing a 'giant man' with his family close up to Yuendumu. Someone else saw the enormous tracks of these people near the big dam. They have photographs to prove it (figure 14). She forwards me the pictures that are being bluetoothed around Yuendumu's mobile phones. Was this picture 'real, or the internet', my friend asks?

Figure 15:
Lizzy Napurrurla Ross:
*Myself, walking along
the road, thinking*,
Yuendumu 2011.

The picture with which I shall close this exploration of drawing is the one that most strikingly stimulates questions of what kind of future Warlpiri see for themselves. The maker of this drawing (figure 15), Lizzy Napurrurla Ross, a thirty-four-year-old woman who completed a high level of school-based education, is widely sought after as an employee across Yuendumu's community organisations. As I finalise this book Lizzy is advised her application for recruitment to the NT police force has been successful. A sometime videomaker and regular radio broadcaster she loves music and has a riotous sense of humour. She communicates her daily dilemmas through regular status updates on Facebook. Lizzy is the daughter of Larry Jungarrayi's adopted daughter, Tess Napaljarri. She is commonly addressed as Lizzy rather than Napurrurla. When invited to draw something from memory, an event from her past life, Lizzy eschews classical iconography and gives us point perspective, the horizon, the lone figure — herself — walking along a road into the setting sun.

The picture calls to mind the idea of Warlpiri women being 'boss for themselves' explored by Diane Bell in her classic ethnography of women's ritual life,[19] but Lizzy's drawing also suggests a break in Warlpiri subjectivity, a break in the primary references through which a person sees their relationship to others and their place in the world. 'Look at me as a creative, independent individual', this picture seems to demand; 'do not presume to characterise me through the prism of kinship and Dreamings; do not look backwards in time in order to understand who I am; I am focused on the future'. Its composition reveals the strong visual influences of European education and Hollywood films. In the wake of the introduction of broadcast television to Yuendumu in the mid-1980s, Eric Michaels wrote with passionate conviction of the need for local control of image making and circulation to secure what he dubbed 'a cultural future' for the Warlpiri. The alternative was a form of cultural genocide, or 'lifestyle future'.[20] But things have not evolved so straightforwardly in subsequent years.

While Lizzy's picture jolts the expectations of the viewer, it must be noted that the direction in which she walks is not towards Alice Springs, but rather westward, into the desert. In this sense, if this picture looks to the future it is a future that is less than clear. Lizzy's description of the drawing refuses to admit finality; she is walking and thinking, not leaving.

This drawing appears to enact a similar sensibility to that which I have suggested characterises Larry Jungarrayi's *The malaka's house*. The confident stride of Lizzy's black figure heading toward the radiant setting sun on the horizon resonates with Jungarrayi's attention to light shining through the window of the superintendent's house. Like Lizzy's thinking figure, Jungarrayi's picture brings the viewer close to a point where we can glimpse but not clearly see the forces behind the screen with which he grapples. Both pictures seem to distil uncertain, future-focused, hope.

* * *

What is the upshot of this journey undertaken via eighty years of Warlpiri drawing? At a basic level, tracking the story of the drawings has enabled us to glean something of the remarkable and turbulent history of Warlpiri experience, a story both highly specific and deeply resonant with the stories of other Aboriginal communities across Australia. Guided by responses to these pictures, this exploration has covered ground not commonly traversed by writing on Aboriginal art. This book closes with questions unanswered; such questions leave an enlarged space for thinking on the nature of Warlpiri creative production across time, and more broadly on what sustains and nourishes persons in the turbulent circumstances of exile. By extension, the journey by way of the drawings has unsettled the expectations we might have of their makers. Holding this sentiment, and in a final act of speculation, through Lizzy's picture of the horizon I invoke the ideas of philosopher Hans-Georg Gadamer. The horizon for Gadamer, is

> the range of vision that includes everything that can be seen from a particular vantage point . . . A person who has no horizon is a man who does not see far enough and hence overvalues what is nearest to him. On the other hand, 'to have an horizon' means not being limited to what is nearby, but to being able to see beyond it.[21]

There is no word for horizon in Warlpiri and the concept sits at odds with Warlpiri ways of reckoning the relationship between sky and land. But I am told it resonates with *mirrlyipindi*, the place where two *kuruwarri*, two ancestral tracks, come together and meet. In Gadamer's use horizon is deployed metaphorically to think through the possibilities of cross-cultural interchange. His optimistic vision for relations between peoples of different backgrounds proposes a new way of seeing brought about by the reciprocal openness of self and other to each other's worldviews, a *fusion* of horizons. If Lizzy's picture makes a demand on the viewer it is this: 'see me in relation to you'.

Warlpiri drawings collected by Mervyn Meggitt, Hooker Creek 1953–54.

This catalogue presents 169 drawings collected by Meggitt at Hooker Creek in 1953–4. It excludes 50 works identified by Warlpiri men in 1980 as inappropriate for public display and circulation. These drawings are #2–20 by Paddy Japaljarri, #22–26 by Abe Jangala, #41, #43, #46, #47, #50, #71 and #92 by Larry Jungarrayi, #118–120 by Ginger Japangardi, #121 and #124 by Wally Japaljarri, #132, #133, #135 and #136 by Alecky I Japaljarri, #142 and #143 by Freddy Jangala, #144–#146 by Jack Jakamarra, #147 and #148 by Louis Jupurrurla, #151 by Paddy Jupurrurla, #154 by Charlie Jupurrurla, #155 by Cookie Jampijinpa.

All works are lumber crayon and/or pencil on paper. Each drawing is identified here by a descriptor taken from Meggitt's documentation, most often place name. Meggitt Collection, AIATSIS, Canberra.

#1
Paddy Japaljarri
Maliki-jarra
(9 x 21 cm)

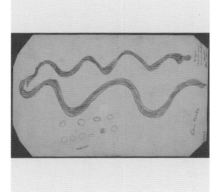

#21
Abe Jangala
Pintinganu
(20 x 31 cm)

#27
Abe Jangala
Jarnpa
(25 x 31 cm)

#28
Abe Jangala
Jarnpa
(25 x 31 cm)

#29
Abe Jangala
Jarnpa
(25 x 31 cm)

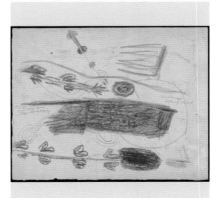

#30
Abe Jangala
Mala
(25 x 31 cm) (verso #31)

#31
Abe Jangala
Mala
(25 x 31 cm) (verso #30)

#32
Abe Jangala
Walpirinpa
(25 x 31 cm)

#33
Abe Jangala
Lungkarrajarra
(25 x 31 cm)

#34
Abe Jangala
Papinya
(25 x 31 cm)

#35
Abe Jangala
Luwindji
(21 x 25 cm)

#36
Abe Jangala
Malungurru
(21 x 25 cm)

#37
Abe Jangala
unidentified country
(21 x 25 cm)

#38
Abe Jangala
Unidentified country
(21 x 25 cm)

#39
Abe Jangala
Pamapardu
(19 x 26 cm)

#40
Abe Jangala
Lungkarra
(19 x 26 cm)

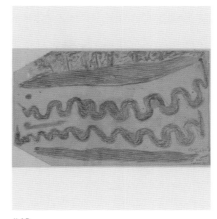

#42
Larry Jungarrayi
Pikilyi
(26 x 32 cm) (verso #41)

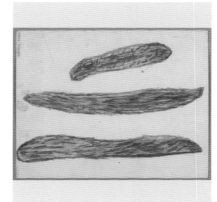

#44
Larry Jungarrayi
Karrinyarra
(26 x 32 cm)

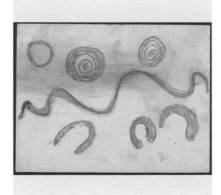

#45
Larry Jungarrayi
Warnayarra
(26 x 32 cm)

#48
Larry Jungarrayi
A spearing at Yuendumu
(25 x 31 cm)

#49
Larry Jungarrayi
Yarripirlangu
(25 x 32 cm)

#51
Larry Jungarrayi
Yarripirlangu
(26 x 32 cm)

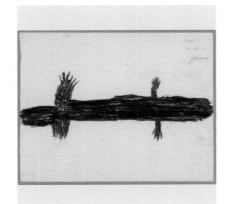

#52
Larry Jungarrayi
Pulalypa
(25 x 31 cm)

#53
Larry Jungarrayi
Jarnpa
(25 x 31 cm)

#54
Larry Jungarrayi
Man walking at night
(25 x 31 cm)

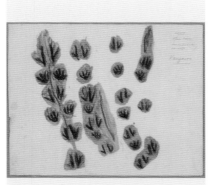

#55
Larry Jungarrayi
Marlu
(25 x 31 cm)

#56
Larry Jungarrayi
Warlawurru
(25 x 31 cm)

#57
Larry Jungarrayi
Trees at Hooker Creek
(25 x 31 cm)

#58
Larry Jungarrayi
Kandangarra
(25 x 31 cm)

#59
Larry Jungarrayi
Wampana
(25 x 31 cm)

#60
Larry Jungarrayi
Kirrirri Creek
(25 x 31 cm)

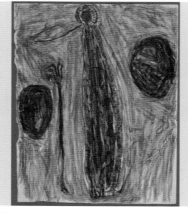

#61
Larry Jungarrayi
Hooker Creek windmill
(25 x 31 cm)

#62
Larry Jungarrayi
Wangarla
(25 x 31 cm)

#63
Larry Jungarrayi
The malaka's house
(25 x 31 cm)

#64
Larry Jungarrayi
Warna
(25 x 31 cm)

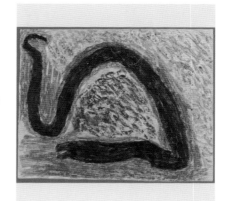

#65
Larry Jungarrayi
Ulayi
(25 x 31 cm)

#66
Larry Jungarrayi
Bush
(25 x 31 cm)

#67
Larry Jungarrayi
Bush
(25 x 31 cm)

#68
Larry Jungarrayi
Bush
(25 x 31 cm)

#69
Lary Jungarrayi
Trees at Hooker Creek
(22 x 24 cm)

#70
Larry Jungarrayi
Trees at Hooker Creek
(20 x 25 cm)

#72
Larry Jungarrayi
Trees at Hooker Creek
(22 x 25 cm)

#73
Larry Jungarrayi
Billabongs near Hooker Creek
(21 x 25 cm)

#74
Larry Jungarrayi
Jarrampayi
(21 x 25 cm)

#75
Larry Jungarrayi
King Billabong
(21 x 25 cm)

#76
Larry Jungarrayi
Trees at Hooker Creek
(21 x 25 cm)

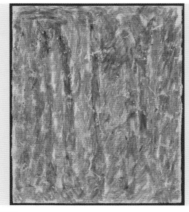

#77
Larry Jungarrayi
Bush
(21 x 25 cm)

#78
Larry Jungarrayi
Country near Hooker Creek
(21 x 25 cm)

#79
Larry Jungarrayi
Country near Hooker Creek
(21 x 25 cm)

#80
Larry Jungarrayi
Yarripirlangu
(21 x 25 cm)

#81
Larry Jungarrayi
Yarripirlangu
(21 x 25 cm)

#82
Larry Jungarrayi
Unidentified country
(21 x 25 cm) (verso #83)

#83
Larry Jungarrayi
Pirrpirrpakanu
(21 x 25 cm) (verso #82)

#84
Larry Jungarrayi
Bush
(22 x 25 cm) (verso #85)

#85
Larry Jungarrayi
Kanyala
(22 x 25 cm) (verso #84)

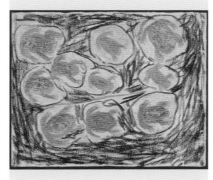

#86
Larry Jungarrayi
Jalji
(21 x 25 cm)

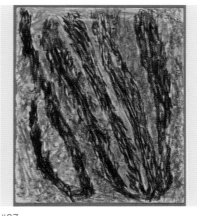

#87
Larry Jungarrayi
Bush
(21 x 25 cm) (verso #88)

#88
Larry Jungarrayi
Wurrkali
(21 x 25 cm) (verso #87)

#89 Larry Jungarrayi
Bush
(21 x 25 cm) (verso #90)

#90
Larry Jungarrayi
Yankirri
(21 x 25 cm) (verso #89)

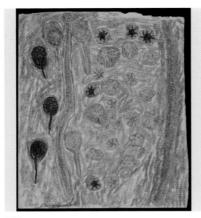

#91
Larry Jungarrayi
Ngarrka
(21 x 25 cm) (verso #92)

#93
Alecky II Japaljarri
Ngarrarri
(21 x 25 cm)

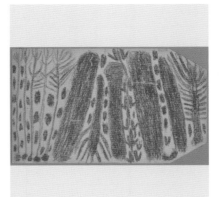

#94
Alecky II Japaljarri
Dalgiri
(21 x 25 cm)

#95
Alecky II Japaljarri
Ngalyipi
(21 x 25 cm)

#96
Alecky II Japaljarri
Warlawurru
(21 x 25 cm)

#97
Alecky II Japaljarri
Wampana
(25 x 31 cm) (verso #98)

#98
Alecky II Japaljarri
Ngalyipi
(25 x 31 cm) (verso #97)

#99
Alecky II Japaljarri
Ngalyipi
(25 x 31 cm) (verso #100)

#100
Attributed to Alecky II Japaljarri and Abe
Jangala
Unidentified subject
(25 x 31 cm) (verso #99)

#101
Clem Jungarrayi
Country near Tanami
(21 x 35 cm)

#102
Clem Jungarrayi
Unidentified country
(20 x 23 cm)

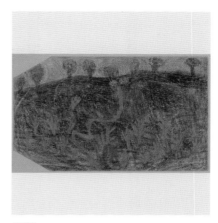

#103
Clem Jungarrayi
Country west of Hooker Creek
(20 x 23 cm)

#104
Clem Jungarrayi
Country in the Tanami area
(19 x 27 cm)

#105
Clem Jungarrayi
Country near Tanami
(20 x 33 cm)

#106
Clem Jungarrayi
Country near The Granites
(20 x 33 cm)

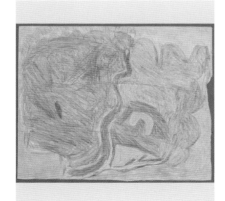

#107
Clem Jungarrayi
Country near The Granites
(21 x 25 cm)

#108
Clem Jungarrayi
Kura
(21 x 25 cm)

#109
Clem Jungarrayi
Country near Tanami
(21 x 25 cm)

#111
Bulbul Japaljarri
Yurlpawanu
(21 x 25 cm)

#112
Bulbul Japaljarri
Mina Mina
(23 x 25 cm)

#113
Bulbul Japaljarri
Karnta
(22 x 25 cm)

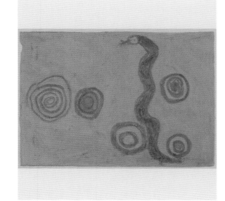

#110
Clem Jungarrayi
Maliki-jarra
(9 x 20 cm)

#114
Bulbul Japajarri and Clem Jungarrayi
Warnayarra
(19 x 27 cm)

#115
Ginger Japangardi
Larrara
(21 x 25 cm)

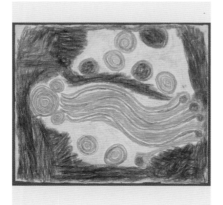

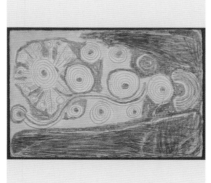

#116
Ginger Japangardi
Larrara
(21 x 25 cm)

#117
Ginger Japangardi
Larrara
(16 x 24 cm)

#122
Wally Japaljarri
Karltarrangu
(21 x 25 cm)

#123
Wally Japaljarri
Karltarrangu
(18 x 19 cm)

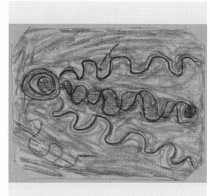

#125
Wally Japaljarri
Ngalyipi
(21 x 25 cm) (verso #126)

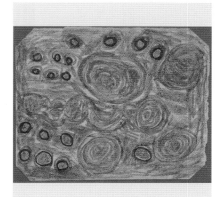

#126
Wally Japalajarri
Ngalyipi
(21 x 25 cm) (verso #125)

#127
Tony Jungarrayi
Lawandja
(21 x 25 cm)

#128
Tony Jungarrayi
Wirnparrku
(21 x 25 cm)

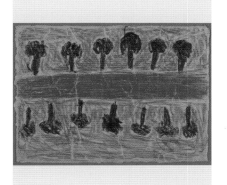

#129
Tony Jungarrayi
King billabong
(20 x 27 cm)

#130
Tony Jungarrayi
Wampana
(16 x 28 cm)

#131
Tony Jungarrayi
Tiri
(21 x 25 cm)

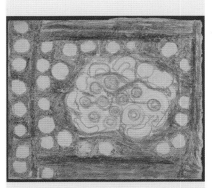

#134
Alecky I Japaljarri
Kulungalipa
(22 x 25 cm)

#137
Norman Jampijinpa
Unidentified country
(21 x 25 cm)

#138
Norman Jampijinpa
Country near Yuendumu
(21 x 25 cm)

#139
Norman Jampijinpa
Lukurri
(21 x 25 cm)

#140
Norman Jampijinpa
Kirrirrdi
(21 x 25 cm)

#141
Norman Jampijinpa
Country south of Yuendumu
(21 x 25 cm)

#149
Willy Japangardi
House at Hooker Creek
(25 x 31 cm)

#150
Willy Japangardi
House at Hooker Creek
(25 x 31 cm)

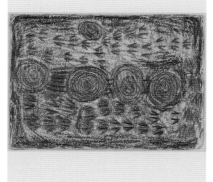

#152
Paddy Jupurrurla
Wampana at Yuendumu
(19 x 27 cm)

#153
Charlie Jupurrurla
Unidentified country
(19 x 26 cm)

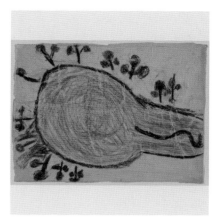

#156
Jimmy Jampijinpa
Wampana
(20 x 20 cm)

#157
Billy Jampijinpa
Kurlpulurnu
(20 x 25 cm)

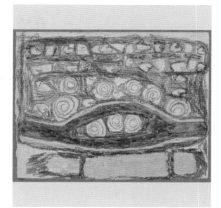

#158.
Silent Jampijinpa
Walpajirri
(21 x 26 cm)

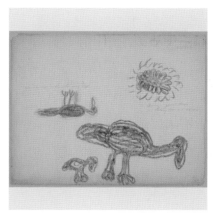

#159
Lucy Nakamarra
Yinalingi
(25 x 31 cm)

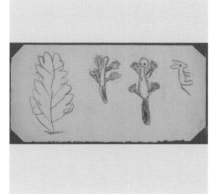

#160
Lucy Nakamarra
Donkey
(16 x 31 cm) (verso #161)

#161
Lucy Nakamarra
Camel
(16 x 31 cm) (verso #160)

#162
Lucy Nakamarra
Unidentified country
(25 x 31 cm) (verso #63)

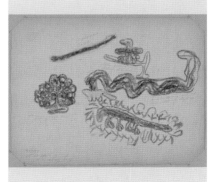

#163
Lucy Nakamarra
Bush foods
(25 x 31 cm) (verso #162)

#164
Elizabeth Napanangka
or Annie Nungarrayi
Unidentified fruit tree
(18 x 32 cm) (verso #165)

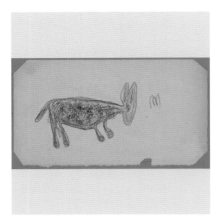

#165
Elizabeth Napanangaka
or Annie Nungarrayi
Donkey
(18 x 32 cm) (verso #164)

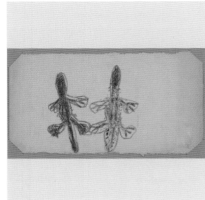

#166
Elizabeth Napanangka
Goannas
(18 x 32 cm) (verso #167)

#167
Elizabeth Napanangka
Stockmen's campfire
(18 x 32 cm) (verso #166)

#168
Abe Jangala and Annie Nungarrayi
Unidentified snake
(25 x 31 cm) (verso #169)

#169
Annie Nungarrayi
Unidentified fruit trees
(25 x 31 cm) (verso #168)

Notes

Preface

1 Jon Altman, pers. comm., May 2001.
2 Swartz (2012).

Introduction

1 Joan Meggitt, in discussion with Melinda Hinkson, Canberra, 16 November 2012.
2 Meggitt, n.d., unpublished documentation for MEGGITT.MI.CS, AIATSIS.
3 In the tradition of Appadurai (1986).
4 Mitchell (2005).
5 Hall (1997); Mitchell (2005); Mirzoeff (2011); Lydon (2012).
6 Berger (2005); Ingold (2007); Carter (2009); Taussig (2011).
7 Berger (2005: 4).
8 ibid: 71.
9 Wild (1980).
10 ibid.
11 Munn (1972).
12 Geertz (1973).
13 Joan Meggitt in discussion with Melinda Hinkson, Canberra, 16 November 2012.
14 Fabian (2002).
15 Munn (1973).
16 Mountford (1937: 21). See also Berndt, Berndt and Stanton (1982: 33).
17 Michaels (1994 [1986]: 2).
18 Cecilia Alfonso, pers. comm., 20 November 2013.
19 Langton (1993); Hinkson (2010).
20 Gutman, Sodaro and Brown (2010: 1) observe a scarcity of scholarship on the relationship between memory and future-focused action and aspiration. Recent brain research suggests a 'common brain network underlies both memory and imagination' Schacter et al. (2012).
21 See, for example, Stanner (1979 [1968]).
22 See Carter (1996: Part 1), (2009: Chapter 4); Mitchell (1994: 420).

Interlude I

1 Campbell (2006).

Chapter 1

1 Meggitt (n.d.: 3).
2 Berndt, Berndt and Stanton (1982: 37).
3 Mountford (1951: 6).
4 Meggitt (n.d.).
5 ibid: 6, emphasis added.

6 Mountford (1951: 6); Tindale quoted in Jones (2012: 6).
7 Berndt (1958: 28).
8 ibid.
9 Jones (1988: 165–6); Sayers (1994: 81–5).
10 Sayers (1994: 81).
11 ibid: 82.
12 ibid: 70.
13 Cooper (1994: 102).
14 Sayers (1994: 71).
15 ibid: 69–70.
16 This passage is adopted from Hinkson (2009).
17 Sayers (1994: 2).
18 Berger (2005: 129).
19 See Jones (1995).
20 Jones (2012: 37).
21 ibid: 43, 49.
22 Thomas (2012) citing Sally May.
23 Mountford (1951, emphasis added).
24 Meggitt (n.d.: 3–4).
25 Berndt, Berndt and Stanton (1982: 40–1).
26 Berndt (1958: 26–43).
27 Quoted in Jones (2012: 34).
28 See Hinkson (2008).
29 Keen (2008).
30 See also McGregor (2011: 26–7).
31 Strehlow (1964).
32 Henson (1994: 54); Carter (1996: 31).
33 Carter (1996); Hill (2002).
34 Long (1992: 46–7).
35 Berger (2005, 2011); Ingold (2007).
36 Berger (2011: 150).
37 ibid.
38 Berger (2005); Ingold (2007); Taussig (2011).
39 Benjamin (1979 [1933]; 2008 [1936]).
40 Benjamin (1979 [1933]: 66).
41 Berndt (1958: 41–2).
42 ibid: 40.
43 Munn (1973: 185–6); Dubinskas and Traweek (1984: 24).
44 Berger (2011: 72).
45 Munn (1973: 214).
46 ibid.
47 ibid: 217.
48 Ingold (2007: 46).
49 ibid: 81.
50 Glowczewski (1991: 123).
51 Ingold (2007: 70–5).
52 Neville Japangardi Poulson in discussion with Melinda Hinkson, Yuendumu, 9 February 2011.
53 Meggitt (1962: 34).
54 Biddle (2007).
55 Berndt, Berndt, and Stanton (1982: 138–9).
56 Mountford (1948: 14).
57 Young (2011: 361).

58 ibid: 356–60.
59 ibid: 361.
60 Strehlow (1951: 5–6).
61 ibid.
62 Battarbee (1951: 54).
63 Carter (1996: 45).
64 ibid.
65 See Rowse (1992) for Hermannsburg; Morphy (1983, 1991) for Yirrkala.
66 Myers (1989: 5, 2004).
67 Stanton (n.d.) makes this argument for the crayon drawings collected by the Berndts.
68 See, for example, Michaels (1985).

Interlude II

1 This is a transcribed and lightly edited version of Olive Pink, 'A picnic with stone-age people. South of The Granites track, Cen. Aus', unpublished manuscript, 1934, AIATSIS MS2368 BCc (6) 1.

Chapter 2

1 Baume (1994 [1933]: 92).
2 ibid, emphasis added.
3 ibid.
4 ibid: 57–8.
5 Peterson (2006).
6 Rowse (1998); McGregor (2012).
7 McGrath (1987: 97).
8 Baume (1994 [1933]: 92).
9 Hartwig (1960).
10 Campbell (2006: 137–8).
11 Paul Burke's (2013) study of the Warlpiri diaspora looks to periodise the emergence of key figures of intercultural brokerage, including the figure of the stockman.
12 Campbell (2006).
13 Rowley (1976: 285); Berndt and Berndt (1987).
14 Hartwig (1960: 8).
15 ibid: 9.
16 ibid: 5–7.
17 Rowley (1974: 230).
18 Powell (2009: 161).
19 Rowley (1974: 259).
20 Hartwig (1960: 28).
21 McGrath (1987: 14).
22 Baume (1994 [1933]); Campbell (2006).
23 Hartwig (1960: 11).
24 ibid: 11.
25 McGrath (1987: 15).
26 Marcus (2001: 229).
27 Meggitt (1962: 21).
28 Part of Rosie Nungarrayi's testimony as told to and translated by Petronella Vaarzon-Morel, see Vaarzon-Morel (1995: 45).

29 As documented by Hannah Quinliven.

30 Hartwig (1960: 31).

31 ibid: 45.

32 CH Noblett, Chief Protector of Aborigines to the Government Resident, JC Cawood, Alice Springs, 1 December 1928, NAA A431 1950 / 2768, Part 1, emphasis added.

33 I thank Mandy Paul for helping me clarify this point. See, for example, Reynolds (2013).

34 Rowse (1998: 63).

35 Watts and Fisher (2000).

36 Hartwig (1960: 4).

37 Watts and Fisher (2000: 111–16).

38 ibid: 160.

39 ibid: 183–4.

40 ibid: 186.

41 ibid.

42 Elias (2001: 80).

43 ibid.

44 ibid: 82–3.

45 Long (1992: 49); Marcus (2001: 239).

46 Watts and Fisher (2000: 206).

47 Jangala (1977: 2).

48 Elias (2001).

49 Watts and Fisher (2000: 206).

50 ibid.

51 ibid.

52 *Courier Mail*, 12 October 1946; Henson (1994: 178).

53 Long (1992: 98).

54 Marcus (2001: 137–8).

55 ibid: 138.

56 ibid: 237.

57 ibid: 212.

58 Rowley (1974: 233–4).

59 Long (1992).

60 Gray (2007: 167–9).

61 Braitling to NT Administrator, 24 January 1946, 1945/271, National Archives of Australia, Darwin.

62 Application by Frederick Coin and M Ey for grazing licence 1150, 18 March 1946, 1945/271, National Archives of Australia, Darwin.

63 Howard Vaughan solicitor, acting for Directors of Bokhara Pastoral Company to the Administrator of the NT, 20 March 1946, 1945/271, National Archives of Australia, Darwin.

64 WL Clough to the Chief Clerk, Lands, 1 April 1946, 1945/271, National Archives of Australia, Darwin.

65 Chief Veterinary Office AL Ross to Director of Lands, 4 November 1947, 1945/271, National Archives of Australia, Darwin.

66 AS Bingle, Manager, Australian Investment Agency Pty Ltd to Hon CLA Abbott, Administrator, 7

67 September 1945, 1945/157, National Archives of Australia, Darwin.

67 Long (1992: 33).

68 AS Bingle to Director of Native Affairs, 11 January 1946, 1945/157, National Archives of Australia, Darwin.

69 VG Carrington, Acting Director of Native Affairs to AS Bingle, 16 January 1946, 1945/157, National Archives of Australia, Darwin.

70 AS Bingle to Director of Native Affairs, 23 January 1946, 1945/157, National Archives of Australia, Darwin.

Chapter 3

1   Hooker Creek Day Journal 1951–52, 7 February 1952, 1952/771, National Archives of Australia, Darwin.

2   Hooker Creek Day Journal 1951–2, 1952/771, parts 1 and 2, National Archives of Australia, Darwin.

3   Mirzoeff (2011: 3).

4   ibid.

5   ibid.

6   Spencer and Gillen quoted in Peterson (2006: 18).

7   See Keys (1999).

8   ibid.

9   Reser (1979).

10 Heppell (1979: 55).

11 Keys (1999) and Reser (1979) detail these factors for Central Australian and Arnhem Land communities.

12 Hooker Creek Day Journal 1953–4, 23 February entries, 1954/792, National Archives of Australia, Darwin.

13 ibid, 21 and 22 April 1953.

14 ibid, 23 December 1953.

15 Pholeros and Lea (2010: 187–209).

16 Robin Japanangka Granites and Neville Japangardi Poulson quoted in Hinkson (1999: 18.)

17 Musharbash (2008).

18 Stanner (1979 [1968]: 230).

19 Dolly Nampijinpa Daniels translated by Petronella Vaarzon-Morel in University of South Australia Art Museum (1994: 23).

20 Vaarzon-Morel (1994: 12).

21 Ned Hargraves, quoted in 'Voices from the heart', *The Australian*, 22 October 2007.

22 Jackson (1995: 84).

23 Musharbash (2008).

24 Bachelard (1969: 6, 17).

25 Reser (1979: 83); Ross (1979: 69).

26 Ross (ibid: 70).

27 Patrol Officer BD Greenfield to the Acting District Superintendent, 1 October 1952, 1952/943, National Archives of Australia, Darwin.

28 Long (1992: 99).

29 Hooker Creek Day Journal 1951–52, January entries, 1952/771, part 1, National Archives of Australia, Darwin.

30 ibid, February–March entries.

31 ibid.

32 Welfare Branch, 1952/943, National Archives of Australia, Darwin.

33 Hooker Creek Day Journal 1951–52, March, April, May entries, 1952/771, part 1, National Archives of Australia, Darwin.

34 Mahood (1995: 26).

35 ibid: 27.

36 ibid: 20.

37 ibid: 19.

38 Hooker Creek Day Journal 1951–52, January and February entries, 1952/771, part 1, National Archives of Australia, Darwin.

39 ibid, 7 February.

40 ibid, January and February entries.

41 Hooker Creek Day Journal 1953–54, 31 March 1954, 1954/792, National Archives of Australia, Darwin.

42 Goffman (1961).

43 Romanyshyn (1989: 42); see also Friedberg (2009).

44 Bachelard (1969: 34).

Interlude III

1   Recorded by Melinda Hinkson, Lajamanu, 25 November 2011.

Chapter 4

1   See Altman and Hinkson (2007, 2010) for a variety of interpretations of and responses to the Northern Territory National Emergency Response.

2   Hinkson (2010); McCallum (2009). The figure of the suffering child made a regular appearance in the writings of Noel Pearson in the opinion pages of *The Australian* newspaper this period; see also Sutton (2009).

3   Musharbash (2010); Vaarzon-Morel (2012).

4   This bush trip is similarly explored in Hinkson (2013).

5   Benjamin (1979 [1933]: 66).

6   ibid.

7   Mitchell (2005).

8   Darby Jampijinpa Ross quoted in Warlpiri Media Association (1984).

9   See, for example, Swain (1993).

10 Hughes (2007); Johns (2011).

11 Scott (1990: 2).

12 A number of anthropologists working in land rights and native title contexts

have written about this in various ways, see for example Merlan (1998); Povinelli (2002).

13 Myers' (1986) discussion of the Pintupi concept of 'looking after' which resonates strongly with the way Warlpiri people deploy this notion.

14 Meggitt (1955).

15 ibid: 378.

16 ibid: 379.

17 ibid: 383–4.

18 ibid: 384.

19 ibid.

20 Farmer (1996).

21 Comaroff and Comaroff (1999).

22 Gluckman citing Evans-Pritchard, in Comaroff and Comaroff (ibid: 283).

23 Munn (1973: 158).

24 Munn (1996).

25 Mitchell (2005: 105).

Interlude IV

1 Beckett (2005: 16); see also Tonkinson (2005).

2 Beckett (2005: 118).

3 ibid.

4 Joan Meggitt in conversation with Melinda Hinkson via telephone, 2 December 2013.

5 Joan Meggitt in conversation with Melinda Hinkson, 23 November 2012, Canberra.

6 Beckett (2005: 119).

7 ibid: 118.

8 Meggitt (1964: 169).

9 Meggitt (1965).

10 Beckett (2005: 117).

11 ibid.

12 Meggitt (1966: 302).

Chapter 5

1 I am grateful to Petronella Vaarzon-Morel for this insight and for her generous and thoughtful engagement and comments on an earlier version of this chapter.

2 Levi-Strauss (1966).

3 Berger (2005: 48–9).

4 See, among others, Michaels (1985); Swain (1993); Jackson (1995); Vaarzon-Morel (1995).

5 And others have observed, only certain trees of any species come to acquire qualities of sacred power, see Merlan (1982); Peterson (2011).

6 Michaels (1987).

7 Again I thank Petronella Vaarzon-Morel for this insight.

8 See Attwood and Marcus (1997).

9 The notions of dis-embedding and re-embedding are taken from Giddens (1991).

10 Wild (1987).

11 ibid: 12.

12 Jangala (1977: 2).

13 ibid: 2–3.

14 ibid: 4.

15 My embrace of the indeterminate responses to these drawings, of a research journey that generates questions rather than explanation, shares ground with Michael Jackson's anthropology of experience (Jackson 1995).

16 Stanner (1979 [1968]: 49).

17 ibid: 63.

18 Benjamin (2008 [1936]: 25–7).

19 Berger (2005: 3).

20 ibid.

21 ibid: 51.

22 ibid: 143.

Chapter 6

1 Native Settlement Yuendumu School, File 51/797, National Archives of Australia, Darwin.

2 I am grateful to David Brooks and Nicolas Peterson for thoughtful discussions of this drawing.

3 Meggitt discusses penalties faced by law-breakers including three causes of death — that caused by non-human agency, human sorcery and physical attack. See Meggitt (1962: 258).

4 Munn (1973).

5 Ricoeur (2004: 505).

6 'Remembering the Coniston Massacre', SBS Radio 9 September 2013, podcast available at http://www.sbs.com.au/podcasts/Podcasts/radionews/episode/287555/Remembering-the-Coniston-Massacre (accessed 22 September 2013).

7 Chlanda (2013).

8 See the comments that follow Chlanda's report at http://www.alicespringsnews.com.au/2013/08/02/violence-must-stop-forgiveness-must-rule/ (accessed 20 August 2012).

9 Warnayaka Art Centre files; *The Age*, 7 August, 2002.

10 See comparative data for remote Aboriginal Australian art centres in Office of the Registrar of Indigenous Corporations (2012).

11 See Warlukurlangu Aboriginal Artists of Yuendumu website at http://warlu.com/.

12 Memmott (1997).

13 Stephen Wanta Jampijinpa Patrick, in conversation with Melinda Hinkson, 26 May 2013.

14 Jeannie Hungarrayi Herbert, in conversation with Melinda Hinkson, Lajamanu, 26 November 2011.

15 See for example Sutton (1989); Ryan (1990); Taylor (1996); Bardon and Bardon (2004); Myers (2004); Morphy (2008).

16 Hinkson (2005: 157–68).

17 David Tunley in conversation with Melinda Hinkson, 14 March 2013, Torquay.

18 Frank Baarda in conversation with Melinda Hinkson, 6 February 2011, Yuendumu.

19 Bell (1983: 7).

20 Michaels (1987).

21 Gadamer (1997 [1960]: 302).

References

Altman, Jon and Hinkson, Melinda (eds), 2007, *Coercive reconciliation: stabilise, normalise, exit Aboriginal Australia*, Arena Publications, Carlton North.

—— 2010, *Culture crisis: anthropology and politics in Aboriginal Australia*, UNSW Press, Sydney.

Anderson, Christopher and Dussart, Françoise, 1988, 'Dreamings in acrylic: contemporary Western Desert art', in Peter Sutton (ed.), *Dreamings: art from Aboriginal Australia*, Braziller Publishers, New York, pp. 89–142.

Appadurai, Arjun (ed.), 1986, *The social life of things*, Cambridge University Press, Cambridge.

Attwood, Bain and Markus, Andrew, 1997, *The 1967 Referendum, or, When Aborigines didn't get the vote*, Aboriginal Studies Press, Canberra.

Bachelard, Gaston, 1969, *The poetics of space*, Grossman Publishers, Toronto.

Bardon, Geoffrey and Bardon, James, 2004, *Papunya: a place made after the story*, Miegunyah Press, Melbourne.

Battarbee, Rex, 1951, *Modern Australian Aboriginal painting*, Angus and Robertson, Sydney.

Baume, FE, 1994 [1933], *Tragedy track: the story of The Granites*, North Flinders Mines Ltd and Hesperian Press, Perth.

Beckett, Jeremy, 2005, 'Mervyn Meggitt, 1924–2004', *The Australian Journal of Anthropology*, 16 (1): 116–19.

Bell, Diane, 1983, *Daughters of the Dreaming*, Allen and Unwin, Sydney.

Benjamin, Walter, 1979 [1933], 'Doctrine of the similar', *New German Critique*, 17: 65–9.

—— 2008 [1936], 'The work of art in the age of its technological reproducibility: Second version', in Walter Benjamin, *The work of art in the age of its technological reproducibility and other writings on media*, Harvard University Press, Cambridge and London, pp. 19–55.

Berger, John, 2005, *Berger on drawing*, Jim Savage (ed.), Occasional Press, Cork.

—— 2011, *Bento's sketchbook*, Verso, London.

Berndt, Ronald, 1958, 'Some methodological considerations in the study of Australian Aboriginal art', *Oceania*, 29: 26–43.

———— 1987, *End of an era: Aboriginal labour in the Northern Territory*, Australian Institute of Aboriginal Studies, Canberra.

——, Berndt, Catherine and Stanton, John, 1982, *Aboriginal australian art: A visual perspective*, Methuen, Sydney.

Biddle, Jennifer, 2007, *Breasts, bodies, canvas*, UNSW Press, Sydney.

Burke, Paul, 2013, 'Warlpiri in the Pacific: Ideas for an intercultural history of the Warlpiri', *Anthropological Forum*, 23 (4): 414–27.

Campbell, Liam, 2006, *Darby: one hundred years of life in a changing culture*, ABC Books, Sydney.

Carter, Paul, 1996, *The lie of the land*, Faber and Faber, London.

—— 2009, *Dark writing: geography, performance and design*, University of Hawaii Press, Honolulu.

Chlanda, Erwin, 2013, 'Violence must stop, forgiveness must rule', *Alice Springs News*, 4 August 2013, available at http://www.alicespringsnews.com.au/2013/08/02/violence-must-stop-forgiveness-must-rule/ (accessed 7 August 2013).

Comaroff, Jean and Comaroff, John, 1999, 'Occult economies and the violence of abstraction: Notes from the South African postcolony', *American Ethnologist*, 26 (2): 279–303.

Cooper, Carol, 1994, 'Traditional visual culture in south-east Australia', in Andrew Sayers, *Aboriginal artists of the nineteenth century*, Oxford University Press, Oxford, pp. 91–109.

Dussart, Françoise, 1999, 'What an acrylic can mean: The meta-ritualistic resonances of a Central Desert painting', in Howard Morphy and Margo Smith Boles (eds), *Art from the land: Dialogues with the Kluge-Ruhe collection of Australian Aboriginal art*, University of Virginia, Charlottesville, pp. 193–221.

—— 2006, 'Canvassing identities: Reflecting on the acrylic art movement in an Australian Aboriginal settlement', *Aboriginal History*, 30: 1–13.

Elias, Derek, 2001, Golden dreams: people, place and mining in the Tanami Desert, unpublished PhD Thesis, School of Archaeology and Anthropology, Australian National University, Canberra.

Fabian, Johannes, 2002, *Time and the Other: How anthropology makes its object*, Columbia University Press, New York.

Farmer, Paul, 1996, 'On suffering and structural violence: A view from below', *Daedalus*, 125 (1): 261–83.

Friedberg, Anne, 2009, *The virtual window: from Alberti to Microsoft*, MIT Press, Cambridge.

Gadamer, Hans-Georg, 1997 [1960], *Truth and method*, Continuum, New York.

Geertz, Clifford, 1973, *The interpretation of cultures*, Basic Books, New York.

Giddens, Anthony, 1991, *Modernity and self-Identity: self and society in the late modern age*, Stanford University Press, Stanford.

Glowczewski, Barbara, 1991, Between two images, *Yapa: peintres Aborigénes de Balgo at Lajamanu*, Galerie Baudoin Lebon, Paris, pp. 117–123.

Goffman, Irving, 1961, *Asylums: essays on the social situation of mental patients and other inmates*, Doubleday Books, New York.

Gray, Geoffrey, 2007, *A cautious silence: The politics of Australian anthropology*, Aboriginal Studies Press, Canberra.

Gutman, Yifat, Sodaro, Amy and Brown, Adam D, 2010, 'Introduction: Memory and the future: why a change of focus is necessary', in Yifat Gutman, Amy Sodaro and Adam D Brown (eds), *Memory and the future: transnational politics, ethics and society*, Palgrave Macmillan, London, pp. 1–14.

Hall, Stuart, 1997, *Representation: cultural representations and signifying practices*, Sage, London.

Hartwig, MC, 1960, The Coniston killings, unpublished Honours Thesis, Department of History, University of Adelaide, Adelaide.

Henson, Barbara, 1994, *A straight-out man: FW Albrecht and Central Australian Aborigines*, Melbourne University Press, Melbourne.

Heppell, Michael, 1979, 'Introduction: Past approaches and future trends in Aboriginal housing', in Michael Heppell (ed.), *A black reality: Aboriginal camps and housing in remote Australia*, Aboriginal Studies Press, Canberra, pp. 1–64.

Hill, Barry, 2002, *Broken song: TGH Strehlow and Aboriginal possession*, Knopf, Sydney.

Hinkson, Melinda, 1999, Warlpiri connections: new technology, new enterprise and emergent social forms at Yuendumu, unpublished PhD Thesis, Department of Sociology and Anthropology, La Trobe University, Melbourne.

—— 2005, 'New media projects at Yuendumu: towards a history and analysis of intercultural engagement', in Luke Taylor et al. (eds), *The power of knowledge, the resonance of tradition*, Aboriginal Studies Press, Canberra, pp. 157–68.

—— 2008, 'Journey to the source: Fitzmaurice rock art and the high culture', in Melinda Hinkson and Jeremy Beckett (eds), *An Appreciation of difference: WEH Stanner and Aboriginal Australia*, Aboriginal Studies Press, Canberra, pp. 102–14.

—— 2009, 'Seeing more than black and white: picturing Aboriginality at Australia's National Portrait Gallery', *Australian Humanities Review*, 49: 5–28.

—— 2010, 'Media images and the politics of hope', in Jon Altman and Melinda Hinkson (eds), *Culture crisis: anthropology and politics in Aboriginal Australia*, UNSW Press, Sydney, pp. 229–47.

—— 2013 'Back to the future: Warlpiri encounters with drawings, country and others in the digital age', *Culture, Theory and Critique*, 54 (3): 301–17.

Hughes, Helen, 2007, *Lands of shame*, Centre for Independent Studies, Sydney.

Ingold, Tim, 2007, *Lines: a brief history*, Routledge, London.

Jackson, Michael, 1995, *At home in the world*, HarperCollins, Sydney.

Jangala, Abe, 1977, *Stories from Lajamanu*, translated by P. Jangala, Northern Territory Department of Education, Darwin, pp. 1–4.

Johns, Gary, 2011, *The whiteman's dream*, Connor Court, Adelaide.

Jones, Philip, 1988, 'Perceptions of Aboriginal art: a history', in Peter Sutton (ed.), *Dreamings: the art of Aboriginal Australia*, Viking in association with The Asia Society Galleries, New York, pp. 165–6.

—— 1995, 'NB Tindale: an obituary', *Records of the South Australian Museum*, 28 (2): 159–76.

—— 2012, 'Inside Mountford's tent: Paint, politics and paperwork', in Martin Thomas and Margo Neale (eds), *Exploring the legacy of the 1948 Arnhem Land expedition*, ANU EPress, Canberra, pp. 33–54.

Keen, Ian, 2008, 'Religion, magic, sign and symbol in Stanner's *On Aboriginal religion*', in Melinda Hinkson and Jeremy Beckett (eds), *An appreciation of difference: WEH Stanner and Aboriginal Australia*, Aboriginal Studies Press, Canberra, pp. 126–34.

Keys, Catherine, 1999, The architectural implications of Warlpiri jilimi, unpublished PhD Thesis, Department of Architecture, The University of Queensland, Brisbane.

Langton, Marcia, 1993, *Well I heard it on the radio, and I saw it on the television*, Australian Film Institute, Sydney.

Levi-Strauss, Claude, 1966, 'The science of the concrete', in Claude Levi-Strauss, *The savage mind*, University of Chicago Press, Chicago, pp. 1–34.

Long, Jeremy, 1992, *The go-betweens: patrol officers in Aboriginal Affairs administration in the Northern Territory 1936–74*, North Australian Research Unit, Australian National University, Darwin.

Lydon, Jane, 2012, *The flash of recognition*, NewSouth Books, Sydney.

Mahood, Marie, 1995, *Icing on the damper*, Central Queensland University Press, Rockhampton.

Marcus, Julie, 2001, *The indomitable Miss Pink*, UNSW Press, Sydney.

McCallum, Kerry, 2009, 'News and local talk: conversations about the "crisis of Indigenous violence" in Australia', in SE Bird (ed.), *The Anthropology of News and Journalism*, University of Indiana Press, Evansville, pp. 151–67.

McGrath, Ann, 1987, *Born in the cattle*, Allen and Unwin, Sydney.

McGregor, Russell, 2011, *Indifferent inclusion: Aboriginal people and the Australian nation*, Aboriginal Studies Press, Canberra.

Meggitt, Mervyn, n.d., 'Interpretive and representational drawings by Walbiri people, collected by Mervyn Meggitt 1953–1954', unpublished transcript, edited by Peter Hamilton, MEGGITT.MI.CS, Australian Institute of Aboriginal and Torres Strait Islander Studies, Canberra.

—— 1955, 'Djanpa among the Walbiri', *Anthropos* 50: 375–403.

—— 1962, *Desert people*, Angus and Robertson, Sydney.

—— 1964, 'Forms of government among Australian Aborigines', *Bijdragen toj de Taal, Land en Volkenkunde*, 120 (1): 163–80.

—— 1965, 'The association between Australian Aborigines and dingoes', in Anthony Leeds and Andrew Vayda (eds), *Man, culture and animals: the role of animals in human ecological adjustments*, American Association for the Advancement of Science, Washington, pp. 7–26.

—— 1966, 'Gadjeri among the Walbiri Aborigines of Central Australia', *Oceania Monographs*, 14, University of Sydney Press, Sydney.

Memmott, Paul, 1997, 'Aboriginal signs and architectural meanings', *Architectural Theory Review*, 2 (1): 38–64.

Merlan, Francesca, 1982, 'A Mangarrayi representational system: environment and cultural symbolization in northern Australia', *American Ethnologist*, 9 (1): 145–66.

—— 1998, *Caging the rainbow: places, politics and Aborigines in a north Australian town*, University of Hawaii Press, Honolulu.

Michaels, Eric, 1985, 'Constraints on knowledge in an economy of oral information', *Current Anthropology*, 26: 505–10.

—— 1986, *The Aboriginal invention of television: Central Australia 1982–86*, Australian Institute of Aboriginal Studies, Canberra.

—— 1987, *For A cultural future: Francis Jupurrurla makes TV at Yuendumu*, Art and Text, Sydney.

—— 1992, 'Afterword: Yuendumu doors and postmodernism', in Warlukurlangu Artists, *Yuendumu doors — Kuruwarri*, Aboriginal Studies Press, Canberra, pp. 133–43.

—— 1994 [1986], 'A primer of restrictions on picture-taking in traditional areas of Aboriginal Australia', in Eric Michaels (ed.), *Bad Aboriginal art: tradition, media and technological horizons*, Allen and Unwin, Sydney, pp. 1–18.

Mirzoeff, Nicholas, 2011, *The right to look: A counterhistory of visuality*, Duke University Press, Durham.

Mitchell, WJT, 1994, *Picture theory: essays on verbal and visual representation*, Chicago University Press, Chicago.

—— 2005, *What do pictures want? The lives and loves of images*, Chicago University Press, Chicago.

Morphy, Howard, 1983, '"Now you understand": An analysis of the way Yolngu have used sacred knowledge to retain their autonomy', in Nicolas Peterson and Marcia Langton (eds), *Aborigines, land and land rights*, Australian Institute of Aboriginal Studies, Canberra, pp. 110–33.

—— 1991, *Ancestral connections: art and an Aboriginal system of knowledge*, Chicago University Press, Chicago.

—— 2008, *Becoming art: exploring cross-cultural categories*, UNSW Press, Sydney.

Mountford, CP, 1937, 'Aboriginal crayon drawings from the Warburton Ranges in Western Australia relating to wanderings of two ancestral beings, the Wati Kutjara', *Records of the South Australian Museum*, 6: 6–28.

—— 1948, *Brown men and red sand*, Sun Books, Melbourne.

—— 1951, 'Aboriginal crayon drawings', *Records of the South Australian Museum*, 6: 1–28. South Australian Museum Archives, Series AA346/20, 1951, available at http://archives.samuseum.sa.gov.au/aa346/AA346-20.htm (accessed 7 April 2014).

Munn, Nancy, 1972, 'The spatial presentation of cosmic order in Walbiri iconography', in Anthony Forge (ed.), *Primitive art and society*, Oxford University Press, London and New York.

—— 1973, *Walbiri iconography: graphic representation and cultural symbolism in a Central Australian society*, Cornell University Press, Ithaca and London.

—— 1996, 'Excluded spaces: The figure in the Australian Aboriginal landscape', *Critical Inquiry*, 22 (3): 446–65.

Musharbash, Yasmine, 2008, *Yuendumu everyday*, Aboriginal Studies Press, Canberra.

—— 2010, 'Warlpiri fears/whitefella fears: ways of being in Central Australia seen through an emotion', *Emotion, Space and Society*, 3: 95–102.

Myers, Fred, 1986, *Pintupi country, Pintupi self: sentiment, place and politics among Western Desert Aborigines*, University of California Press, Berkeley.

—— 1989, 'Truth, beauty and Pintupi painting', *Visual Anthropology*, 2: 163–95.

—— 2004, *Painting culture: the making of an Aboriginal high art*, Duke University Press, Durham.

Office of the Registrar of Indigenous Corporations, 2012, *At the heart of art*, available at http://www.oric.gov.au/Content.aspx?content=publications/mediareleases/oricmr112-46_aboriginal_tsi_corp_report.htm (accessed 20 October 2013).

Peterson, Nicolas, 2006, 'Visual knowledge: Spencer and Gillen's use of photography in *The native tribes of Central Australia*', *Australian Aboriginal Studies*, 1: 12–22.

—— 2011, 'Is the Aboriginal landscape sentient? Animism, the new animism and the Warlpiri', *Oceania*, 81 (2): 167–79.

Pholeros, Paul and Lea, Tess, 2010, 'This is not a pipe: The treacheries of indigenous housing', *Public Culture*, 22 (1): 187–209.

Povinelli, Elizabeth, 2002, *The cunning of recognition: Aboriginal alterity and the making of Australian multiculturalism*, Duke University Press, Durham.

Powell, Alan, 2009, *Far country: A short history of the Northern Territory*, Charles Darwin University Press, Darwin.

Reser, Joseph, 1979, 'A matter of control: Aboriginal housing circumstances in remote communities and settlements', in Michael Heppell (ed.), *A black reality: Aboriginal camps and housing in remote Australia*, Aboriginal Studies Press, Canberra, pp. 65–96.

Reynolds, Henry, 2013, *Forgotten war*, NewSouth Books, Sydney.

Ricoeur, Paul, 2004, *Memory, history, forgetting*, Chicago University Press, Chicago.

Romanyshyn, Robert, 1989, *Technology as symptom and dreams*, Routledge, London.

Ross, Helen, 1987, *Just for living: Aboriginal perceptions of housing in Northwest Australia*, Aboriginal Studies Press, Canberra.

Rowley, CD, 1974, *The destruction of Aboriginal society*, Penguin, Ringwood.

—— 1976, *The remote Aborigines*, Penguin, Ringwood.

Rowse, Tim, 1992, 'Painting from memory: art, economics and citizenship 1940–60', in Jane Hardy, JVS Megaw and Ruth Megaw (eds), *The heritage of Namatjira: the watercolours of Central Australia*, William Heinemann Australia, Melbourne, pp. 177–201.

—— 1998, *White flour, white power: from rations to citizenship in Central Australia*, Cambridge University Press, Cambridge.

Ryan, Judith, 1990, *Paint up big: Warlpiri women's art from Lajamanu*, National Gallery of Victoria, Melbourne.

Sayers, Andrew, 1994, *Aboriginal artists of the nineteenth century*, Oxford University Press, Oxford.

Schacter, Daniel, Addis, Donna Rose, Hassabis, Demis, Martin, Victoria, Spreng, R Nathan and Szpunar, Karl, 2012, 'The future of memory: remembering, imagining and the brain', *Neuron*, 677–94.

Scott, James, 1990, *Domination and the arts of resistance: hidden transcripts*, Yale University Press, New Haven.

Stanner, WEH, 1965, 'Religion, totemism and symbolism', in Ronald Berndt and Catherine Berndt (eds), *Aboriginal man in Australia: essay in honour of Emeritus Professor AP Elkin*, Angus and Robertson, Sydney, pp. 207–37.

—— 1979 [1958], 'Continuity and change among the Aborigines', in *White man got no dreaming: essays 1938–1973*, Australian National University Press, Canberra, pp. 41–66.

—— 1979 [1968], 'After the dreaming', in *White man got no dreaming: essays 1938–1973*, Australian National University Press, Canberra, pp. 198–249.

Stanton, John, n.d., 'Before the dots, before Papunya: Australian Aboriginal crayon drawings from Birrundudu, NT', available at http://actesbranly.revues.org/350 (accessed 6 October 2013).

Strehlow, TGH, 1951, 'Foreword', in Rex Battarbee, *Modern Australian Aboriginal painting*, Angus and Robertson, Sydney, pp. 5–6.

—— 1964, 'The art of circle, line and square', in Ronald Berndt (ed.), *Australian Aboriginal art*, Ure Smith, Sydney, pp. 44–59.

Sutton, Peter (ed.), 1989, *Dreamings: the art of Aboriginal Australia*, Viking in association with The Asia Society Galleries, New York.

—— 2009, *The politics of suffering: Indigenous Australia and the end of the liberal consensus*, Melbourne University Press, Melbourne.

Swain, Tony, 1993, *A place for strangers: towards a history of Australian Aboriginal being*, Cambridge University Press, Cambridge.

Swartz, Stephen M, 2012, *Warlpiri–English dictionary*, 2nd edn, AuSIL Dictionary Series, A–3, Charles E Grimes (series ed.), Australian Society for Indigenous Languages, Darwin, available at http://ausil.org/Dictionary/Warlpiri/lexicon/index.htm (accessed 14 February 2014).

Taussig, Michael, 2011, *I swear I saw this: drawings in fieldwork notebooks, namely my own*, Chicago University Press, Chicago.

Taylor, Luke, 1996, *Seeing the Inside*, Oxford University Press, Oxford.

Thomas, Martin, 2012, 'Expedition as time capsule: introducing the American–Australian Expedition to Arnhem Land', in Martin Thomas and Margo Neale (eds), *Exploring the legacy of the 1948 Arnhem Land expedition*, ANU EPress, Canberra, pp. 1–32.

Tonkinson, Robert, 2005, 'Mervyn J Meggitt, 1924–2004', *Australian Aboriginal Studies*, 1: 127–8.

University of South Australia Art Museum, 1994, *Ngurra (camp/home/country): Dolly Nampijinpa Daniels and Anne Mosey*, exhibition catalogue, Adelaide.

Vaarzon-Morel, Petronella, 1994, 'Ngurra (camp/home/country)', catalogue essay, in *Ngurra (camp/home/country): Dolly Nampijinpa Daniels and Anne Mosey*, University of South Australia Art Museum, pp. 9–12.

—— 1995 (ed.), *Warlpiri women's voices: our lives our histories*, IAD Press, Alice Springs.

—— 2012, 'Pointing the phone: transforming technologies and social relations among Warlpiri', unpublished paper presented at the Australian Anthropological Society conference, Brisbane, September 2012.

Warlpiri Media Association, 1984, 'We been talking and talking about TV', local video recording, edit of Remote Aboriginal Telecommunications Meeting, Warlpiri Media Association Archives, VHS video tape no. 0495, Yuendumu.

Watts, Lisa and Fisher, Simon Japangardi, 2000, Pikilyi: water rights — human rights, unpublished thesis submitted for the degree of Master of Aboriginal and Torres Strait Islander Studies, Faculty of Aboriginal and Torres Strait Islander Studies, Northern Territory University, Darwin.

Wild, Stephen, 1980, 'Commentary on "Interpretive and representational drawings by Walbiri people, collected by Mervyn Meggitt 1953–1954"', unpublished ms, MEGGITT.MI.CS, Australia Institute of Aboriginal and Torres Strait Islander Studies, Canberra.

—— 1987, 'Recreating the Jukurrpa: adaptation and innovation in songs and ceremonies in Warlpiri society', in Margaret Clunies Ross, Tamsin Donaldson and Stephen Wild (eds), *Songs of Aboriginal Australia*, University of Sydney, Sydney, pp. 97–120.

Young, Diana, 2011, 'Mutable things: colours and material practice in the northwest of South Australia', *Journal of the Royal Anthropological Institute*, 17 (2): 356–76.

General Index

Note: page numbers in italics indicate a drawing or painting, and in bold indicate a photograph. A list of artists and their works appears in a separate index.

Artists' Index

Note: page numbers in italics indicate a drawing or painting, and in bold indicate a photograph.